THE POETICAL WORKS OF
SIR JOHN DENHAM

THE POETICAL WORKS OF
SIR JOHN DENHAM

EDITED WITH NOTES AND INTRODUCTION

BY THEODORE HOWARD BANKS

SECOND EDITION

ARCHON BOOKS

1969

SBN: 208 00155 7
LIBRARY OF CONGRESS CATALOG CARD NUMBER: 69-11555
PRINTED IN THE UNITED STATES OF AMERICA

TO MY FATHER

PREFACE TO THE SECOND EDITION

THE fact that this is a photo-offset printing has dictated the way in which the first edition has been corrected. The following changes should be noted:

1. The addition in Appendix A of eleven new ms. poems, which I am able to print through the courtesy of Mr. James M. Osborn, Yale University. These poems have no literary value but help to complete the Denham canon.

2. A table of Denham's ms. errata and addenda in his *1668* edition. These include six new lines in Cooper's Hill.

3. A revision of pp. *50-53,* which deal with the editions of Cooper's Hill *and possible sources for the "Thames couplets."*

4. A table of my own errata and addenda.

T. H. B.

Middletown, Connecticut
   October, 1968

PREFACE

THIS, the first critical edition of the poetical works of Sir John Denham, is based upon the only edition appearing in his lifetime, Poems and Translations, 1668. Subsequent collected editions are merely reprints of this, as are those included in the various series of British Poets, save that in these last there are occasional omissions. I have attempted an exact reproduction of the 1668 text, corrected in accord with its table of errata. The second and third editions of 1671 and 1684, have been collated with this, as have such separate editions or MSS. of individual poems as I could find.

Poems not included in the 1668 edition have been gathered from various sources, thus affording for the first time an opportunity to estimate Denham's work as a whole. I believe that Denham, though by no means a great poet, deserves more attention than has as yet been given to him, as influencing his own and the Augustan periods.

An attempt has been made to determine the authorship of certain doubtful poems, which either originally appeared under Denham's name or were later ascribed to him. Two of his poetical works are not included in this edition: his version of the Psalms, and his translation of an act of Corneille's Horace, done in collaboration with Katherine Philips.

I have not followed the 1668 edition in the haphazard order in which the poems were there printed, but have separated original poems from translations, and have further grouped the original poems under three heads: miscellaneous, political, elegies and eulogies; within these headings the poems are printed in chronological order. This arrangement is somewhat artificial, but was adopted to call attention to the main divisions of Denham's work, and their relative bulk.

I have gathered in appendices references to the whole poem

of Cooper's Hill, *and allusions to, and imitations of his apostrophe to the Thames, but all other echoes of particular passages by later poets I have included in the footnotes, feeling that the reader's convenience was served by having the parallels immediately before him. I should like to make it quite clear that in all the above categories I make no pretence at completeness. The references represent merely what I have come upon in my own reading, and what have been supplied by the kindness of friends. Doubtless any student of seventeenth- or eighteenth-century literature will be able to add to them.*

A final word is perhaps necessary to explain the abbreviations of the collated texts of Cooper's Hill. *1642 and 1655 are the editions of* Cooper's Hill *appearing in those years; MS. H. 837, and MS. H. 367 are the versions in the Harleian Manuscripts in the British Museum.*

The present edition owes its origin to work done in fulfillment of the requirements for the degree of Doctor of Philosophy at Yale University, and is the result of a number of years' work. I am only too conscious, however, of the gaps I have been unable to fill. Should any of my readers fill these, or point out to me any errors or omissions which I may have inadvertently made, I would appreciate their courtesy.

T. H. B., Jr.

New Haven, Connecticut,
 January, 1928

CONTENTS

CONTENTS

* First printed in the 1668 edition.
† Not included in the 1668 edition.

EDITOR'S ERRATA AND ADDENDA

THERE is an ms. poem of Denham which I was not able to buy and could not get permission to publish. It is an eighteen-line poem in very halting anapaests addressed to D'Avenant and written in the flyleaf of a copy of the 1651 edition of D'Avenant's *Gondibert*. In 1933 it was in the possession of a New York bookseller, Mr. B. J. Beyer, 5 East 52nd St. The poem has no literary value, but the fact of its existence should be recorded.

p.3   n.10   "Oxonienses" for "Oxoniensis" So throughout:

            p.3   n.12,15.
            p.4   n.16.
            p.5   n.28.
            p.6   n.35.
            p.13   n.64.
            p.16   n.80.
            p.21   n.112.
            p.100   n.1.
            p.139   n.16.
            p.147   n.1.

p.69   n.8   *"Philip[pa]"* for *"Phillip[pa]."*

p.100 n.2   Substitute: Perhaps because he lived in Louvain during the exile.

p.102 n.8   Substitute: Robert Wisdom (d. 1568), archdeacon of Ely, was the author of a metrical version of certain Psalms and other verses. His Psalms were sung by criminals at Tyburn before their execution.

p.102 l.11   The devil who drove the swine into the sea.
      n.9   Matt 8:31-32.

p.111 n.1   "1654?" for "1652."

p.119 n.10   Substitute: Translating the proverb "Corruptio optimi pessima."

p.123 l.1   The text should probably read: "You see the King embraces" [no punct.].

p.136 n.3　　Substitute: Pay up; cash down. See the O.E.D.

p.139 n.17　　"Hagley Park" for "Hughley Park."

p.153 n.1　　A variant of the Egerton manuscript version is to be found in the National Library of Scotland (Advocates Manuscript 19.3.8). This is a ms. of Sir James Balfour of Denmilne, an antiquary. The changes are merely differences in spelling and a few obvious slips in transcription. However, this ms. indicates that the Egerton ms. is no later than April 1643. Hamilton, H. L., *Lines by Denham,* T. L. S., Sept. 22, 1966, p.888.

p.157 l.2　　"his" for "this."

p.157 l.4　　Perhaps an echo of Randolph's: The best of tutours to the worst of Kings (See p.53).

p.160 l.13　　"sit" for "fit."

p.180 n.1　　"foras" for "soras."

p.210 l.109　Period for comma.

p.211 l.133　The text *"Sabinium"* is a misprint for *"Sabinum."* Cf. p.218 l.63.

p.232 n.1　　Cancel section of note dealing with the 1642 edition.

p.328 l.3　　"Aitkin" for "Aikin."

p.335　　　　Dryden.
　　　　　　　"Cooper's Hill, a poem which your Lordship knows for the majesty of the style, is, and ever will be, the exact standard of good writing."
　　　　　　　　　　Epistle Dedicatory to *The Rival Ladies,* 1664

p.339　　　　Manning, Francis.
　　　　　　　Greenwich Hill, 1697. Both general and specific imitation of *Cooper's Hill.*

p.342　　　　Wood.
　　　　　　　Add [from Dryden. q.v.]

p.344　　　　Eddy, Clyde.
　　　　　　　Voyaging down the Thames, 1938. Thames couplets quoted in the Dedication.

p.346   Manning, Francis.
               "O could I rise like thee, and make thy Height
               The graceful measure of my Muse's flight!
               Rounded tho' wide, tho' wild, yet full of State,
               High without Force, without aspiring Great."
                                        Greenwich Hill, 1697

p.349   Randolph.
               See p.53.

p.353   1751.   POEMS/AND/TRANSLATIONS;/WITH
               THE/SOPHY,/A TRAGEDY/WRITTEN BY
               THE HONOURABLE/SIR JOHN DENHAM,
               KNIGHT   OF   THE   BATH./GLASGOW:/
               PRINTED BY ROBERT AND ANDREW
               FOULIS/MDCCLI.

FROM the copy of the 1668 edition in the Osborn collection. See Appendix A. The ms. abbreviations are expanded. Most of the ms. changes duplicate those recorded in the printed Table of Errata in the 1668 edition. Additional changes are printed here.

p.71 l.97 "Grandchild" for "Grandsire." The reference is probably to Henry V's victories in France, notably Agincourt. Henry V was the greatgrandson of Edward III.

p.77 l.3 Between ll. 3 and 4 insert:
> "Rome only conquerd halfe the world, but trade
> One commonwealth of that and her hath made
> And though the sun his beame extends to all
> Yet to his neighbour sheds most liberall
> Least God and Nature partiall should appeare
> Commerse makes everything grow everywhere"

p.100 l.7 "With" for *"Will."*

p.100 n.3 "We three" (See n.4) would then be Denham, Mennis, and Aubrey, 20th Earl of Oxford.

p.100 l.8 Canceled by a pen stroke.

p.109 l.8 Canceled by a pen stroke.

p.179 l.6 "Why all" cancelled. "which ayre" inserted after "Tributes."

p.196 l.198 Between ll. 198 and 199 insert:
> "Who pursues every man with flattering praise
> The fame of good and bad alike doth raise."

l.202 Between ll. 202 and 203 insert:
> "And the detractor who at all doth bite
> Both vice and vertue equally doth slight.
> Detraction yet without designe offends
> But flattry by base waies seeks baser ends.

> What's Sweet delights the tast, but who digest
> Them both shall find the bitter, wholesomest."

p.307 l.592 "They" for "Then."

l.601 "in my bones" canceled by a pen stroke.

THE POETICAL WORKS OF
SIR JOHN DENHAM

JOHN DENHAM

A FAMOUS poet, a renowned wit, a prominent courtier in the eyes of his own and succeeding generations, Sir John Denham has become for us a curiously indistinct figure. We know the main outline of the events of his life, but little that brings his individuality before us. Few personal letters or manuscripts remain; his wit, save for one retort upon Wither, has perished; and he is known to us as a man chiefly through the gossip aroused by his unfortunate second marriage, his madness, and his wife's supposedly violent death.

As the husband of one of the Duke of York's mistresses, Denham certainly does not occupy a dignified position; as a man thought to have been driven mad by jealousy, his case is hardly better. He was, moreover, exposed to ridicule by not being fully qualified for the official position he held at court, that of Surveyor General. Evelyn did not think highly of his abilities as an architect, and Butler regarded him as not only incompetent but dishonest. He gambled inveterately. He is spoken of as vain and irreligious.

Yet it is Denham's misfortune that his weaknesses are so thrust upon our attention. The charge of gambling we must admit at once. The charge of vanity may or may not be true. With regard to religion, Johnson says, "As he appears, whenever any serious question comes before him, to have been a man of piety, he consecrated his poetical powers to religion, and made a metrical version of the psalms of David."[1] To support Johnson we might adduce the tone of many of his serious poems, such as *Cato Major* (including the preface), *Justice*, *Prudence*, *The Progress of Learning*, and others of less bulk, and the fact that in his will he bequeathed £100 and all his fees as "Surveyor General for the rebuilding of St. Paul's" for the furtherance of "that noble and pious work."[2]

Indeed, Denham has qualities, hardly mentioned by his contemporaries, that make him a figure worthy of some respect. His loyalty to the cause of the Stuarts throughout the whole period of the Civil

[1] Johnson, *Lives of the Poets* (ed. Waugh), I, 87-88.
[2] *Prerogative Court of Canterbury*, 57 Penn.

War is admirable. Of his numerous estates, many were confiscated by
Parliament, because of his support of his King. He was of active as-
sistance during the period of open hostilities; was constantly engaged
in the plotting of the Royalists during the Commonwealth; and
though he was never among the foremost of Charles I's advisers, or
of the exiles in the court of Charles II, yet he executed many less
important missions with faithfulness and success. After the Restora-
tion, Charles conferred upon him the honor of Knight of the Bath, and
while we cannot but feel that this was partly because Denham had
"diverted the evil hour of his banishment"[3] with his poetry, yet we
may well admit that the quality and amount of his services were such
as to deserve reward.

From Aubrey we learn something of his physical appearance. "He
was of the tallest, but a little incurvetting at his shoulders, not very
robust. His haire was but thin and flaxen, with a moist curle. His
gate was slow, and was rather a stalking (he had long legges) which
was wont to putt me in mind of Horace, *De Arte Poetica:*—

> Hic, dum sublimes versus ructatur et errat
> Si veluti merulis intentus decidit auceps
> In puteum foveamve.

His eie was a kind of light goose-gray, not big; but it had a strange
piercingness, not as to shining and glory, but (like a Momus) when
he conversed with you he look't into your very thoughts."[4] He was
lame,[5] and "unpolished with the small-pox; otherwise a fine com-
plexion."[6] "He delighted much in bowles, and did bowle very well."[7]

Of Denham's family comparatively little is known.[8] They may

[3] See *Epistle Dedicatory*, p. 60.
[4] Aubrey, *Brief Lives* (ed. A. Clark), I, 220.
[5] William Oldys's note in the British Museum copy of Gerard Langbaine, *An Account of the English Dramatic Poets*, p. 125. Butler, Samuel, *A Panegyric Upon Sir John Denham's Recovery from his Madness,* l. 29.
[6] Aubrey, *Brief Lives* (ed. A. Clark), I, 216.
[7] *Ibid.,* I, 220.
[8] For genealogy see Appendix C. For account of family arms, monumental in-
scriptions, etc., at Egham, see *Surrey Archaeological Collections,* XXX, 1;
XXXIII, 6.

have come originally from the west of England,[9] but the line cannot be traced back with certainty beyond his grandfather, William Denham, a goldsmith of London. The poet's father was Sir John Denham, an eminent lawyer and judge, who at the time of the poet's birth was the Chief Baron of the Exchequer in Ireland and one of the Lords Justices or Commissioners. His mother was Sir John's second wife, Eleanor Moore, the daughter of Sir Garret Moore, Baron Mellefont and Viscount Drogheda. When the poet was four years old, his mother died in giving birth to a child who died also.[10]

John Denham was born in Dublin in 1615; but in 1617, "before the Foggy Air of that Climate, could influence, or any way adulterate his Mind, he was brought from thence"[11] to England, where his father had been made one of the Barons of the Exchequer. Just where he went to school is uncertain, as both Wood and Aubrey are ignorant of this detail.[12] An examination of the extant records of the London schools then in existence does not reveal his name.

He was apparently early destined to follow his father in a legal career, for we find his name entered on the register of Lincoln's Inn on the twenty-sixth of April, 1631.[13] With this provision made for his future, he went to Oxford, and became a gentleman commoner of Trinity College November 18, 1631.[14] He continued at Oxford about three years, and in 1634 was "examined in the public schools for the degree of Bach. of Arts."[15] There is, however, no record of his taking a degree.

At Oxford his career was undistinguished. His life was that of the average undergraduate, more play than work, and he gave no indi-

[9] "Sir John told me his family was originally westerne." Aubrey, *Brief Lives* (ed. A. Clark), I, 221.

[10] Wood, Anthony, *Athenae Oxoniensis*, 1721, II, 422. Manning, Rev. Owen, *History and Antiquities of the County of Surrey*, 1804, III, 259.

[11] Langbaine, Gerard, *English Dramatic Poets*, 1691, p. 126.

[12] Wood, *Athenae Oxoniensis*, 1721, II, 422. Aubrey, *Brief Lives* (ed. A. Clark), I, 217.

[13] *Records of the Society of Lincoln's Inn. Admissions*, 1896, I, 213. This date is erroneously given as the twenty-eighth of April by Sir Sidney Lee in the *Dictionary of National Biography*.

[14] Foster, Joseph, *Alumni Oxoniensis*.

[15] Wood, *Athenae Oxoniensis*, 1721, II, 422.

cations of future ability. "Being looked upon as a slow and dreaming young man by his seniors and contemporaries, and given more to cards and dice than his study, they could never then in the least imagine that he could ever inrich the world with his fancy, or issue of his brain, as he afterward did."[16] Nor was he more prompt than the average undergraduate in paying his debts, if Aubrey's account may be trusted. "Sir John Denham had borrowed money of Mr. Whistler, the recorder, and, after a great while, the recorder askt him for it again. Mr. Denham laught at it, and told him he never intended that. The recorder acquainted the President, who at a lecture in the chapell, rattled him, and told him, 'Thy father haz hanged many an honester man.' "[17] At college, too, his love of gambling manifested itself. "I have heard Mr. Josias Howe say that he was the dreamingest young fellow; he never expected such things from him as he haz left the world. When he was there he would game extremely; when he had played away all his money, he would play away his father's wrought rich gold cappes."[18]

On June 25, 1634, he married, at the church of St. Bride's, in Fleet Street, Anne Cotton of Whittington, County Gloucester.[19] Of his wife's family little is known, save that they had held the manor of Whittington from the time of Henry VII. The male line failed soon after 1600, Anne being the last heir.[20] Denham's own family consisted of a son, who died in 1638,[21] and two daughters. The elder, Ann, married Sir William Morley of Halnaker, County Sussex;[22] the younger, Elizabeth,[23] married Sir Thomas Price, Bart., of Park Hall,

---

[16] Wood, *Athenae Oxoniensis*, 1721, II, 422.

[17] Aubrey, *Brief Lives* (ed. A. Clark), II, 18. It might be well to state that Aubrey's gossipy remarks are, in general, to be received with caution.

[18] *Ibid.*, I, 217.

[19] *Marriage Register of St. Bride's.*

[20] Atkyns, Sir Robert, *The Ancient and Present State of Glocestershire*, 1768, p. 428.

[21] *Parish register of Egham.*

[22] For a short account of Sir William, see *Sussex Archaeological Collections*, XXXI, 5, n. 3.

[23] I have determined the relative ages of the daughters as follows: Elizabeth was "about 21" in 1675. Cokayne, G. E., *Complete Baronetage*, 1903, III, 19. This would make the year of her birth about 1654, but we know from other evidence that this date is too late. Denham in 1647 refers to an estate

County Warwick.[24] Elizabeth had no children, and of Ann's five children only one had a child, who died an infant.[25] The direct line of descent fails, therefore, in three generations. The date of the death of Denham's first wife is unknown. It is certain, however, that it falls within the period between 1643 and 1647.[26]

From Oxford Denham went to Lincoln's Inn, where he applied himself seriously to the study of law, without, however, being able to discontinue his habits of gambling. Here too he seems to have been a normal young man, with his powers as a poet and a wit as yet undeveloped. "He was as good a student as any in the house. Was not suspected to be a witt."[27] "Tho' he followed his study very close to the appearance of all persons, yet he would game much, and frequent the company of the unsanctified crew of gamesters, who rook'd him sometimes of all he could wrap or get."[28] Once Denham indulged in an escapade that would do credit to a modern student. Aubrey tells the story amusingly. "He was generally temperate as to drinking; but one time . . . having been merry at the taverne with his camerades, late at night, a frolick came into his head, to gett a playsterer's brush and a pott of inke, and blott out all the signes between Temple-Barre and Charing-crosse, which made a strange confusion the next day, and 'twas in Terme time. But it happened that they were discovered, and it cost him and them some moneys. This I had from R. Estcott, esq. that carried the inke-pott."[29]

His father not unnaturally objected to Denham's gambling propensities, and John, to prove his reformation, and incidently to make

of his "late wife," so that Elizabeth must have been born in or before that year. *State Papers, Domestic*, LXXX, 171. There is no direct mention of Ann's age, but as we know that her mother was confined in 1643 (see p. 9) it is permissible to infer that Ann was born in that year.

[24] For a short account of Sir Thomas, see Cokayne, G. E., *Complete Baronetage*, 1903, III, 19.

[25] Berry, William, *County Genealogies, Pedigrees of the Families of the County of Sussex*, 1830, p. 76.

[26] See note 23 above.

[27] Aubrey, *Brief Lives* (ed. A. Clark), I, 217.

[28] Wood, *Athenae Oxoniensis*, 1721, II, 422.

[29] Aubrey, *Brief Lives* (ed. A. Clark), I, 220.

sure of his patrimony, wrote *The Anatomy of Play*, a pamphlet which exposes with admirable lucidity the evils of gambling.

In August, 1638, his son died, and was buried in the church at Egham, County Surrey, on the twenty-eighth, and on January 6 of the following year his father died.[30]

Denham inherited a considerable property: "2,000 or 1,500 li. in ready money, 2 houses well furnished, and much plate,"[31] and probably the numerous estates (exclusive of those held in right of his wife) that he possessed after the outbreak of hostilities. These were in Surrey, Essex, Bucks., and Suffolk. His favorite seat, and the one that he made his home, was that of Egham in Surrey. How sincere was the repentance that preserved this inheritance may be gathered from Aubrey's statement that "shortly after his father's death . . . the money was played away first, and next the plate was sold."[32]

He was called to the bar on January 29, 1639.[33] How much of a success he would have made of his legal career is, of course, a matter of speculation, but that he had strong literary leanings was evident. He had already written the *Destruction of Troy*, a translation in heroic couplets of the second book of the *Aeneid*, and perhaps a first draft of *Cooper's Hill*;[34] but he first came openly before the public in 1641 with his play of *The Sophy*, a tragic melodrama in blank verse. This "took extremely much, and was admired by all ingenious men, particularly by Edm. Waller of Beaconsfield, who then said of the author, that he broke out like the Irish Rebellion, threescore thousand strong, when no body was aware, or in the least suspected it."[35]

The outbreak of open war between Charles and the Parliament now interrupted Denham's pursuits, both legal and literary. He was, indeed, no extreme Royalist; of this we can find many indications in his poetry: (1) His elegy on Judge Crooke (see p. 156), one of the judges who opposed the sweeping claims of the King in the fa-

---

[30] *Parish Register of Egham.*

[31] Aubrey, *Brief Lives* (ed. A. Clark), I, 217-218.

[32] *Ibid.*

[33] *Records of the Society of Lincoln's Inn. The Black Books*, 1898, II, 350.

[34] There is strong reason to believe that he had made a complete translation of Books II to VI, inclusive. See p. 41.

[35] Wood, *Athenae Oxoniensis*, 1721, II, 423.

mous ship-money case, is perhaps indicative of Denham's attitude toward the royal prerogative; (2) in the 1642 edition of *The Sophy* there occurs a passage which is significantly omitted in the collected edition of 1668 (Act I, sc. ii, ll. 48 ff.). The Persian King, Abbas, wishes to raise additional supplies of money for his son who is at the wars. A Lord replies:

> Sir, your treasures
> Are quite exhausted; the exchequer's empty.

Abbas retorts:

> Talke not to me of treasures or exchequers.
> Send for five hundred of the wealthiest burgers—
> Their shops and ships are my exchequer,

And Abdall, another courtier, remarks aside:

> 'Twere better you could say their hearts.

This is clearly a reference, and an unfriendly one, to Charles's high-handed policy in the matter of ship-money. Motives of prudence no doubt prompted Denham to cancel this passage in 1668. Charles II would not have relished the allusion. (3) The concluding passage of the 1642 edition of *Cooper's Hill* runs as follows:

> Thus kings by grasping more then they could hold
> First made their subjects by oppression bold.
> And popular sway by forcing kings to give
> More then was fit for subjects to receive
> Ran to the same extreame, and one excesse
> Made both by striving to be greater lesse;
> Nor any way but seeking to have more
> Makes either lose what each possest before.
> Therefore their boundless power tell princes draw
> Within the channell and the shores of law,
> And may that law which teaches kings to sway
> Their scepters, teach their subjects to obey. (p. 87.)

From these passages it is clear that Denham had no sympathy with the doctrine that the sovereign was above the law, or his acts above criticism. Moreover, when we notice the curious absence from his poems of an elegy to Charles I, we cannot but wonder how far

Denham was influenced by motives of personal affection and loyalty
to the King.

Yet the legal mind that could not approve arbitrary and tyrannical
acts on the part of the King was still less able to sympathize with a
rebellion against the constitutional office of kingship. In the 1642 text
of *Cooper's Hill* we read:

> For armed subjects can have no pretence
> Against their princes but their just defence,
> And whether then or no I leave to them
> To justifie, who else themselves condemne.
> Yet might the fact be just, if we may guesse
> The justness of an action from successe. (p. 84.)

The actual murder of the King, an act plainly against the established
order, fills him with horror. In his elegy on Henry, Lord Hastings,
we find that the beheading was

> that impious stroke
> That sullied earth, and did heaven's pity choke. (p. 145.)

Whatever Denham's attitude may have been toward previous royal
acts, therefore, when open warfare began he did not hesitate to es-
pouse the King's cause, and remained faithful to it until the end.

Appointed High Sheriff for Surrey, and Governor of Farnham
Castle, Denham, with the Commissioners of Array for Surrey, col-
lected about a hundred soldiers, and took possession of the castle.[36]
The poet, George Wither, had a low opinion of this troop's fighting
qualities. "I should almost have scorned," he says, "to have de-
sired the aid of above two squadrons of my troop to have scattered
that despicable rout wherewith Sheriff Denham . . . and other
such like leaders of the same countie first robbed my house and
afterward seized the said castle, and victualled the same with my
stores as I purposed to have done,"[37] Wither's estimate of the Royal-
ists seems to have been correct, for, on December 1, Sir William
Waller had little difficulty in forcing them to surrender. He had

---

[36] Rushworth, J., *Historical Collections of Private Passages of State*, 1721, V, 81-82.
[37] Wither, George, *Se Defendendo*, p. 10.

only a small number of horse and dragoons,[38] but "within the space of three houres forced their approach so neare the castle-gates that with a petard they blew open one of them, and most resolutely made forcible entrance thereinto. Whereupon the Cavaleers within threw their Armes over the wall, fell downe upon their knees, crying for *Quarter,* (not so much as having once offered or desired to treat of any honourable conditions, to depart like Souldiers, before the castle was entered) which Sir *William* gave them. There was taken in this castle, one Master *Denham* the new high Sheriffe of *Surrey,* Captaine *Hudson,* Captaine *Brecknox,* a Brewer in *Southwarke,* a most desperate Malignant against the Parliament, and divers other prisoners of quality, with about an hundred vulgar persons, together with all the Armes and Ammunition in the castle, and about 40000 pounds in money and plate, as was credibly informed; besides that the common Souldiers had good pillage for themselves to a good value."[39] Although this is the enemy's version of the affair, Denham's part cannot be considered brilliant. He was sent prisoner to London, probably arriving there on December 3.[40] How long he remained in captivity we do not know, perhaps until after March 15, for on "this day Parson Keeley and some others of the Cavaliers that were taken at Farnham Castle were brought to the Lords House, but in regard of other weighty affairs of the kingdom they were ordered to come againe another day."[41] Upon being released, he rejoined the King at Oxford.

This seems to have involved considerable sacrifices on his part. His estates had, of course, been confiscated by Parliament, that of Egham falling to the poet Wither; but it would appear that now, in addition, he was forced to leave his wife, who was with child, to the mercies of his enemies. On May 11, 1643, the House empowered the Committee for Sequestration "to deliver unto her [Anne Denham]

[38] *A Perfect Diurnall of the Passages in Parliament* (printed for I. Okes and F. Leach), No. 25.
[39] Vicars, John, *Jehovah-Jireh . . . Englands Parliamentarie Chronicle,* 1644, p. 223.
[40] *A Perfect Diurnall of the Passages in Parliament* (printed for I. Okes and F. Leach), No. 25.
[41] *Ibid.* (printed for Cook and Wood), No. 41.

childbed linen, and such other necessaries as they shall think fit,"[42] and later approved her petition to return to Egham for her lying in. George Wither, the poet, complains bitterly of this: "I seized by the said order . . . some part of the goods and estates of . . . Master John Denham . . . The goods which were Master Denham's are by an order of some sequestrators taken out of my hands, and put into the possession of his wife, who (as do many other delinquents) findes much more favour then I, who have been ever faithful to the state. For when my wife and children had been cruelly driven out of their habitation, and robbed of all they had by her husband and his confederates, enemies to the Parliament, and when by virtue of the fore-mentioned order, I justly entred upon the house of the said Denham, purposing to harbour my said wife and children therein, Mistress Denham, having long before deserted the house, and left there only some tables, with such-like household stuffe, (though her husband sought, and yet seekes the destruction of the kingdome) was, upon false suggestions, put againe by order into possession of that house; because as her charitable petition alledged, shee was, forsooth, a gentlewoman, big with childe, and had a fancie to the place."[43] We know nothing further of the birth of this child, but it was probably Denham's eldest daughter, Ann.[44]

The paths of the two poets crossed once more, when Wither was later captured by the Royalists, and Denham wittily interceded for his life. "It [happened] that G[eorge] W[ither] was taken prisoner, and was in danger of his life, having written severely against the king &c. Sir John Denham went to the king, and desired his majestie not to hang him, for that whilest G[eorge] W[ither] lived he should not be the worst poet in England."[45]

Denham's circumstances must now have been greatly reduced. Most of his estates were lost; and such of his goods as the Parliament could lay hold of were sold in London on June 19, 1644.[46]

[42] *Journals of the Commons.*
[43] Wither, *Se Defendendo,* pp. 13-14.
[44] See p. 4, n. 23.
[45] Aubrey, *Brief Lives* (ed. A. Clark), I, 221.
[46] *Mercurius Aulicus, the 26th Weeke, ending June 29, 1644,* p. 1050.

Yet during this period his poetical reputation was rapidly increasing, because an edition of *Cooper's Hill*, the poem upon which his fame chiefly rests, appeared in London in 1642, and the first of the many reprints at Oxford in 1643.[47] Here too belong several of his satirical poems on the military and political events of the day.

Of Denham's part in the war from 1643 to 1646 we know nothing. Yet he was apparently of some influence and importance in the ranks of the Royalists, for we find in November, 1644, during the fruitless negotiations for a peace, that Parliament includes him in the group of persons they wish excluded from the King's counsels.[48] (He is also excluded in the proposals for the Treaty of Newport, 1648.)[49]

Apparently during this period he was separated from his wife and family, for we find in a petition of Anne Denham to the Committee for Sequestrations of November 25, 1645, the statement that "she hath ever lived in the parliament quarters."[50]

In January, 1645/6, he was in Dartmouth during the siege and capture of that town, and, with the Earl of Newport, was instrumental in inducing the governor to surrender the castle after the city itself had been taken.[51] Newport and Denham were sent prisoners to London in the custody of Hugh Peters, where they arrived January 23.[52] On February 4 orders were issued by the House of Commons for Denham's exchange with Major Harris,[53] who was held prisoner by the Royalists at Exeter.[54]

He therefore went to this city, and remained there as a member of the garrison during the siege by Fairfax. After the surrender of Exeter on April 9, 1646, the Royalists were permitted to leave the country or to retire to their homes on condition of not engaging fur-

[47] For editions of this poem see Appendix F, Part II.
[48] *Journal of the Lords*, Nov. 8, 1644.
[49] *Ibid.*, Oct. 17, 1648.
[50] *State Papers, Interregnum, B*, 11.
[51] For a full account of the capture of Dartmouth, see Sir Thomas Fairfax's *Letter to Both Houses more exactly and fully relating the storming and taking of Dartmouth*.
[52] *Journal of the Commons*, Jan. 23, 1645/6.
[53] *Ibid.*, Feb. 4, 1645/6.
[54] *Journal of the Lords*, May 4, 1646.

ther in the war. Generous terms were offered to them if they wished to compound.

Denham, however, appears to have encountered difficulties. There were civil actions against him for debt, and he found himself again in London, a prisoner. On April 27 the Committee for Prisoners ordered his discharge, but Sir John Lenthall refused to permit it, believing that it was illegal. Denham, therefore, petitioned the Lords for a habeas corpus, and on May 4 this was issued.[55] On the same day the Lords voted to approve the action of the Commons of February 4 in exchanging him for Major Harris. On May 11 he appeared before the Lords, was arrested by his creditors before he left the precincts of Parliament, and on the Lords' order was at once released.[56]

In accordance with the terms of his surrender at Exeter, Denham left at once for France, where he joined Queen Henrietta Maria. Here he remained for nearly a year, until, at her command, he returned to England. He gave as his ostensible reason his wish to compound with Parliament for his delinquency, and for this purpose a pass was granted to him on March 24, 1646/7,[57] but his real motive was to join Sir Edward Ford in the attempt to intercede between the King and Parliament. His friendship with Mr. Hugh Peters, "a preacher and a powerful person in the army,"[58] which he had contracted when in prison the year before, was probably an inducement for the Queen to send him. Through the help of Peters, he gained his admission to the King. He was not, however, considered sufficiently influential for this mission, and Sir John Berkeley was sent after him, because it was "necessary to employ some to the Army, that might be supposed to have greater Trust both with the Queen in *France*, and with the King in *England* than either Sir *Edward Ford* or Mr. *Denham* had."[59] In the negotiations that fol-

---

[55] *Journal of the Lords*, May 4, 1646. *Historical MSS. Commission, Report 6*, p. 115.

[56] *Journal of the Lords*, May 11, 1646.

[57] *Ibid.*, March 24, 1646/7.

[58] Berkeley, Sir John, *Memoirs of Sir John Berkeley*, 1699, p. 4.

[59] *Ibid.*, p. 5.

lowed, Denham played but a small part, though he was once, with several others, called into consultation by the King.[60]

For the next few months he was either in attendance on Charles or in London. In November the King escaped from his confinement at Hampton Court, and in this Denham may have had some share. He was suspected of being in the plot, as we learn from a letter describing the King's escape. "This day his Majesty . . . spent most part of this day in writing . . . After supper one of them knocking, his Majesty answered not . . . it seems his Majesty was gone through the garden and park and so away. . . . some gentlemen passed this night over Kingston bridge, supposed to be his Majesty, with Sir Edward Ford, Sir John Bartlet [Berkeley?], Mr. Ashburnham and Mr. Denham."[61] Moreover, when he says in the dedication of the 1668 edition, "at his [the King's] departure from *Hampton Court* he was pleased to command me to stay privately at London," he seems to imply that he was present on that occasion.

Denham remained in London, and the following month petitioned Parliament to be allowed to compound for his delinquency, obtaining from Fairfax a certification of his presence in Exeter in order to take advantage of the terms of the articles of surrender of that city.[62] Under cover of this he busied himself in the Royalist ciphered correspondence and intrigues, as we know from his statement in the preface to the 1668 collected poems, and from references to him, in letters of January, February, 1647/8, and of April 1648.[63] On April 21 the Duke of York escaped from his confinement in St. James Palace. Just what part Denham had in this is uncertain. Wood says that "he conveyed or stole away James, Duke of York, . . . and carried him into France to the Prince and the Queen Mother."[64] Clarendon, on the other hand, does not mention him in this connection, and Denham himself says that he remained in London about nine months after the

[60] Berkeley, Sir John, *Memoirs of Sir John Berkeley*, 1699, p. 37.

[61] A letter from Edward Helaw to Commons, Nov. 11, 1647. *The kings Majesties most gratious message, with a perfect narrative of the manner of his Majesties going from Hampton Court*, 1647.

[62] *Calendar of the Committee for Compounding*, p. 1790.

[63] Carte, Tho., *A Collection of Original Letters*, 1739, II, 351-352. Camden Society Publications, *Hamilton Papers*, pp. 148, 153.

[64] Wood, *Athenae Oxoniensis*, 1721, II, 423.

King's departure from Hampton Court, or until about July.[65] It is probable that Denham's share in the Duke's escape was, at most, but a small one. It is indicated, perhaps, in the following: the Duke "stole away . . . alone, but was soone mett by some that stayed for him, the Chief whereof is thought to be Collonel Bamfield."[66] In May the Prince of Wales writes to the Marquis of Hertford that Denham will relate the proceedings in England,[67] and in June the Prince instructs one Humfrey Boswell to report to Denham in London, and "proceed in all things by his advice."[68] In July the Royalist correspondence was discovered "by their knowledge of Mr. Cowley's hand,"[69] and Denham fled to France. At this time his wife was dead, and his children probably under the guardianship of Colonel Fielder.[70]

For the next four years, 1648-1652, Denham lived abroad in attendance on Charles, and employed in various missions. In September, 1648, he was sent by the Prince to Scotland, to investigate the general condition of the country, and to determine the strength of the Stuart cause there. He was to remain in Scotland until recalled, but when this occurred we do not know.[71]

In March, 1649, he left the court of Charles II at the Hague and went with the Duke of York into France to the Queen,[72] and in May returned with instructions from her.[73] Early in August, 1649, Charles appointed him and William Crofts ambassadors to Poland,[74] to treat for supplies, and to raise money from the King's Scottish subjects in that country. He succeeded, he tells us, in collecting £10,000. He must have been absent on this mission until

[65] *Epistle Dedicatory*, p. 60.
[66] *Sydney Papers, consisting of . . . original letters of Algernon Sydney*, 1825 (ed. Blencowe), pp. 33-34.
[67] *Historical MSS. Commission, Pepys MS.*, p. 279.
[68] *Ibid.*, p. 211.
[69] *Epistle Dedicatory*, p. 60.
[70] Colonel Fielder was, at any rate, their guardian in 1650. *Calendar of the Committee for Compounding*, p. 1790.
[71] *Historical MSS. Commission, Pepys MS.*, p. 227.
[72] *Ibid., Popham MS.*, p. 10.
[73] *Letters of Queen Henrietta Maria*, 1857 (ed. M. A. E. Green), p. 361.
[74] *Perfect occurrences of Every Daies journall in Parliament, Aug. 3-10, 1649*.

May or June 1651,[75] when he undoubtedly returned to the court of Charles. To this period of his life we can assign the poems *On my Lord Croft's and my Journey into Poland, On Mr. Tho. Killigrew's return from his Embassie from Venice, and Mr. William Murray's from Scotland*, and perhaps one or two others.

On May 13, 1652, Sir Edward Nicholas, Secretary of State to Charles, writes to Mr. Smith [Lord Hatton] from The Hague: "Mr. Denham hath here lately had very ill luck at play, which hath made him (I am told) in great want at present. He talks of going for England, but it is thought intends not to adventure it, more for fear what his creditors than the rebels there will do against him."[76]

Denham's affairs were indeed desperate. All his lands were lost, having been either sold by him or confiscated by Parliament. He owed large sums of money.[77] Yet early in 1653 he ventured back. Soon after his arrival, he was called up before a Parliamentary committee to be examined,[78] but appears to have escaped further molestation, even by his creditors. This is probably due to the fact that he returned under the protection of the Earl of Pembroke, who was a member of Cromwell's council of state for that year and a person of importance in the Commonwealth, and who may well have made himself responsible for Denham's good behavior.

By 1650 Denham's composition for his estate had been completed; one fifth was allowed him, which was to be paid to Colonel Fielder, member of Parliament for St. Ives Cornwall, the guardian of his children, and trustee of his estate, undoubtedly for the support of the children.[79]

With Pembroke, Denham remained for about a year at the Earl's estate at Wilton, and in London. He had now presumably more ease and leisure than he had had for some years previously, and he evidently cultivated it in a more extensive writing of poetry, for to this

[75] *On my Lord Croft's and my Journey into Poland*, p. 107.
[76] Camden Society Publications, *Nicholas Papers*, I, 300.
[77] Aubrey, *Brief Lives* (ed. A. Clark), I, 218. *Journals of the Commons*, July 1, 1651. *Acts & Ordinances of the Interregnum*, II, 545. *Calendar for Committee on Compounding*, I-III, *passim*.
[78] *Calendar State Papers, Domestic, 1652-1653*, p. 193.
[79] *Calendar of the proceedings of the Committee for Compounding*, p. 1790.

period we can assign some translations of Virgil,[80] and in addition, perhaps, the revised version of *Cooper's Hill*, published in 1655. Yet if his material circumstances were now low, his poetical reputation was high. In a letter of intelligence to Thurloe from Paris of September 20, 1653, we read: "I have sent this enclosed song [a French drinking song] which if Englished by one Denham, I hear to be the state's poet, truly it will be much to the instruction of the youth of our country."[81]

We hear nothing of Denham for the next two years, save that he visited Evelyn on April 6, 1654;[82] but early in June, 1655, he was arrested in London, together with a number of other Royalists.[83] All of them except Denham were committed to the Tower or to the custody of the Serjeant at Arms, but in his case it was ordered that he "be confined to a place chosen by himself, not within 20 miles of London."[84] Where that was we do not know, nor do we know why he was treated with this special consideration. Perhaps it was again due to the Earl of Pembroke. Denham was at this time, as also, no doubt, during his whole stay in England, aiding the Royalist cause to the best of his ability by corresponding with the court of Charles, keeping him informed of conditions in England, and by conveying dispatches, instructions, etc., to the Stuart adherents in England.[85] He went on such a mission to the Earl of Carbery in Wales some time in 1655.[86] By the beginning of 1656 he was back in England, for on January 5 he again visited Evelyn.[87]

Our knowledge of his movements once more fails until June, 1657, when he appears in Brussels, cognizant of the Duke of Buckingham's movements, who was "believed to be in England, upon some desperate design, for a rising in the city or against the Protector's

[80] Wood, *Athenae Oxoniensis*, 1721, II, 423. Aubrey, *Brief Lives* (ed. A. Clark), I, 218.

[81] Thurloe, John, *A Collection of State Papers*, 1742, I, 471.

[82] Evelyn, *Diary*.

[83] *Calendar State Papers, Domestic, 1655*, p. 204. (See *Verses on the Cavaliers*, p. 135.)

[84] *Ibid.*

[85] *Ibid.*, pp. 193, 212.

[86] *Calendar of the Clarendon State Papers*, 1872, III, 58.

[87] Evelyn, *Diary*.

person."[88] We do not know when Denham had left England, but he must have returned by March, 1658, for on the eleventh of that month a license was granted him by Cromwell to live in Bury, County Suffolk.[89] Whether he took advantage of this permission is not known.[90] His friend, John Pooley (see p. 103) was living in the manor house of the family at Boxstead, some nine or ten miles from Bury. Denham may therefore have selected this locality in order to visit or to be near Pooley.

In September he again left England, this time with the official sanction of the Commonwealth. On the fourteenth, a pass was granted to William Lord Herbert, Mr. Denham and five servants to go beyond seas.[91] As Lord Herbert was the eighteen-year-old son and heir of the Earl of Pembroke, this indicates that Denham went abroad as guardian and companion of the boy, perhaps to make the grand tour, and suggests that the relations between Denham and the Earl of Pembroke were close. Unfortunately most of the family papers of the Herberts have been destroyed by fire, and those that remain contain no information about the poet.[92]

In the stir and confusion preceding the Restoration, Denham's loyalty and services to the Royalist cause did not pass unnoticed. One Mr. Broderick writes to Hyde, who was now Lord Chancellor, on January 13, 1660: "Of Mr. Denham there is at this time an universal good opinion, and if your Lordship would engage him by a letter, or induce his Majesty to write, I know not anything absolutely in your own power so advantageous. The man I know full well, his former intrigues, dependencies, expectations, his present condition, temper and reputation; and though I have ever wished it might be achieved by your own dependents, I must now propose his

---

[88] *Calendar State Papers, Domestic, 1657-1658*, p. 6. *Calendar of the Clarendon State Papers*, III, 307. The "desperate design" was to marry the daughter of Fairfax, in which he succeeded.

[89] *Calendar State Papers, Domestic, 1657-1658*, p. 552.

[90] A few miles from Bury there is the village of Denham, but I have been able to find no connection between the family who lived there and the poet's. In any case the manor passed out of their possession in the fourteenth century.

[91] *Ibid., 1658-1659*, p. 580.

[92] A letter of the Earl of Pembroke to me.

adoption into that number as the last remedy (if I were to speak my last) I could upon the most sober thought I am capable of deliver to you. . . . Many objections I have made to myself, his familiarity with the Duke of Bucks. George Porter &c, but sure I am they will be as much strangers to his business as acquainted with his diversions."[93] The value of this testimony is uncertain, since I have been able to discover nothing about the writer, but his chief point, that Denham would make a conscientious servant of the King, seems borne out by Denham's previous and subsequent conduct.

Denham hardly needed this strong recommendation to the King, for Charles had already promised him the reversion of the post of Surveyor of the Works upon the death of Inigo Jones (which occurred in 1651), and on June 30, 1660, officially confirmed his promise.[94]

This appointment met with a protest from John Webb, the deputy of Jones, and his nephew, who petitioned the King for the place for himself, advancing the argument that "though Mr. Denham may, as most gentry, have some knowledge of the theory of architecture, he can have none of the practice, but must employ another."[95] Webb, although unsuccessful in dislodging Denham, secured the promise of the reversion of the post and became his assistant. Yet Christopher Wren, who was appointed sole deputy to Denham on March 6, 1669,[96] succeeded him on his death, which occurred shortly after. It is probable that Webb's estimate of Denham's architectural abilities was not far from correct; it was, at any rate, shared by Evelyn. "I went," he says, "to London to visite my Lord of Bristoll, having been with Sir John Denham (his Maties surveyor) to consult with him about the placing of his palace at Greenwich, which I would have had built between the river and the Queene's house, so as a large square cutt should have let in ye Thames like a bay; but Sir John was for setting it on piles at the very brink of the water, which I did not assent to, and so came away, knowing

[93] Clarendon, State Papers Collected by Edward, Earl of, 1786, III, 644-645.
[94] Calendar State Papers, Domestic, 1660-1661, p. 72.
[95] Ibid., 1660-1661, p. 76.
[96] Ibid., 1668-1669, pp. 224, 227.

Sir John to be a better poet than architect, tho' he had Mr. Webb (Inigo Jones's man) to assist him."[97] Samuel Butler also thought little of him as an architect, for he remarks,

> For had the stones, like his [Amphion], charmed by your verse,
> Built up themselves they could not have done worse;[98]

and, in addition, accuses him of cheating the King in a variety of ways. Yet Denham was active in his office, and we have a record of several important buildings put up under his supervision, among them Burlington House, and Greenwich Palace.[99] His offices and house (which he also built) were in Scotland Yard. During the great fire of 1666 these were "uncovered and defaced for preventing the further spreading thereof," and were not repaired for nearly two years.[100]

However good or bad he may have been as an architect, there is at least one substantial practical achievement to his credit, an improvement in the condition of the pavements of London. Evelyn, in dedicating his translation of Freart's treatise on architecture to Denham, speaks of this in glowing terms: "But neither here must I forget what is alone due to you, Sir, for the reformation of a thousand deformities in the streets, as by your introducing that incomparable form of paving, to an incredible advantage of the publick, when that which is begun in Holburn shall become universal, for the saving of wheels and carriages, the cure of noysom gutters, the deobstruction of encounters, the dispatch of business, the cleanness of the way, the beauty of the object, the ease of the infirme, and the preserving of both the mother and the babe; so many of the fair sex and their offspring having perished by mischances (as I am credibly inform'd) from the ruggedness of the unequal streets."[101]

Charles's honors to Denham did not stop with the granting of the

---

[97] Evelyn, *Diary*, Oct. 19, 1661.

[98] Butler, Samuel, *A Panegyric upon Sir John Denham's Recovery from his Madness*, ll. 45-46.

[99] Pepys, *Diary*, Sept. 28, 1668.

[100] *Calendar Treasury Books, 1667-1668*, p. 598.

[101] Freart, Roland, *A Parallel of the Antient Architecture with the Modern*, 1664, Dedication.

surveyorship. At his coronation he made Denham a Knight of the Bath, and later bestowed other favors: the office of "Clerk of the Works in the Tower of London and in all his majesty's honors, castles etc. reserved for his abode";[102] valuable grants of land and leases in London and Norfolk;[103] the authorization (together with the Marquis of Ormond and O'Neille, a groom of the bedchamber) "to prosecute any person who had injured the royal castles or parks during the commonwealth, and to keep three parts of the money collected for their own use";[104] and from time to time specific sums of money.[105] Nor was he favored by the King alone, for on April 29, 1661, he was returned as member of Parliament for Old Sarum, County Wilts.[106] and on May 20, 1663, was elected a member of the Royal Society.[107]

For the first five years after the Restoration, Denham is not conspicuous among the courtiers, and we hear little or nothing of him aside from the routine of official business. At the coronation, April, 1661, he superintended, doubtless *ex-officio*, the paving of Westminster, and the construction of a throne and other necessities.[108] On March 22, 1663, he and Waller are appointed censors for a certain play;[109] in the same year we find him performing a small act of charity.[110] To this period belongs a letter of introduction which he wrote to Sir George Lane, secretary to the Duke of Ormonde. It is of little interest in itself, but we may be justified in reproducing it, as it is the nearest approach to a personal letter of Denham's that has as yet been discovered. "The bearer herof,"

[102] *Calendar Treasury Books, 1660-1667,* p. 375.

[103] *Calendar State Papers, Domestic, passim.*

[104] *Egerton MS. 2551,* p. 137.

[105] *Calendar State Papers, Domestic, 1660-1661,* p. 452: *1667,* p. 116: *1667-1668,* p. 176. *Calendar Treasury Books, 1667-1668,* p. 161.

[106] *Parliament, 1878. House of Commons Accounts & Papers,* vol. 62, part I, p. 531. Old Sarum was one of the most notorious of the "rotten boroughs." I have not been able to discover who had the gift of the seat at this time.

[107] *The Record of the Royal Society. Chronological Register of Fellows.*

[108] *Calendar Treasury Books, 1660-1667,* p. 232. *Calendar State Papers, Domestic, 1663-1664,* p. 238.

[109] *Calendar State Papers, Domestic, 1663-1664,* p. 83.

[110] *Ibid.,* p. 423.

he writes, "my kinsman, Dr. Denham, is the gentleman concerning whom I spoke to you at London, who, when you have some knowledge of him will recomend himselfe better to you then I can. What his pretentions are I know not, but whether they concerne the(y) body naturall, or the body politick, he is very capable of serving his Grace in either, and if for your favour to him I can make you a returne of any service here, I shall thinke myself very happy to have it in my power to do it, being most unfeinedly Sir, your most affectionate kinsman and most faithfull servant."[111]

On May 25, 1665, at Westminster Abbey he married for the second time, and at once became a prominent figure in the gossip and slander of the next three years. His wife was Margaret Brooke, third daughter of Sir William Brooke, K.B., by his second wife Penelope, daughter of Sir Moses Hill.[112] The match was unequal in many respects. Lady Denham was young (being only twenty-three) and beautiful, and soon became notorious as the mistress of the Duke of York; while Denham was fifty, and must have looked older, as Aubrey describes him as "ancient and limping,"[113] and Grammont gives his age as seventy-nine.[114]

A year later Denham became mad. This "first appeared," says Aubrey, "when he went from London to see the famous free-stone quarries at Portland in Dorset, and when he came within a mile of it, turned back to London again, and did not see it. He went to Hownslowe and demanded rents of lands he had sold many yeares before; went to the king and told him he was the Holy Ghost."[115] On March 3, 1666, the King, on Denham's behalf, summoned Valen-

111 Historical MSS. Commission, *Ormonde MS., New Series* (1904), III, 19-20. I have not been able to establish the kinship of either Dr. Denham or Sir George Lane.
112 Wood, *Athenae Oxoniensis*, 1721, II, 423. Chester, J. L., *Marriage, Baptism & Burial Register of Westminster*, 1876, p. 4.
113 Aubrey, *Brief Lives* (ed. A. Clark), I, 219.
114 Grammont, *Memoirs* (ed. Sir Walter Scott), p. 185. A poem of Waller's on the marriage, referring to the disparity of ages and Denham's lameness, is printed by G. Thorn-Drury in *A Little Ark, containing Seventeenth Century Verse*, 1921, p. 33.
115 Aubrey, *Brief Lives* (ed. A. Clark), I, 219.

tine Greatrakes, "the Irish stroker," but his efforts were ineffectual.[116] Denham's final collapse seems to have been sudden. We find a record in Wood's journal for April 8, 1666, that he was dead, which was subsequently corrected to "not yet dead, but distracted."[117] On April 9, Sir Paul Neile writes to H. Slingesby: "Sir John Denham is very sick, if not dead, in Somersetshire. His wife went hence late on Saturday night to travel night and day to see him before he died if she could.—Thus far was written on Monday, and since then there is nothing new; for we hear nothing more of Sir John Denham, and therefore I hope he will scape the fit."[118] On April 14 Sir Stephen Fox writes to Sir George Lane: "Sir John Denham, that great master of wit and reason, is fallen quite mad, and he who despised religion, now in his distraction raves of nothing else."[119] On April 17, George Walsh writes to Henry Slingesby: "Sir John Denham is now stark mad, which is occasioned (as is said by some) by the rough striking of Greatrakes upon his limbs; for they say that formerly having taken the fluxing pills in Holland, and they not working, they rubbed his shins with mercury, but . . . they supposed it lodged in the nerves till the harsh strokes caused it to sublimate."[120] On April 24 Sir Paul Neile writes to Slingesby: "Sir John Denham did not die, but is fallen violently mad, and so is likely to continue: he is now at one Dr. Lentall's house at the Charter House. The doctor is one that pretends to cure those in this condition, and to him Dr. Fraiser and the rest sent him: what that means you can safely imagine. Hugh May execute[s] his place during his infirmity,[121] and it is no hard thing to guess at the meaning of that neither."[122]

How long his madness lasted we do not know, but that it could not have been of long duration is proved by the fact that in September,

---

[116] *Calendar State Papers, Ireland, 1666-1669*, p. 52.
For an account of the man and his remarkable cures, see the *Dictionary of National Biography*.
[117] *The Life and Times of Anthony Wood*, 1892 (ed. A. Clark), II, p. 75.
[118] *Historical MSS. Commission, Report 6*, p. 339.
[119] *Ibid., Ormonde MS., New Series* (1904), III, 217.
[120] *Ibid., Report 6*, p. 339.
[121] *Calendar State Papers, Domestic, 1665-1666*, p. 354.
[122] *Historical MSS. Commission, Report 6*, p. 339.

1666, when Parliament reassembled, he is recorded as continuing his duties as a member of various committees and otherwise.[123] He remained in regular attendance during the sessions of 1666 and 1667.[124]

Yet, though not insane, he was still noticeably eccentric. Lord Lisle in a letter to Sir William Temple, dated September 26, 1667, says: "Poor Sir John Denham is fallen to the ladies also. He is at many of the meetings at dinners, talks more than ever he did, and is extremely pleased with those that seem willing to hear him; and from that obligation exceedingly praises the Duchess of Monmouth and my Lady Cavendish; if he had not the name of being mad, I believe in most companies he would be thought wittier than ever he was. He seems to have few extravagancies, besides that of telling stories of himself, which he is always inclined to. Some of his acquaintance say, that extreme vanity was a cause of his madness, as well as it is an effect."[125]

There is little doubt that his insanity was due to a form of paresis, arising from early excesses.[126] Yet the opinion seems to have been general that he went mad through jealousy of his wife's intrigue with the Duke of York, the coincidence in dates making this interpretation natural.[127] The affair was notorious. Many verses were printed referring derisively to Denham as a cuckold.[128] In a number of frank comments, Pepys indicates the progress of the affair. On June 10, 1666, he writes: "He [Pierce, the surgeon] tells me further how the Duke of Yorke is wholly given up to his new mistresse, my Lady Denham, going at noon-day with all his gentlemen with him to visit her in Scotland Yard; she declaring she will not be his mistresse as Mrs. Price, to go up and down the privy-stairs, but will be owned publicly; and so she is."[129] On September 26, 1666: "Here [White-

---

[123] *Journal of the Commons*, September 21, 22, 24.

[124] See T. W. Baldwin, *Sir John Denham and Paradise Lost, Modern Language Notes*, December, 1927, p. 508.

[125] Temple, Sir William, *Works*, 1814, I, 459.

[126] Pepys, Diary, Aug. 15, 1664.

[127] So Wood and Aubrey.

[128] Thorn-Drury, G., *A Little Ark, containing Seventeenth Century Verse*, 1921, p. 33. *Historical MSS. Commission, Report 6*, p. 458. Marvel, *Last Instructions to a Painter*, ll. 151-154.

[129] Pepys, *Diary*, June 10, 1666.

hall] I had the hap to see my Lady Denham . . . and the Duke of Yorke taking her aside and talking to her in the sight of all the world, all alone; which was strange, and what also I did not like. Here I met with good Mr. Evelyn, who cries out against it, and calls it bitchering, for the Duke of Yorke talks a little to her, and then she goes away, and then he follows her again like a dog."[130]

The scandal took a new turn in November, 1666, when Lady Denham fell ill, and the rumor at once became current that she was poisoned. Pepys remarks on November 10: "This afternoon . . . I hear that my Lady Denham is exceeding sick, even to death, and that she says and every body else discourses, that she is poysoned."[131] On November 15, H. Muddiman writes to George Powell: "Lady Denham is recovering; some have raised strange discourses about the cause of her sickness, but the physicians affirm it to have been *iliaca passio*."[132] Her improvement was but temporary. She continued sick for two months,[133] and died on January 6, 1667. On the seventh Pepys says: ". . . my Lady Denham is at last dead. Some suspect her poisoned, but it will be best known when her body is opened, which will be to-day, she dying yesterday morning. The Duke of Yorke is troubled for her; but hath declared he will never have another public mistress again."[134]

The autopsy revealed no trace of poison,[135] but the gossip continued unchecked. The number of people accused of administering the drug is remarkable. The very fact that the suspicion was so widely scattered proves better than anything else how unfounded it was, but the gossip is interesting for its own sake. On January 8, 1667, Lord Conway writes to Sir George Rawdon: "My Lady Denham died poisoned, as she said herself, in a cup of chocolate."[136] Marvel makes several references to the affair:

[130] Pepys, *Diary*, Sept. 26, 1666. See also Oct. 8, 13, 15, 1666.
[131] *Ibid.*, Nov. 10, 1666.
[132] *Calendar State Papers, Domestic, 1666-1667*, pp. 262-263.
[133] Pepys, *Diary*, Dec. 12, 1666.
[134] *Ibid.*, Jan. 7, 1667.
[135] Boyle, Roger, *First Earl of Orrery, A Collection of the State Letters of*, 1742, p. 219.
[136] Bramhall, John, *The Rawdon Papers, consisting of Letters . . . to and from Dr. John Bramhall*, 1819, p. 227.

> What frosts to fruits, what arsnick to the rat,
> What to fair Denham mortal chocolat,
> What an account to Carteret, that and more
> A Parliament is to the Chancellor.[137]

Again:

> Express her [the Duchess of York] studying now, if china clay
> Can, without breaking, venom'd juice convey:
> Or how a mortal poison she may draw
> Out of the cordial meal of the cacoa.[138]

The Duchess of York was also suspected of accomplishing her design by means of "powder of diamond."[139] Aubrey states that she was "poysoned by the hands of Co. of Roc[hester] with chocolatte."[140]

Denham himself did not escape suspicion. Grammont has a picturesque but incredible version of his own: "Old Denham, naturally jealous, became more and more suspicious . . . he had no country house to which he could carry his unfortunate wife. This being the case, the old villain made her travel a much longer journey without stirring out of London . . . as no person entertained any doubt of his having poisoned her, the populace of his neighborhood had a design of tearing him in pieces, as soon as he should come abroad; but he shut himself up to bewail her death, until their fury was appeased by a magnificent funeral, at which he distributed four times more burnt wine than had ever been drunk at any burial in England."[141]

As a final touch we learn that the Duchess of York was soon afterward "troubled with the apparition of the Lady Denham, and through anxiety bit off a piece of her tongue."[142]

Denham profited by the remission of his disease sufficiently to

[137] Marvel, *Last Instructions to a Painter*, ll. 341-344. See also *Clarendon's House Warming*, stanza 7.

[138] Marvel, *Last Instructions to a Painter*, ll. 65-68.

[139] *A Key to Grammont's Memoirs*, annexed to 1719 edition, note on "old D—m."

[140] Aubrey, *Brief Lives* (ed. A. Clark), I, 219.

[141] Grammont, *Memoirs* (ed. Sir Walter Scott), pp. 207-208.

[142] Sir Sidney Lee in the *Dictionary of National Biography* gives this as "according to Henry Newcome." I have been unable to trace or verify this reference.

write his eulogy of Cowley, one of his best poems. This, together with the translation of Mancinus (see p. 189), occupied the summer of 1668 when he was at Epsom. He had not, however, long to live. On March 6, 1669, Wren was appointed Deputy Surveyor "at the request of Sir John Denham . . . on account of his weakness."[143] He died at his office on March 10, 1669,[144] probably of apoplexy. There was apparently some hesitation as to the disposition of his body, for his friend Mr. Christopher Wase, in *An Elegy upon Sr John Denham, Kn^t of ye Bath, Lately deceased,* indignantly demands:

> What means this silence, that may seeme to doome
> Denham to have an undistinguished tombe?
> Is it astonishment? or deep respect
> To matchlesse witt? it cannot be neglect.
> What e'er th' excuse, it must not be allow'd
> In loathed oblivion so much worth to shrowd.[145]

Yet Wase's estimate of Denham's worth and abilities was shared by the authorities, and Denham received the highest honor that can fall to the lot of an English poet. He was buried, on March 23, in the Poets' Corner of Westminster Abbey.

When we turn from his life to his poetry, we find that he has "become a name." His reputation, which once made him one of the foremost English poets, has steadily declined, and he now does little more than share with Waller a paragraph in a History of Literature as the father of the Augustan closed couplet. I cannot say that the judgment of time is not in the main just. Nevertheless, his poetry deserves study, if only to throw light on the poetical tastes and tendencies of his day.

"Lord Dorset," says Pope, ". . . and Lord Rochester should be considered as holiday-writers; as gentlemen that diverted themselves now and then with poetry, rather than as poets. . . . There is no

---

[143] *Calendar State Papers, Domestic, 1668-1669,* p. 227.

[144] Blount, Sir T. P., *De Re Poetica, Characters & Censures,* 1694, p. 66.

[145] *State Papers, Domestic, Charles II,* vol. 270, p. 182. For Wase, see p. 39, note 173.

one of our poets of that class, that was more judicious than Sir John Denham."[146] Southey, after denying Denham's title to a reformer of the verse of his time, continues: ". . . but it was easy to avoid the more obvious faults of inferior authors; and in this he succeeded, just so far, as not to be included in 'the mob of gentlemen who wrote with ease'; nor consigned to oblivion with the 'Persons of Quality' who contributed their vapid effusions to the miscellanies of those days. His proper place is among those of his contemporaries and successors who called themselves Wits, and have since been entitled Poets by the courtesy of England."[147] These two criticisms are the only ones I have come upon that attempt to fix Denham's place among his contemporaries. Pope considers him a holiday-writer, Southey a wit; but neither regards him as qualified for the high title of poet.

It is perfectly true that Denham was not a poet in Pope's sense of the word, a man who made the writing of verse the chief business of his life. Many of his poems, as he himself says in his dedication to Charles II, were written "to divert and put off the evil hours of our banishment." He was a courtier and a wit. Yet when we subtract the numerous light and occasional verses from his work—and it is significant to observe that almost all of them fall within the period of the Civil War and the Commonwealth, when Denham was actively engaged in the Royalist cause—there remains a sufficient body of serious poetry to make both Pope's and Southey's classification misleading.

Essentially Denham's poetry is didactic. He has little imagination, little emotion, little beauty of phrase; his strength lies in his thought, in his neatly turned expressions of ethical and moral truisms. If his work is of the same class as Dorset's, Rochester's, and the rest of the wits, it is curious that he wrote no love poetry, or that he undertook anything so exacting as a paraphrase of the Psalms, or extended pieces of translation. His is a dignified position, and however far he may be from a great poet (and the distance is

[146] Spence, Joseph, *Anecdotes*, 1820, pp. 281-283.
[147] Southey, Robert, *The Life and Works of William Cowper*, 1836, II, 130-131.

considerable), we must recognize that he took his calling more seriously than many of his contemporaries.[148] Johnson realized this when he said, "He appears when any serious question comes before him to have been a man of piety."[149] Denham's muse is fundamentally a sober one.

The variety of his work is remarkable; he demands consideration as an original writer of both light and serious verse, as a translator, and as a playwright. Many of his serious poems are elegies or eulogies. While there is a noticeable Royalist bias to some of them, they are, as a whole, greatly superior to the mass of adulatory poetry of the time; they are more restrained, and in better taste. Very few are addressed to the nobility, and many are literary in theme.

Of his light verse, much is satire: political in *A Western Wonder, A Second Western Wonder, To the Five Members, A Speech against Peace,*[150] personal in a *Dialogue between Sir John Pooley and Mr. Thomas Killigrew, Verses on the Cavaliers;* religious in *News from Colchester;* poetical in his verses on Davenant's *Gondibert,* and his mock-laudatory address to Howard. The rest is merely occasional poetry. Of these productions Johnson says: "He appears to have had, in common with almost all mankind, the ambition of being upon proper occasions *a merry fellow,* and in common with most of them, to have been by nature, or by early habits, debarred from it. Nothing is less exhilarating than the ludicrousness of Denham. He does not fail for want of efforts: he is familiar, he is gross; but he is never merry, unless the 'Speech against peace in the Close Committee' be excepted."[151] It is true that many of these poems are without value, yet Johnson's sentence is a little too severe. The *News from Colchester* and the *Dialogue between Sir John Pooley and Mr. Thomas Killigrew* have a strain of humor that at least partly

[148]   'Twas certainly mysterious that the name
            Of Prophets and of Poets is the same;
                                    Progress of Learning, ll. 77-78.

[149] Johnson, *Lives of the Poets* (ed. Waugh), I, 87.

[150] This work is hardly important enough to warrant classing him with Cleveland, Marvel, Butler, and the lesser "party" satirists of the day. *Directions to a Painter* I regard as spurious. See Appendix B.

[151] Johnson, *Lives of the Poets* (ed. Waugh), I, 89.

atones for their indecency, and one or two of his satires and parodies of *Gondibert* are excellent. "For grave burlesque . . . his imitation of Davenant shews him to have been well qualified."[152] Love poetry is notably absent, the only exception being the poem *To his Mistress*.[153]

Denham's reputation rested to a large extent on his style. Dryden and, following him, the eighteenth-century poets and critics praised him as being largely responsible (together with Waller) for the development of the closed couplet. Dryden says, "Even after Chaucer there was a Spencer, a Harrington, a Fairfax, before Waller and Denham were in being; and our numbers were in their nonage till these last appear'd."[154] Johnson says: "As one of Denham's principal claims to the regard of posterity arises from his improvement of our numbers, his versification ought to be considered. It will afford that pleasure which arises from the observation of a man of judgment naturally right forsaking bad copies by degrees, and advancing towards a better practice, as he gains more confidence in himself. In his translation of Virgil, written when he was about twenty-one years old, may be still found the old manner of continuing the sense ungracefully from verse to verse. . . . From this kind of concatenated metre he afterwards refrained, and taught his followers the art of concluding their sense in couplets; which has perhaps been with rather too much constancy pursued."[155]

Denham certainly did not originate the school of classical heroic couplet in England, nor is it at all certain that this claim on Waller's behalf, fostered largely by Gosse, rests upon solid foundations. Before Waller were Drummond of Hawthornden and George Sandys, both directly exposed to French influence, notably that of Malherbe, and both writing, in their early couplets at least, in the strict classical manner.[156] Before them we find tendencies toward closed couplets in

[152] Johnson, *Lives of the Poets* (ed. Waugh), I, 89.

[153] See p. 121.

[154] *Dryden, The Poetical Works of* (Cambridge ed.), *Preface to the Fables*, p. 744.

[155] Johnson, *Lives of the Poets* (ed. Waugh), I, 93-94.

[156] See Henry Wood, *The Beginnings of the Classical Heroic Couplet in England*, 1890.

Beaumont and Fairfax, and Cartwright has, in the midst of meta-
physical conceits, lines of the balance and polish typical of Pope.
We might multiply examples, but these are enough to show that
closed couplets were not the invention of any one man, but were
simply the outcome of a gradual process of prosodical develop-
ment.[157]

Yet though not the first to write closed couplets, we may with
confidence assert that Denham had great influence in increasing
their popularity. In support of this we have not only the statements
of Dryden and Johnson, but the evidence of his influence on the
early poems of Pope, notably *Windsor Forest*, and the evidence of the
numerous seventeenth- and eighteenth-century allusions to him, and
imitations of him. This influence was undoubtedly due to the im-
mense popularity of *Cooper's Hill*, a poem in which the couplets
show a marked tendency toward Augustan conciseness. As Johnson
points out, Denham shows a steady development in the use of the
closed couplet, and in his late translations *Of Prudence* and *Of Jus-
tice* nearly every one is an independent unit. Many of his lines,
moreover, have a balance and antithesis that point directly to
Pope.

Anticipatory of Pope, too, is Denham's ability to turn a thought
neatly, a trait which goes hand in hand with his didacticism. Dryden
praises this in extravagant terms: "Sir George Mackensie . . .
ask'd me why I did not imitate in my verses the turns of Mr. Waller
and Sir John Denham, of which he repeated many to me. I had often
read with pleasure, and with some profit those two fathers of our
English poetry, but had not seriously enough consider'd those
beauties which give the last perfection to their works."[158] By a
"turn" Dryden meant the musical repetition of a word or phrase.
Of course neither Denham or Waller originated "turns," but they
do make frequent use of them. The opening lines of *Cooper's Hill*
will serve as an example:

[157] See the *Writers of the Couplet, Cambridge History of English Literature,*
VII, chap. 3.
[158] *Dryden, The Poetical Works of* (Cambridge ed.), p. 319.

> Sure there are poets which did never dream
> Upon Parnassus, nor did tast the stream
> Of Helicon, we therefore may suppose
> Those made not poets, but the poets those.
> And as courts make not kings, but kings the court,
> So where the Muses and their train resort,
> Parnassus stands; if I can be to thee
> A poet, thou Parnassus art to me.

Yet though alike in this particular the styles of Denham and Waller are distinct; the former is weighty, the latter graceful; indeed, the strength of Denham is as common a phrase as the smoothness of Waller.

> And praise the easy vigour of a line
> Where Denham's strength and Waller's sweetness join.
> > Pope, *Essay on Criticism*, ll. 360-361.
> Hail mighty master of thy mother tongue,
> More smooth than Waller or than Denham strong.
> > Henry Hall, *To the Memory of John Dryden Esq.* (*Luctus Britannici, or the Tears of the British Muses*, 1700, p. 19.)
> Were by soft Waller, manly Denham seen.
> > *Buckingham House*, (*Three New Poems. Viz. I. Family Duty*, . . . 1721, p. 20.)

Again Johnson admirably sums up this characteristic of Denham's poetry: "The 'strength of Denham' which Pope so emphatically mentions, is to be found in many lines and couplets, which convey much meaning in few words, and exhibit the sentiment with more weight than bulk."[159] It is this quality in his work that accounts for the presence of so large a number of quotations from Denham that are to be found in subsequent books of extracts, quotations, etc., a number out of all proportion to the merit of the poems as a whole.

While it is not, strictly speaking, a characteristic of his poetry, we may here consider Denham's literary judgment. This appears to have been, on the whole, sound. Of his predecessors, Chaucer, Spenser, Shakespeare, Jonson, and Fletcher are praised; of his contemporaries, Waller, Cowley, and Fanshawe (for his translation of

---

[159] Johnson, *Lives of the Poets* (ed. Waugh), I, 92. Johnson illustrates by quoting: *Cooper's Hill*, ll. 165-168. See p. 751. *On Mr. Abraham Cowley*, ll. 29-38. See p. 150. *On the Earl of Strafford's Tryal*, ll. 7-18. See p. 153.

Guarini). Howard's *The British Princes* and Davenant's *Gondibert* he satirized. His relations with Wither were personal rather than literary, and undoubtedly influenced his judgment of Wither's poetry, if indeed his remark to Charles I is to be taken seriously.[160]

In connection with his literary judgment occurs one of the most interesting of all the anecdotes concerning him, that which makes him one of the first admirers of Milton's *Paradise Lost*. As the tradition is fairly well known it is, perhaps, necessary to examine it in some detail here. Its source was Jonathan Richardson's *Explanatory Notes and Remarks on Milton's Paradise Lost, 1734*, where we find it in the following form: "Sir George Hungerford, an ancient member of Parliament, told me, many years ago, that Sir John Denham came into the House one morning with a sheet, wet from the press, in his hand. What have you there, Sir John? Part of the noblest poem that ever was wrote in any language, or in any age. This was Paradise Lost. However, 'tis certain the book was unknown till about two years after, when the Earl of Dorset produced it. Dr. Tancred Robinson has given permission to use his name, and what I am going to relate he had from Fleet Shephard, at the Grecian Coffee-house, and who often told the story. My Lord was in Little Britain, beating about for books to his taste. There was Paradise Lost. He was surprised with some passages he struck upon dipping here and there, and bought it. The bookseller begged him to speak in its favour if he liked it, for that it lay on his hands as waste paper. (Jesus!) Shephard was present. My Lord took it home, read it, and sent it to Dryden, who in a short time returned it. 'This man,' says Dryden, 'cuts us all out and the ancients too.' "[161]

Edmund Malone was the first to attack this account, in 1800, in his *Critical and Miscellaneous Prose Works of Dryden*,[162] pointing

---

[160] See p. 10.

[161] Richardson, Jonathan, *Explanatory Notes*, 1734, CXX.

[162] Vol. I, part 1, p. 112. His arguments may be summarized as follows: (1) It is very unlikely that Denham should have had a proof sheet of *Paradise Lost;* these are seen only by the author, or his intimate friends, and there is no evidence of any personal connection between Denham and Milton; (2) when *Paradise Lost* was going through the press, Denham was mad; (3) Denham was never in Parliament; (4) Richardson tells us that Denham's praise had no stimu-

out improbabilities and inconsistencies and reaching the conclusion that it was unworthy of credit.

The discussion is continued by Masson, in his *Life of Milton*, who, although meeting some of Malone's objections, reaches a similar conclusion, and rejects the tradition.[163]

Yet there is no reason to deny Denham's claim to literary discernment. Let us examine once again the objections that have been made to his share in this tradition, ignoring the second part, that concerning Dryden, as irrelevant to our purpose. The objections are as follows: (1) Denham could not have seen a proof sheet; (2) he was mad at the time of the publication of *Paradise Lost;* (3) he was not a member of Parliament; (4) his public praise, celebrated poet though he was, had no stimulating effect on the sale. Passing over,

lating effect on the sale of the book, since, two years after, it was "waste paper"; yet we can prove that by that time most of the edition had been sold. According to his agreement with his publisher, Milton was to receive a second five pounds when 1,300 of the 1,500 copies of the first edition had been sold. He had already received this sum before the date of the Earl of Dorset's visit to the bookshop. This fact cannot be reconciled with Richardson's previous statement that the edition was "waste paper." The whole account, therefore, concludes Malone, should be rejected.

[163] VI, 628 ff. Masson begins by quoting Richardson, and continues by analyzing Malone's arguments. Malone, he says, is somewhat too critical; that while it is true that Denham was never in Parliament, still, as he had recovered from his madness by August, 1667, when *Paradise Lost* appeared, Malone's objection on the ground of Denham's insanity loses its force. Masson continues: "But for the rest one must agree with Malone, and suppose that there was some confusion of memory on the part of the old Parliament man, Sir George Hungerford when he told the story of Denham to Richardson, or on Richardson's part in recollecting what Sir George had said. Even if we waive the question of the place . . . How can we account for his [Denham's] being before all the rest of the world in having access privately to the proof sheets of a forthcoming book by such a political recluse as Milton? And how was his remark so ineffective, the celebrated Sir John Denham though he was, that the book received no benefit from his vast admiration, and its merits had to be re-discovered and re-proclaimed two years afterward? In short the first part of the tradition given by Richardson will not cohere with the second part." Masson then discusses this second part, concerning the Earl of Dorset and Dryden, and succeeds in giving a plausible explanation for the difficulties found there. His conclusion is, therefore, that since the two parts do not agree, and since the second can be better established than the first, the first must be given up and the story of Denham's early recognition of the greatness of *Paradise Lost* rejected. And there the matter has rested until now.

for the moment, the first objection, let us consider the second. That Denham was mad at the time of the appearance of *Paradise Lost* Masson himself denies, and evidence supporting Masson has been added in these pages. Denham had resumed his official duties by September, 1666.[164] The third objection is also groundless. He was returned a member for Old Sarum in 1661.[165] The fourth is stressed by Masson, who, curiously enough, does not see that he at once answers his own objection. Masson says that as 1,300 of 1,500 copies had been sold, the bookseller, when he spoke of *Paradise Lost* as "waste paper," must have meant merely that the copies in his own shop had not been sold. If we thus explain away the waste paper, we at the same time remove the objection that Denham's praise had no effect on the sale. We see that *Paradise Lost had* sold comparatively well, and that Denham might have contributed to this success.

Of the four objections, therefore, only one remains, that Denham could not have seen the proof sheets of the poem. In this connection it would be well to examine the original source once again: "Sir John Denham came into the House one morning with a sheet, wet from the press in his hand. What have you there Sir John? Part of the noblest poem that ever was wrote," etc. It is true that the arguments against Denham's having seen a proof sheet are sound; but we observe at once that in the original *proof* sheet is nowhere mentioned, and that this meaning has been read into the passage by the commentators, who have not seen that it is capable of an entirely different and simple explanation. Denham might have had in his hand a freshly printed sheet of the first edition, yet unbound, which possibly had been hanging up in the book shop to dry when his excited discovery of it induced the bookseller to lend it to him. If we accept this conjecture, the difficulties vanish. There is no reason why Denham, in his right mind, and a member of the House, should not have brought into Parliament an unbound sheet of *Paradise Lost* "wet from the press," and praised it; and as Sir John was a

[164] See above, p. 23.

[165] See above, p. 20. Mr. T. W. Baldwin, in *Modern Language Notes*, December, 1927, p. 508, cites the *Journals of the Commons* to prove his membership in 1667, and brings forward additional and welcome evidence to support this theory.

famous literary figure, there is no reason why his praise may not have been instrumental in assisting the sale of 1,300 copies of the poem within two years.

We should not overlook the fact, moreover, that *Paradise Lost* was a poem that would very naturally arouse Denham's enthusiasm, since its high moral theme was similar in character to his own literary didacticism. We must conclude, therefore, that there is no inconsistency in the tradition, and that it is probable that Denham recognized at once the greatness of *Paradise Lost*. This surely is not his least claim to the regard of posterity.

Of all his contemporaries, however, Denham has been most closely associated with Waller. As we have seen, since the time of Dryden, they have been regarded as the two forerunners of Augustan poetry. A study of the personal and literary relations between them becomes, therefore, of interest. There is a large amount of evidence, though most of it is indirect, that they knew one another personally, and there is direct evidence that Denham's early work was greatly influenced by Waller.

That they were closely associated after the Restoration is certain. Both were members of the House of Commons,[166] both were courtiers; both were favorites. In 1663 they were appointed censors for a play of Killigrew's.[167] By that time, however, each had long established his technique, so that this association is of no special significance.

When they first met cannot be precisely determined, but it is possible that it was about 1635 or 1636.[168] At all events, Denham,

[166] Thorn-Drury, *The Poems of Edmund Waller*, LXIII. See p. 20.

[167] *Calendar of State Papers, Domestic, 1663-1664*, p. 83.

[168] Denham went to Oxford, as we have seen [see p. 3] in 1631. There he must have become acquainted with his first cousin, George Morley, later Bishop of Winchester [see Appendix C], if, indeed, he did not already know him, as seems very probable. Morley had remained at Oxford after his graduation in 1618, and in 1633, when Lucius Carey, second Lord Falkland, retired to his estate at Burford near Oxford, became one of the brilliant group that gathered about that nobleman. To this circle Morley introduced Waller about 1635, with whom he contracted a warm friendship, apparently living with Waller for a time and directing his studies at Waller's house at Beaconsfield [Thorn-Drury, *The Poems of Edmund Waller*, XXII].

It is evident, then, that Morley might well have brought Denham and Waller

by 1642, knew much of Waller's poetry in manuscript, and thought highly of it. In the first edition of *Cooper's Hill* of 1642, Denham, speaking of St. Paul's cathedral says:

> Pauls, the late theme of such a muse whose flight
> Has bravely reach't and soar'd above thy height:
> Now shalt thou stand though sword, or time, or fire,
> Or zeal more fierce than they, thy fall conspire,
> Secure, whilst thee the best of poets sings,
> Preserved from ruine by the best of kings.
>
> ll. 19-24.

A marginal note reads, "Master Waller," and the reference is to Waller's poem *Upon his Majesty's repairing of Paul's*. As none of Waller's poems[169] were published until 1645, Denham must have seen this poem in manuscript. The phrase "the best of poets" as applied to Waller's early work sounds somewhat like the complimentary exaggeration of personal friendship, though doubtless Waller's simplicity and directness appealed to Denham.

But *Cooper's Hill* furnishes still more evidence of familiarity with Waller's verse, as is shown by several parallel passages.[170]

together, either at Beaconsfield, but a short distance from London, where Denham was then studying law at Lincoln's Inn [see p. 5], at London itself, or at Denham's place at Egham, only twelve or fifteen miles from Beaconsfield.

[169] With three exceptions: *To the King on his Return from Scotland,* in *Rex Redux,* 1633; *To Mr. George Sandys,* in Sandys' *Paraphrase upon the Divine Poems,* 1638; and *Upon Ben. Johnson, the most excellent of comick poets,* in *Jonsonus Verbius,* 1638.

[170]   1. "Not to look back so far, to whom this isle
       Owes the first glory of so brave a pile [Windsor]."
                 Cooper's Hill, ll. 65-66.

     "When the first monarch of this happy isle
      Moved with the ruin of so brave a pile,"
            Waller, *Upon his Majesty's repairing of Paul's.* ll. 5-6.

     2. "Nor then destroys it with too fond a stay,
       Like mothers which their infants overlay;"
                 Cooper's Hill, ll. 171-172.

     "As careless dames whom wine and sleep betray
      To frantic dreams their infants overlay:"
            Waller, *The Battle of the Summer Islands,* Canto II: 21-22.

As the exact dates of the writing of all these poems is unknown, it is not impossible that Denham influenced Waller, but it seems far more probable that Denham, then at the beginning of his poetic career, echoed the various poems of the older poet with which he

3. "And thither all the horned hoast resorts
   To graze the ranker mead, that noble heard
   On whose sublime and shady fronts is rear'd
   Nature's great master-piece; to show how soon
   Great things are made, but sooner are undone."

Cooper's Hill, ll. 236-240.

"So we some antique hero's strength
Learn by his lance's weight and length;
As these vast beams express the beast
Whose shady brows alive they dressed."

.   .   .   .   .

"O fertile head! which every year
Could such a crop of wonder bear!
The teeming earth did never bring
So soon, so hard, so huge a thing;"

Waller, On the Head of a Stag, ll. 1-14.

4. "Wearied, forsaken, and pursu'd, at last [the stag]
   All safety in despair of safety plac'd,
   Courage he thence resumes, resolv'd to bear
   All their assaults, since 't is in vain to fear.
   And now too late he wishes for the fight
   That strength he wasted in ignoble flight;
   But when he sees the eager chase renew'd,
   Himself by dogs, the dogs by men pursu'd,
   He straight revokes his bold resolve, and more
   Repents his courage, than his fear before;"

Cooper's Hill, ll. 289-298. (See also ll. 247-289.)

"So the tall stag, upon the brink
Of some smooth stream about to drink,
Surveying there his armed head
With shame remembers that he fled
The scorned dogs, resolves to try
The combat next; but if their cry
Invades again his trembling ear,
He straight resumes his wonted care,
Leaves the untasted spring behind,
And, winged with fear, outflies the wind."

Waller, Of Love, ll. 45-54.

was familiar. In another poem of this period, Denham again echoes Waller's *Upon his Majesty's repairing of Paul's:*

> Our nation's glory and our nation's crime
>   l. 4

In the Egerton MS. 2421 text of *On the Earl of Strafford's Trial and Death* Denham says:

> Our nations glory and our nations hate
>   l. 20

It is certain, therefore, that by 1642 Denham was thoroughly acquainted with Waller's poetry, and it is probable that he knew Waller himself.

In any case, during the years 1648 to 1652 the two men must have been thrown together. In 1648 Waller removed from Rouen to Paris, where he remained, a member of the exiled English court, until his return to England in 1652.[171] In 1648 Denham fled from England, and joined Charles in Paris, with whom he stayed, except for occasional absences on various missions, until he too went back to England in 1653. As Waller and Denham were both favorites at court, and were now both famous poets, it is almost certain that by the time they were again in England they knew one another intimately.

In 1655 we find our next indication of personal relationship. In that year the greatly revised edition of *Cooper's Hill* appeared in which a passage which might have been construed as an unfriendly allusion to Waller was dropped.[172]

[171] Thorn-Drury, *The Poems of Edmund Waller,* LIX ff.
[172] This occurs between lines 36 and 37. In the 1642 text, the poet, speaking of the confusion and tumult of life in London, continued:

> Some study plots, and some those plots t'undoe,
> Others to make 'em, and undoe 'em too,
> False to their hopes, afraid to be secure,
> Those mischiefs only which they make, endure,
> Blinded with light, and sick of being well,
> In tumults seek their peace, their heaven in hell.

Certainly these lines apply very well to Waller's plot, his attempt to seize London on behalf of the King, and his subsequent confessions and exposures before

Finally,[173] in 1658, we come to our last and most convincing evidence. In that year was published *The Passion of Dido for Aeneas . . . Translated by Edmund Waller and Sidney Godolphin*. Waller's portion of this joint work was later published separately in his collected editions, under the title *Part of the Fourth Book of Virgil, Translated*. It is a passage of 134 lines, running in the original from line 437 to line 583.

Denham also translated part of the fourth book of the *Aeneid*. It was first published in the collected edition of 1668, under the title of *The Passion of Dido for Aeneas*. This represents a revision, done about 1653 of a portion of a much earlier complete translation of books II-VI.[174] As in his other translations, he condenses greatly, but in this instance he omits altogether a passage of about 130 lines, save for a few scattered lines to bridge the gap. These lines omitted by Denham are precisely the lines translated by Waller.[175]

The coincidence is too striking to be accidental, and there can, I think, be but one explanation. Denham, having already translated the passage, omits it in revision because Waller has written his version in the meantime, and Denham does not wish to compete with his friend. This failure to make use of his own work seems otherwise unexplain-

the bar of the House of Commons. Whether or not the realization of this unintentional aptness caused Denham's ears to tingle and his hair to stand on end, as Gosse dramatically suggests [Gosse, Edmund, *From Shakespeare to Pope*, p. 90], the lines were dropped in 1655. There is no prosodical reason for this; indeed, the lines are technically good, better than many that he retained. Yet as there must have been some reason for canceling them, it seems a permissible inference that it was a personal one; that he became dissatisfied with them since they could be taken to allude to an episode discreditable to his friend.

[173] Another, though less important, link between the two during the period after their return to England is the fact that they had a common friend in Christopher Wase. In 1652 Waller wrote, highly recommending Wase as a tutor, and in 1654 his poem *To my Worthy Friend Mr. Wase* appeared in Wase's translation of the *Cynegeticon* of Gratius Faliscus. Wase dedicated the book to Lord Herbert, son of the Earl of Pembroke, to whom he was tutor [Thorn-Drury, *The Poems of Edmund Waller*, II, 197, note]. As Denham was at this time living with the Earl, Wase came to know him there. [We learn this from an anecdote supplied to Aubrey, *Brief Lives* (ed. A. Clark), I, 218.]

[174] For a discussion of the original translation and the revision see below.

[175] Waller begins fifteen lines before Denham breaks off. Waller translates 437 to 583; Denham omits 452 to 583.

able. On this occasion, therefore, direct relationship is nearly certainly established.[176]

We see, then, that from 1635 on, Denham's life touched Waller's on numerous occasions, and that the two men were thrown together under circumstances that must have resulted in intimacy.[177] What conclusions in regard to their poetry are we to draw from these facts? Denham, in his most important and one of his earliest poems, *Cooper's Hill*, was clearly influenced by Waller, and it is probable that this was the outcome of personal friendship. There are no further echoes of Waller in Denham's later work, nor has Waller's ever any traces of Denham. Yet Denham, as we have seen, must have kept in touch with Waller's verse, and Waller could not have avoided knowing so famous a poem as *Cooper's Hill*.[178]

Their styles are distinct. Yet each developed a similar technique of the heroic couplet; each, as he matured, wrote couplets more and more closely approaching Augustan cadence and polish. I do not believe that either consciously attempted a revolution in prosody, nor do I believe that either consciously imitated the other. Yet see-

[176] Why Waller translated no more, or why Denham's translation was not printed with Waller's instead of Godolphin's, I do not know. Godolphin's portion shows no trace of Denham's influence, nor does Waller's of Denham's original version.

[177] There is one other possible link between them. In 1650 we find that a Colonel John Fielder is the guardian of Denham's children and trustee of his estate (see p. 14); now Fielder was elected to the Long Parliament as member for St. Ives, Cornwall, when that seat became vacant through the expulsion of Waller! The coincidence is certainly curious, but I have been unable to determine its significance.

[178] There is one possible, though by no means certain, echo of *Cooper's Hill* in Waller's *On the Duke of Monmouth's expedition*, 1679:

". . . his [the mountain's] curled brows
Frown on the gentle stream, which calmly flows,
While winds and storms his lofty forehead beat:
The common fate of all that's high or great."

Cooper's Hill, ll. 219-222.

"But seeing envy, like the sun, does beat
With scorching rays, on all that's high and great,
This, ill-requited Monmouth! is the bough
The Muses send to shade thy conquering brow."

On the Duke, ll. 33-36.

ing that their personal and literary relationships were close, it is a reasonable assumption that their influence was interactive, and even if subconscious, none the less effective.

As a translator, Denham deserves more attention than we can at present give him. Over half the body of his work, excluding *The Sophy*, is translation, and he occupies a conspicuous position among the predecessors of Dryden and Pope, both of whom praise him.[179] He translated from the French, the Greek, and the Latin. His French work is the fifth act of Corneille's *Horace,* the first four being by Mrs. Phillips, and is in his late style of strictly closed couplets; his Greek is a short fragment from the *Iliad*. His Latin work is more important, and consists in its printed form of an epigram of Martial, two poems of Mancinus, part of the second and part of the fourth book of the *Aeneid,* and Cicero's *Cato Major*. It is of interest to note that Dryden clearly made use of the second *Aeneid* in his own translation, even taking over Denham's concluding line without a change.

There is in addition a MS. version of the *Aeneid,* books II-VI inclusive, which differs materially from the printed fragments.[180] The MS. must represent Denham's original translation, for it is in his earliest manner, abounding in run-on couplets, full stops within the

[179] Dryden, *Preface to Ovid's Epistles,* pp. 91 ff., *Dedication of the Aeneid* (Cambridge ed.), p. 514. Pope, see p. 179.

[180] In a letter to the *London Times Literary Supplement* of July 7, 1927, the Rev. Francis E. Hutchinson, of Trinity College, Oxford, England, called attention to this hitherto unknown material, which he has in his possession, and which is contained in a MS. commonplace book of Mrs. Lucy Hutchinson, where it is ascribed to Denham. In this letter, and in subsequent letters to me, the Rev. Hutchinson has kindly furnished me with his reasons for considering the ascription correct. They may be summarized as follows: (1) Mrs. Hutchinson's attributions of other poems in the collection are in all cases correct; (2) she was a contemporary of Denham, and intimate with the literary circle of the day; (3) a collation of the MS. with the versions of books II and IV printed in the 1668 edition, shows that the texts are too close to be the work of someone else, and must be Denham's.

Mr. Hutchinson, though quite properly reserving to himself the right of later editing of this MS., has kindly transcribed for me the MS. versions of Denham's published portions of books II and IV as well as a portion of book VI. A collation of these texts convinces me that the Hutchinson MS. represents Denham's work.

line, and other irregularities. The title-page of *The Destruction of Troy*, 1656 (a portion of book II), states that it was written in 1636. I see no reason to doubt this, or the fact that it applies to the whole MS., since the style is the same throughout (that is, of course, in the parts I have seen).

In the printed form of books II and IV the verse is somewhat tightened and polished, indicating later work. Denham did not complete his revision, either because he had no time, or because he felt that it was not worth the effort. The date of the revision is in all probability about 1653, when he was with the Earl of Pembroke. We know that he then worked on Virgil.[181] As further evidence we have: 1) The relation, discussed above, between Denham's revision of book four and Waller's translation done about this time. 2) the following parallel:

> No unexpected inundations [of the Thames] spoyl
> The mowers hopes, nor mock the plowman's toyl.
>
> *Cooper's Hill*, ll. 175-176.

> [The torrent]
> Bears down th' opposing Oaks, the fields destroys
> And mocks the Plough-mans toil
>
> *Destruction of Troy*, ll. 294-295.

The phrase in *The Destruction of Troy* being changed from its earlier form in the Hutchinson MS. of *And all the oxens toyle*, which is closer to Virgil. About 1653 would be a natural date for this change; Denham very probably then had the text of *Cooper's Hill* freshly in mind, as he published the revised edition in 1655. As this phrase was in the 1642 version of *Cooper's Hill*, I take it he transferred it to Virgil, consciously or unconsciously, when working on both poems at about the same time.

In the seventeenth century a very large number of translations from the classics were produced. In this field it is, of course, difficult to trace literary influence, and the relations between the various translators are ill defined. In general, however, we may say that the

---

181 "Here he translated the . . . booke of Virgil's Aeneis, and also burlesqu't it. He also burlesqued Virgil, and burnt it, saying that 'twas not fitt that the best poet should be so abused."—From Mr. Christopher Wase. Aubrey, *Brief Lives* (ed. A. Clark), I, 218.

earlier attempts were largely word for word, and line for line. Later two other methods arose: more or less free paraphrase, and what was called "imitation." Denham makes his own position clear in his praise of Fanshawe's translation of Guarini:

> That servile path thou nobly dost decline
> Of tracing word by word, and line by line.
> Those are the labour'd births of slavish brains,
> Not the effects of Poetry, but pains;
> Cheap vulgar arts, whose narrowness affords
> No flight for thoughts, but poorly sticks at words.
> A new and nobler way thou dost pursue
> To make Translations and Translators too.
> They but preserve the Ashes, thou the Flame,
> True to his sense, but truer to his fame.
>
> *To Sir Richard Fanshaw*, ll. 15-25.

This poem, Johnson says, ". . . contains a very spritely and judicious character of a good translator: [Quotes above lines] The excellence of these lines is greater, as the truth which they contain was not at that time generally known."[182] Denham treats this same thought more at length in his introduction to *The Destruction of Troy*. In theory, then, Denham is an "imitator," but in practice he is more moderate, and departs no farther from his original than paraphrase. Indeed, his changes consist for the most part in condensing and focusing the thought, a characteristic of his original poems. It is this trait that made his mature translations, *Cato Major*, and *Of Prudence, Of Justice*, favorite fields for the compilers of books of quotations. Denham never goes so far as true "imitation," a triumphant example of which is Pope's *Epistle to Augustus*.

Denham's translation of Virgil clearly illustrates this change toward greater freedom, his 1636 version being considerably closer to the Latin than the revised form of 1653. I might give many illustrations of this, but perhaps one will suffice, since it concerns the famous line,

> . . . timeo Danaos et dona ferentes.

In the Hutchinson MS. this reads:

[182] Johnson, *Lives of the Poets* (ed. Waugh), I, 90.

The Grecians most when bringing guifts I feare.

In *The Destruction of Troy:*

> Their swords less danger carry than their gifts.
>
> l. 48.

That Denham here is ready to sacrifice the full force of so famous a phrase for the sake of greater neatness and antithesis shows unmistakably that to render Virgil literally is no longer so important as to render him attractively.[183]

Denham's translations are not very successful poetically, and are of less significance for the results he obtained than for the methods he followed. Here, as in his original poetry, he points the way toward Dryden and Pope.

Denham's metrical version of the Psalms was one of the hundreds of such versions made in the seventeenth century.[184] "In this attempt," says Johnson, "he has failed; but in sacred poetry who has succeeded?"[185] The task of writing good poetry that was at the same time fitted to church tunes proved too much even for Milton. This being the case, it seems unprofitable to attempt a detailed comparison of Denham's work with that of his rivals. We may content ourselves with one comparison taken at random, and set Denham's version of the twenty-third Psalm against Sternhold's, part of the popular version of Sternhold and Hopkins.

Sternhold:

> My shepeheard is the living Lord
>   Nothing therefore I need;
> In pastures faire with waters calme
>   He set me forth to feede.
> He did convert and glad my soule
>   And brought my mind in frame;
> To walk in pathes of righteousnesse,
>   For his most holy name.

---

[183] Permission to print the foregoing extracts from the Hutchinson MS. has been kindly given by the Rev. F. E. Hutchinson, acting for the actual owner of the MS., the Rev. Charles A. Hutchinson, West Monkton Rectory, Somerset.

[184] Between 1600 and 1653 there were 206 complete metrical versions. Studley, M. H., *Milton and his Paraphrases of the Psalms, Philological Quarterly,* October, 1925, p. 265.

[185] Johnson, *Lives of the Poets* (ed. Waugh), I, 88.

Yea though I walke in vale of death,
  Yet will I feare none ill.
Thy rod and staffe doth comfort me,
  And thou art with me still.
And in the presence of my foes,
  My table thou shalt spread!
Thou shalt O Lord fill full my cup,
  And eke anoint my heade.

Through all my life thy favour is
  So franckly shewed to me:
That in thy house for evermore
  My dwelling place shal be.

Denham:

My Shepherd is the living Lord;
  To me my Food and Ease
The rich luxuriant Fields afford;
  The Streams my Thirst appease.
My Soul restor'd he'l gently lead
  Into the Paths of Peace;
To walk in Shades among the Dead,
  My Hopes, not Fears, increase.

His Rod and Staff are still my Guide,
  He stands before my Foes:
For me a feast he does provide,
  My sparkling Cup o'er-flows.
He with sweet Oil anoints my Head;
  His Mercy, Grace, and Praise,
Have me into his Temple led,
  Where I will end my Days.

The comparison seems to me greatly in Denham's favor.

As a playwright Denham need not detain us long. His only play is *The Sophy,* an early production, and one of no great importance. The story is founded upon historical fact, or at least upon travelers' tales. Herbert, in his *Travels,*[186] recounts among many incidents of the cruelty of the then reigning Shah of Persia, the story of his relations with his son. The Shah, Abbas, having murdered his elder brother and his father in order to mount the throne, becomes jealous of the great fame of his son and heir, Mirza; accuses him of plotting rebellion; has him blinded and thrown into prison. Yet he retains

---

[186] Herbert, Thomas, *Some Yeares Travels into Divers Parts of Asia and Afrique,* . . . 1638, pp. 174 ff. The first edition was in 1634.

the greatest affection for Mirza's seven-year-old daughter Fatyma. Mirza, enraged by his father's cruelty, obtains a terrible revenge by strangling Fatyma in order to deprive Abbas of the delight of her society. He then poisons himself. Not long after, Abbas dies, leaving Mirza's young son, Sophy, as his successor.

Upon this foundation Denham has built his play. He increases the dramatic value of the story by having the King's mind poisoned against his son by his trusted favorite, Haly, who is jealous of Mirza, and ambitious to set up a new dynasty which he can dominate. Denham, seeing the unfitness of the original for stage presentation, has Mirza tempted to kill Fatyma, but relent at the last moment and allow her to escape. He also departs from Herbert by having both the King and Mirza poisoned by Haly, who in turn falls when his confidant confesses under torture by Mirza's partisans.

Denham's play lacks sufficient complication of plot to make it effective, but it contains numerous well-phrased moral, philosophical and political maxims characteristic of his work, and exhibits a not altogether feeble power of psychological analysis. He seems to have been largely influenced by Shakespeare and the later Elizabethans. The theme is strongly reminiscent of Othello; Haly is a faint echo of Iago, who, after he has succeeded in ruining both the King and his son, goes smiling to his torture and death; he is even called "honest Haly." There are a number of Shakesperian echoes in the verse, and the metaphorical style is characteristically Elizabethan. Prosodically it presents some interesting features. Aside from one passage of highly finished couplets[187] the play is in slipshod blank verse, which seems to be more an unskillful attempt to write in Shakespeare's late manner, or in Fletcher's, than anything else. The five-foot line is the standard, but the verse wavers sadly; six-foot and four-foot lines are common; feminine and double-feminine endings abound; the speeches almost always begin and end with half-lines that refuse to match; and from time to time the verse degenerates into prose pure and simple.[188]

[187] Act IV, ll. 16-66.

[188] This same story upon which *The Sophy* is founded was employed later by Robert Baron in his *Mirza*, published about 1647. Baron states that he was

Denham does not appear to have been influenced by any of the other Eastern plays of the period, printed or acted, most of which seem to have been of slight importance. However, in 1632 Massinger's *Emperor of the East,* a Turkish play, and in 1637 Suckling's *Aglaura,* a Persian play, were both successful, and may have encouraged Denham to choose an Eastern theme.

Perhaps the most interesting thing about *The Sophy* is the fact of its success, for which we have Wood's testimony, and the evidence of the 1642 prologue that it was given at court. Produced in 1641, when the rights and privileges of kingship were topics of supreme importance, the play could easily have been interpreted by the spectators as more or less of an allegory of political England; it would not be difficult for them to see in the Persian king, Charles cut off from his people and surrounded by his "evil counsellors," or in the contemptible Caliph, those clergy against whom the "root and branch" bill was aimed, specifically, perhaps, Archbishop Laud. It is further evidence of his interest in fundamental ethical and moral problems that the passage upon which Denham has obviously bestowed most care, attacks the abuses of the ministerial office, both the pride that makes religion the "spur" rather than the "curb" of tyranny, and the improper boldness that unites the cause of religion to popular discontent with kingship.[189]

There remains for our consideration *Cooper's Hill,* incomparably the most important of Denham's writings. "He seems to have been, at least among us, the author of a species of composition that may be denominated *local poetry,* of which the fundamental subject is some particular landscape, to be poetically described, with the addition of such embellishments as may be supplied by historical retro-

---

ignorant of Denham's work until he had completed three acts of his own play, which was modeled on Jonson's *Catiline,* and that he continued because he found the two plays very different. An examination of Baron's play, of extreme length and never acted, confirms his statement. Baron follows Herbert without change in the main story, and, moreover, has a far more complicated plot than Denham. I can find no definite verbal parallels, the plays having only such general similarities as are due to their common source.

[189] *The Sophy,* Act IV, ll. 16-66.

spection, or incidental meditation."[190] This is best seen by summarizing the poem.

After an invocation to *Cooper's Hill*, the poet looks from its "auspicious height" and sees London and St. Paul's Cathedral in the distance. He admires the vastness of the Cathedral and reflects on the life in a city, contrasting its tumult with the serenity of private life. Then, looking nearer, he sees Windsor Castle, which moves him to give an account of some of the famous kings of whom Windsor can boast, Edward III, the Black Prince, etc., ending with a compliment to Charles I and Henrietta Maria. Next to Windsor a ruined abbey, Chertsey, provokes a sharp satire on Henry VIII, and a condemnation of both religious lethargy and religious zeal. The poet then turns to the Thames itself, but gives not so much a physical description as a discussion of its beneficial effects on agriculture, its commerce, etc. Next he describes in general terms the valley's scenery, whose mixture of stream, wood, mountain, and meadow gives delight. Through the meadow Charles I often passes toward the hunt. This leads the poet to a spirited description of a stag hunt in which the quarry falls beneath the King's shaft. The scene of this hunt, Runnymede, was also the scene of another more weighty struggle, which resulted in the yielding of arbitrary power by the signing of Magna Charta. Finally, the poet discusses the privileges and responsibilities of kingship, and the relations between the King and his people with which the poem ends.

It is evident that the nature description is relatively unimportant, being to a large extent conventional or vaguely general, and serving merely as a peg on which to hang ethical and philosophical reflections. The stag hunt is, perhaps, an exception to this rule; it is more spirited and its movement is less impeded by reflective passages than the rest of the poem, but a stag hunt is, after all, hardly nature description.

There are, of course, earlier poems about local scenery: Drayton's *Polyolbion*, Jonson's *Penshurst*, and others; but all of these lack the didactic element that is characteristic of *Cooper's Hill*, and that marks it as the original of a distinctive type. It has also been stated

---

[190] Johnson, *Lives of the Poets* (ed. Waugh), I, 90.

that *Cooper's Hill* is "obviously after the model of the *Mosella* of Ausonius,"[191] but the same objection holds; Ausonius, unlike Denham, gives the physical descriptions merely for their own sake.

In Denham's day the originality of the poem was attacked from a somewhat different angle; he was accused of not being the author, and of having bought the poem from another. Samuel Butler says:

> And now expect far greater matters of ye
> Than the bought Cooper's-Hill or borrow'd Sophy,[192]

and the anonymous author of *The Session of the Poets:*[193]

> Then in came *Denham,* that limping old Bard,
> Whose fame on the *Sophy* and *Cooper's Hill* stands;
> And brought many Stationers who swore very hard,
> That nothing sold better, except 'twere his Lands.

> But *Apollo* advis'd him to write something more,
> To clear a suspicion which possess'd the Court,
> That *Cooper's Hill,* so much bragg'd on before,
> Was writ by a Vicar who had forty pound for't.[194]

This is all the charge amounts to, and it cannot be said to weaken Denham's claim to the authorship. Johnson dismisses it by remarking that the poem "had such reputation as to excite the common artifice by which envy degrades excellence."[195] Denham's place in literature as the originator of a type of poetry which was long popular remains secure.

On the question of the style, there is little to be added here to what has already been said of Denham's style in general. It has obvious characteristics and the obvious criticisms have been well made.[196] Its prosody is important, since the poem's popularity affected not only the subject matter, but the manner of versification, of subsequent poetry, and contributed largely toward the development of the couplet into its Augustan form. The couplets show a

---

[191] Courthope, W. J., *A History of English Poetry,* 1903, III, 282.

[192] *A Panegyric upon Sir John Denham's Recovery from his Madness,* l. 16.

[193] This is not to be confused with Suckling's *A Session of the Poets.*

[194] *Poems on Affairs of State, from the Time of Oliver Cromwell to the Abdication of King James the Second,* 1697, I, 210.

[195] Johnson, *Lives of the Poets* (ed. Waugh), I, 85.

[196] See Appendix D.

marked tendency to break up into units, or at least pairs; there are almost no full stops within the line; and many of the couplets have a conciseness and antithesis that point toward Pope.[197] In this respect *Cooper's Hill* is strikingly different from the earlier *Destruction of Troy*, with its overflow. This change may be due to the influence of Waller, who at that time was associated with Denham's cousin, George Morley, as we have seen. At all events, it is important to see that Denham's development had proceeded so far as to throw the weight of *Cooper's Hill* on the side of the closed rather than the open couplet.

Cooper's Hill is of interest to us in another respect. It offers us our chief opportunity of estimating how far Denham may be considered a conscious artist, though on a smaller scale we may do so in his poem *On the Earl of Strafford's Tryal*, and one or two others. This leads us to consideration of the various texts.[198]

These present a difficult problem, which was convincingly solved by Professor O Hehir.[199] His conclusions can only be summarized here. Copies are extant of editions of 1642, 1643, and 1650. The texts of all three, except for obvious printer's errors and the inevitable differences in spelling, are identical. In 1655 another edition appeared. In the preface J. B. says: "You have seen this Poem often and yet never: for, though there have been Five Impressions, this now in your hand is the onely true Copie. Those former were all but meer Repetitions of the same false Transcript . . ." If we assume that the 1655 text was one of these five impressions, then there were four earlier ones. Three have been accounted for above. The fourth was probably another 1650 edition which has disappeared.[199a] The impression given by J. B. that the 1655 edition is more authentic than the earlier ones is false. Denham was responsible for all of them, but the 1655 edition was so radical a revision that he was anxious to have the previous texts

[197] See *Cooper's Hill*, ll. 127-130; 165-168; 333-334.
[198] For the editions of Cooper's Hill, see Appendix F., Part II.
[199] O Hehir, Brendan P., *John Denham's "Cooper's Hill,"* PMLA., vol. LXXIX (June, 1964), pp. 242-253.
[199a] An edition dated 1660 is probably a "ghost," 1660 being a misprint for 1650. See Appendix F. Part II, p. 354.

superseded. It differs in only a few minor details from the 1668 text, which is the final form except for six additional ms. lines.[199b]

In addition to these printed texts there are two manuscripts in the British Museum, MS. Harley 367, which lacks the first sixty-five lines, and MS. Harley 837. These are practically identical, and represent a state of the text very similar to that of 1642. In only two significant instances do the mss. differ. These will be discussed later.

The text of the mss. differs both from the 1642 (1643, 1650) text, and from the 1655 (1668) text and represents a version intermediate between them. This would account for their only differences; MS. Harley 837 inserts a couplet found nowhere else,[200] and MS. Harley 367 expands a four-line simile to eight lines.[201] Both of these are manuscript experiments that were later canceled.

The chief variations of the mss. text from that of 1642 are as follows.[202]

1. A passage of the 1642 edition is dropped in MS. Harley 837 (MS. Harley 367 being defective) and does not reappear in 1655. This is an allusion to men making and unmaking plots, and there is some reason to suppose that Denham canceled it on the discovery of Waller's plot in 1643,[203] The passage would therefore not occur in any subsequent text based on his ms., but would continue to appear in reprints of the 1642 edition.

2. A four-line comparison of the river Thames to a lover forsaking his mistress is expanded in MS. Harley 367 to eight lines.[204] Denham had sufficient taste to reject both versions of the simile altogether in the 1655 edition.

3. In both mss. a six-line simile between a stag at bay and a sinking ship is introduced, which does not appear in 1642, and which recurs in a condensed and improved form in 1655.[205]

[199b] See Denham's Ms. Addenda.
[200] See p. 76.
[201] See p. 74.
[202] See pp. 62ff.
[203] See pp. 38 and 64.
[204] See p. 74.
[205] See p. 84.

The long variant (9-30) in MS. Harley 837 consists almost entirely of transposition of lines.[206]

When we turn to the 1655 edition, we find that Denham has made many changes from the earlier text. In it perhaps unnecessary to analyse these in detail. In general they are for the better: passages are condensed and given added conciseness; various weak couplets, one or two political passages, and several poor similes are omitted. These revisions, which won Pope's praise,[207] show that Denham's artistic sense was sufficiently acute to enable him to improve his work.

The most important of all these differences is the first appearance in the 1655 text of the famous apostrophe to the Thames, upon which Denham's fame now chiefly rests:

> Oh could I flow like thee, and make thy stream
> My great example as it is my theme!
> Though deep, yet clear; though gentle yet not dull;
> Strong without rage; without o'erflowing, full.

These lines are his finest achievement, and many attempts have been made to find a source for them.[208] A passage of one of Roger Ascham's letters is produced: "Est enim in verbis deligendis tam peritus . . . suavis ubique sine fastidio, gravis semper sine molestia: sic fluens ut nunquam redundet, sic sonans ut nunquam perstrepat, sic plenus ut nunquam turgescat; sic omnibus perfectus numeris, ut nec addi ei aliquid, nec demi quicquid, mea opinione, possit."[209] Yet the parallel, while interesting, is by no means conclusive.

A far more probable source is indicated by William Oldys[210] in a marginal note in a volume in the British Museum:[211] "Den-

---

[206] See p. 62.

[207] Spence, Joseph, *Anecdotes,* 1820, pp. 281-283.

[208] Gosse insinuates that Waller may be the author, but admits that there is no evidence to support such a suggestion. Ward, T. H., *The English Poets,* 1880, II, 280.

[209] *Notes and Queries,* Fourth Series, XII, p. 493.

[210] Oldys (1696-1761) was an antiquary and the author of the *Harleian Miscellany.*

[211] Langbaine, Gerard, *An Account of the English Dramatic Poets,* 1691.

ham's fine lines to the Thames from Cartwright or Randolph, or
both, or Fletcher."

In Cartwright we find:

> But thou still putst true passion on; dost write
> With the same courage that try'd captaines fight;
> Giv'st the right blush and colour unto things;
> Low without creeping, high without losse of wings;
> Smooth, yet not weake, and by a thorough care,
> Bigge without swelling, without painting faire.
>
> *In Memòry of the most worthy Benjamin Johnson*

This poem first appeared in *Jonsonus Verbius,* 1638, a collection
of elegies on Jonson, and was reprinted in Cartwright's collected
works in 1651.[211a]

And in Randolph we find:

> I meane the stile, being pure and strong and round,
> Not long but Pythy: being short breath'd, but sound.
> Such as the grave, acute, wise, *Seneca* sings
> That best of Tutours to the worst of Kings.
> Not long and empty; lofty but not proud;
> Subtle but sweet, high but without a cloud.
>
> *To Mr. Feltham on his booke of Resolves*

This was first printed in Randolph's collected poems in 1638.[211b]
Since these two poems appeared in the same year, it is clearly im-
possible to determine whether one author influenced the other. It is
reasonable to suppose that their common source is Fletcher, since
Oldys is not likely to have been wrong in finding a similarity there.
However, I could discover no appropriate passage in any of the
four possible Fletchers: Giles the elder, Giles the younger, Phineas,
or John. I can only assume that I have overlooked it. As to Den-
ham, as Oldys remarked, he may be indebted to any one of the
earlier writers for the phrasing and movement of the verse in his
famous lines. Yet his essential originality is not seriously weak-

---

[211a] *Comedies, Tragi-Comedies with other poems.* See also Goffin, R.C.,
The Life and Poems of William Cartwright, 1918, p. 198n.

[211b] *Poems; with the Muses Looking-glasse.* See also Thorn-Drury, G.,
The Poems of Thomas Randolph, 1929, p. 77, and p. 202n.

ened. His verses are metrically superior to the others', and the
objects compared in the simile are different, which, of course,
changes the whole thought, and makes Denham's a far more
poetical one. Moreover, Denham had already expressed the under-
lying thought in 1642. There we read:

> O could my verse freely and smoothly flow
> As thy [Thames] pure flood, heaven should no longer know
> Her old Eridanus; thy purer streame
> Should bathe the gods, and be the poet's theme.

In MSS. Harley 367 and 837 this had become

> O could my lines fully and smoothly flow, etc.,

where the change from *freely* to *fully* brings us one step nearer the
final form, and may have suggested the rhyme word *full*. In addition,
the distinguishing features of Denham's couplets, the beauty of
the comparison of the flow of the verse to the flow of the stream,
and the simultaneous illustration of the simile in the skillful ono-
matopoeia, stamp the lines as his alone. There can be no serious
doubt, therefore, of his originality in writing the quatrain, that ad-
mits him on this one occasion to the ranks of authentic poets, and
that "must be numbered among those felicities which cannot be
produced at will by wit and labour, but must arise unexpectedly in
some hour propitious to poetry."[212]

The quatrain became immensely famous. Yet, fine as it is, its
reputation was not due solely to its intrinsic merits. In the dedica-
tion of his translation of the *Aeneid*, in 1697, Dryden offers it as a
test of poetical insight. "I am sure," he says, "there are few who
make verses have observ'd the sweetness of these two lines in
Cooper's Hill [quotes last two lines]. And there are yet fewer who
can find the reason of that sweetness."[213] Thus challenged, the
critics set themselves to solve the riddle, an effort which resulted in
such long analyses as those of Lord Monboddo, Hughes, Say, John-
son, etc., and in an increased fame for the poem. Following Dryden
there began a steady stream of quotations, imitations, and allusions

[212] Johnson, *Lives of the Poets* (ed. Waugh), I, 92.
[213] *Dryden, The Poetical Works of* (Cambridge ed.), p. 512.

to these lines that has continued almost to the present, the latest reference that I have come upon being in Meredith's *Diana of the Crossways*.[214]

Dryden's belief that no one before him had called attention to these lines is probably correct. In 1657 Poole[215] includes five quotations from *Cooper's Hill*, but omits the quatrain; in 1666 an anonymous poem appeared, entitled *St. Leonard's Hill*.[216] This is a close imitation of the general plan of *Cooper's Hill*, and has several long passages which are hardly more than rewritings of Denham's verse, but these lines to the Thames are unnoticed.

Yet the fame of *Cooper's Hill* did not depend entirely on this single passage. Its blend of description and reflection was new; its didacticism appealed to the minds of Denham's contemporaries and successors; the movement of its verse appealed to their ears. As we have seen, it at once became popular. First printed in 1642, it went through four editions before 1655; it found its way into a book of quotations by 1657; an imitation of it appeared by 1666. For more than a century it was one of the most famous poems in the language. From 1642 to 1826 it was published twenty-four times (including two editions of a Latin translation), separately or in collections,[217] and was of course included in the collected editions of Denham's poems, of which there were nineteen up to 1857.[218] There are, in addition, indications of several more editions that have disappeared. Vaughn, Herrick, Swift, Addison, Goldsmith, as well as other lesser writers, refer to it; Pope was largely influenced by it.

The fame of *Cooper's Hill* endured until late in the eighteenth century. In 1766 appeared COOPER'S HILL./A/POEM./ADDRESS'D TO/Sir WATKIN WILLIAMS WYNNE, Bart./LON-

---

[214] See Appendix E. These unquestionably represent only a small fraction of the allusions actually made. That they must have been numerous is shown by Swift's allusion. I ignore such books as general histories of English literature, or works of modern scholarship such as Goffin, mentioned elsewhere.

[215] Poole, Joshua, *The English Parnassus: or a Helpe to English Poesie.*

[216] St. LEONARD'S/HILL./A POEM./Written by R. F. Gent./Licensed, May the 14th. 1666/*Roger L'Estrange.*/ (Device)·/*LONDON*, Printed for *John Simms*, at the/Cross-keyes in *Cornhill*, near the Royal/Exchange. 1666.

[217] See Appendix F, Part II.

[218] See Appendix F, Part I.

DON:/Printed for W. WOOD, in WARWICK-LANE,/AND/M.
HINGESTON, near TEMPLE BAR./(Price TWO SHILLINGS
and SIX-PENCE.);[219] aside from the title, this poem is evidently in-
fluenced by Denham's *Cooper's Hill*, as it has several passages in imi-
tation of it. In 1767 appeared COOPER'S WELL./(Quotation.
Horace.)/A/FRAGMENT,/WRITTEN BY THE HONOUR-
ABLE/Sir JOHN DENHAM, Knight of the BATH,/AND/AU-
THOR of the Celebrated Poem of COOPER'S HILL,/found amongst
the Papers of a late Noble LORD. Dated/in the Year 1667./LON-
DON:/Printed for the AUTHOR;/And Sold by C. MORAN, in the
Great Piazza, Covent Garden./MDCCLXVII.[220] This is a close
and highly indecent parody of Denham's poem. In 1785 John
Scott[221] published a long critical analysis of the original, and, in
attacking it, speaks of it as a poem which everyone has been taught
to admire for its beautiful descriptions, interesting histories, and
rational sentiments.

Yet the importance of *Cooper's Hill* is measured not only by the
number of editions, references, etc., but also by the great number
of poems that sprang up in imitation of it: the earliest was, as we
have seen, *St. Leonard's Hill* in 1666, and following this came
Pope's *Windsor Forest*, Waller's *St. James Park*, Garth's *Claremont*,
Dyer's *Grongar Hill* and many others. Havens cites forty-six "hill"
poems up to 1821,[222] and we cannot doubt that most of them were
inspired directly or indirectly by *Cooper's Hill*. Johnson says that
the smaller poets, following Denham, "have left scarce a corner of
the island not dignified either by rhyme, or blank verse,"[223] and
"The Gentlemen's Magazine complained in 1788 that 'readers have
been used to see the Muses labouring up . . . many hills since

[219] My authority for the date of publication is Watt, *Bibliotheca Britannica*.
I can find no other evidence, internal or otherwise, to support this. The only
copy of the poem I have seen is in my possession.

[220] For a discussion of the authorship of *Cooper's Well*, see under Denham
in the printed catalogue of the Wrenn Library, Texas University.

[221] *Critical Essays on some of the poems of several English poets.*

[222] Havens, R. D., *The Influence of Milton on English Poetry*, 1922, Appen-
dix C.

[223] Johnson, *Lives of the Poets* (ed. Waugh), I, 91.

Cooper's and Grongar, and some gentle Bard reclining on almost every mole-hill.' "[224]

Cooper's Hill is Denham's chief title to fame. Most of his occasional poetry is of no permanent value; his only play is an amateurish example of an outworn mode; his translations are of significance only as serving as models for Dryden and Pope. But in writing *Cooper's Hill* he attained a lasting place in the history of English literature. By this poem he established a new and long popular type of descriptive poetry in which he surpassed all his imitators, and established himself as one of the famous poets of England for more than a hundred years; by it he influenced the development of the heroic couplet, aiding largely in its evolution into the closed Augustan form. Finally, in *Cooper's Hill* he was visited with the gift of tongues, and for four lines attained that finished utterance that is the goal of all who write.

[224] Havens, R. D., *The Influence of Milton on English Poetry*, 1922, p. 248.

TO THE KING

Sir,

AFTER *the delivery of your Royal Father's Person into the hands of the Army,*[225] *I undertaking to the Queen Mother, that I would find some means to get access to him, she was pleased to send me, and by the help of* Hugh Peters[226] *I got my admittance, and coming well instructed from the Queen (his Majesty having been long kept in the dark) he was pleased to discourse very freely with me of the whole state of his Affairs: But Sir, I will not lanch into a History, instead of an Epistle. One morning waiting on him at* Causham,[227] *smiling upon me, he said he could tell me some news of my self, which was that he had seen some Verses of mine the evening before (being those to Sir* R. Fanshaw) *and asking me when I made them, I told him two or three years since; he was pleased to say, that having never seen them before, He was afraid I had written them since my return into* England, *and though he liked them well, he would advise me to write no more, alleging, that when men are young, and have little else to do, they might vent the overflowings of their Fancy that way, but when they were thought fit for more serious Employments, if they still persisted in that course, it would look, as if they minded not the way to any better.*

Whereupon I stood corrected as long as I had the honour to wait upon him, and at his departure from Hampton Court,[228] *he was*

---

[225] On June 2, 1647, Joyce, a cornet in the Parliamentary army, rode to Holmby where Charles I was staying, guarded by a detachment from the army of Scotch Presbyterians, and on June 4 forced the King to accompany him to the English army at Newmarket.

[226] Hugh Peters, a graduate of Cambridge, was a Nonconformist minister. During the war he became prominent as a fighter and a preacher, and was in high favor with the Parliamentary leaders. On Nov. 28, 1646, he was given an estate of £200 a year by Parliament for his "great and faithful services performed unto this kingdom." He was executed after the Restoration for urging the death of Charles I, though he was not one of the actual regicides. For a full account of him, see Neal, Daniel, *History of the Puritans*, 1844, II, 518 ff.

[227] Causham is the phonetic spelling of Caversham, a village on the Thames opposite Reading, where, at Lord Craven's house, Charles I stayed from July 3 to August 24, 1647.

[228] The King escaped from his guards at Hampton Court, Nov. 11, 1647.

pleased to command me to stay privately at London, *to send to him and receive from him all his Letters from and to all his Correspondents at home and abroad, and I was furnisht with nine several Cyphers in order to it: Which trust I performed with great safety to the persons with whom we corresponded; but about nine months after being discovered by their knowledge of* Mr. Cowleys[229] *hand, I happily escaped both for my self, and those that held correspondence with me; that time was too hot and busie for such idle speculations, but after I had the good fortune to wait upon your Majesty in* Holland *and* France, *you were pleased sometimes to give me arguments to divert and put off the evil hours of our banishment, which now and then fell not short of your Majesties expectation.*

After, when your Majesty, departing from St. Germayns *to* Jersey,[230] *was pleased freely (without my asking) to confer upon me that place wherein I have now the honour to serve you,[231] I then gave over Poetical Lines, and made it my business to draw such others as might be more serviceable to your Majesty, and I hope more lasting. Since that time I never disobeyed my old Masters commands till this Summer at the Wells,[232] my retirement there tempting me to divert those melancholy thoughts, which the new apparitions of Forreign invasion, and domestick discontent gave us: But these clouds being now happily blown over, and our Sun cleerly shining out again, I have recovered the relapse, it being suspected that it would have proved the Epidemical disease of age, which is apt to fall back into the follies in [233] youth, yet* Socrates, Aristotle, *and* Cato *did the same, and* Scaliger *saith that Fragment of* Aristotle, *was beyond any thing that* Pindar *or* Homer *ever wrote.[234] I will not call this a Dedication, for those Epistles are commonly greater absurdities than any that come after, for what Author can reasonably believe, that fixing the great name of some eminent Patron*

---

[229] Abraham Cowley.

[230] About the middle of September, 1649. Clarendon, *History of the Rebellion,* V, 66.

[231] Surveyor General.

[232] This summer is 1667. On June 13 of that year DeRuyter attacked Chatham and sailed up the Thames. The Treaty of Breda was signed July 21. The "Wells" is probably Epson. See p. 189, note 2.

[233] Of?

[234] I have been unable to locate this reference.

in the forehead of his book can charm away censure, and that the
first leafe should be a curtain to draw over and hide all the deformities
that stand behind it? neither have I any need of such shifts, for
most of the parts of this body have already had Your Majesties
view, and having past the Test of so cleer and sharp-sighted a Judg-
ment, which has as good a Title to give Law in Matters of this
Nature as in any other, they who shall presume to dissent from Your
Majesty, will do more wrong to their own Judgment, then their
Judgment can do to me: And for those latter Parts which have not
yet received Your Majesties favourable Aspect, if they who have
seen them do not flatter me, (for I dare not trust my own Judgment)
they will make it appear, that it is not with me as with most of
mankind, who never forsake their darling vices, till their vices for-
sake them; and that this Divorce was not Frigiditatis causâ, *but an*
Act of Choice, and not of Necessity. Therefore, Sir, I shall only call
it an humble Petition, that Your Majesty will please to pardon this
new amour to my old Mistress, and my disobedience to his Com-
mands, to whose memory I look up with great Reverence and Devo-
tion, and making a serious reflection upon that wise Advice, it carries
much greater weight with it now, than when it was given, for when
age and experience has so ripened mans discretion as to make it fit
for use, either in private or publick Affairs, nothing blasts and cor-
rupts the fruit of it so much as the empty, airy reputation of being
Nimis Poeta, *and therefore I shall take my leave of the Muses, as*
two of my Predecessors did, saying

> Splendidis longum vale dico nugis,
> Hic versus & cætera ludicra pono.[235]

> Your Majesties most faithful
> and loyal Subject, and most
> dutiful and devoted servant

> *Jo. Denham.*

[235] Denham has taken two independent lines from two different authors, and
combined them, thus taking leave of the Muses as two of his predecessors did.
The first line is used by Sir Philip Sidney as a motto for his sonnet, "Leave me,
O love which reachest but to dust." The original source of the line I have been
unable to discover. The second line is a corruption of "Nunc itaque et versus
et cetera ludicra pono." Horace, *Epistles*, Bk. I, i, 10.

MS.H.837 *1642* 1: Sure we have Poets, that did never dreame

1655 If there be Poets, which did never dreame

MS.H.837 *1642* 3: . . . and therefore I suppose

1655 . . . we justly may suppose

MS.H.837 *1642* 6: . . . Muses and their Troopes resort,

MS.H.837 9-30: Whose topp when I ascend I seem more high,
More boundlesse in my Fancye then myne eye
As those, who rais'd in Bodye or in thought,
Above the Earth, or the Ayre's middle vault,
Behould how wyndes and stormes and Meteors growe,
How cloudes condense to rayne, congeale to snowe,
And see the thunder form'd before it teare
The Ayre, secure from daunger, and from feare;
Soe, to this height exalted, I looke downe
On Paules, as Men from thence uppon the towne:
Paules, the late Theame, of such a Muse, whose flight
Hath bravely reacht, and soar'd above thy height;
Nowe shalt thou stand, though tyme or sowrd, or fyre
Or, zeale, more feirce than they, thy fall conspire,
Secure, while thee the best of poetts singes:
Preserv'd from ruyne by the best of Kinges.
Then London, where my eye the plane, the crowde,
My mynd surveyes, wrap't in a thicker cloude
Of busines, than of smoake, where Men lyke Ants,
Toyle, to prevent imaginarye wants,
Yett all in vayne, increasinge with their store
Their vast desires, butt make their wants the more.
As foode, to unsounde Bodyes, though it please
The Appetite, feedes only the disease

1642 13-18: Exalted to this height, I first looke downe
On *Pauls,* as men from thence upon the towne.

1655 18: . . . or a falling cloud

1642 20: Hath . . .

COOPER'S HILL[1]

Sure there are Poets which did never dream
Upon *Parnassus,* nor did tast the stream
Of *Helicon,* we therefore may suppose
Those made not Poets, but the Poets those.
And as Courts make not Kings, but Kings the Court,
So where the Muses & their train resort,
Parnassus stands; if I can be to thee
A Poet, thou *Parnassus* art to me.
Nor wonder, if (advantag'd in my flight,
By taking wing from thy auspicious height)   10
Through untrac't ways, and aery paths I fly,
More boundless in my Fancy than my eie:
My eye, which swift as thought contracts the space
That lies between, and first salutes the place
Crown'd with that sacred pile, so vast, so high,
That whether 'tis a part of Earth, or sky,
Uncertain seems, and may be thought a proud
Aspiring mountain, or descending cloud,
Pauls, the late theme of such a Muse whose flight
Has bravely reach't and soar'd above thy height:[2]   20

[1] First printed in 1642.
For bibliography of references to this poem see Appendix D.
[2] The reference is to Waller's poem, *Upon His Majesty's Repairing of Paul's.*

1642 21: . . . though Time, or Sword, or Fire,
1642 25-30: As those who rais'd in body, or in thought
Above the Earth, or the Ayres middle Vault,
Behold how winds, and stormes, and Meteors grow,
How clouds condense to raine, congeale to snow,
And see the Thunder form'd, before it teare
The ayre, secure from danger and from feare,
So rais'd above the tumult and the crowd
I see the City in a thicker cloud
Of businesse, then of smoake, where men like Ants
Toyle to prevent imaginarie wants;
Yet all in vaine, increasing with their store,
Their vast desires, but make their wants the more.
As food to unsound bodies, though it please
The Appetite, feeds onely the disease,

1642 Between 36-37 (Omitted in MS. Harley 837):
Some study plots, and some those plots t' undoe,
Others to make 'em, and undoe 'em too,
False to their hopes, afraid to be secure
Those mischiefes onely which they make, endure,
Blinded with light, and sicke of being well,
In tumults seeke their peace, their heaven in hell.

1642 41-60: Into my eye, as the late married Dame,
MS.H.837 (Who proud, yet seems to make that pride her shame)
When Nature quickens in her pregnant wombe
Her wishes past, and now her hopes to come:
With such an easie, and unforc'd Ascent,
Windsor her gentle bosome doth present;
Where no stupendious Cliffe, no threatning heights
Accesse deny, no horrid steepe affrights,
But such a Rise, as doth at once invite
A pleasure, and a reverence from the sight.
Thy Masters Embleme, in whose face I saw
A friend-like sweetnesse, and a King-like aw,
Where Majestie and love so mixt appeare,
Both gently kinde, both royally severe.

Now shalt thou stand though sword, or time, or fire,
Or zeal more fierce than they, thy fall conspire,
Secure, whilst thee the best of Poets sings,
Preserv'd from ruine by the best of Kings.
Under his proud survey the City lies,
And like a mist beneath a hill doth rise;
Whose state and wealth the business and the crowd,
Seems at this distance but a darker cloud:
And is to him who rightly things esteems,
No other in effect than what it seems: 30
Where, with like hast, though several ways, they run
Some to undo, and some to be undone;
While luxury, and wealth, like war and peace,
Are each the others ruine, and increase;
As Rivers lost in Seas some secret vein
Thence reconveighs, there to be lost again.
Oh happiness of sweet retir'd content!
To be at once secure, and innocent.
Windsor the next (where *Mars* with *Venus* dwells.
Beauty with strength) above the Valley swells   40
Into my eye, and doth it self present
With such an easie and unforc't ascent,
That no stupendious precipice denies
Access, no horror turns away our eyes:
But such a Rise, as doth at once invite
A pleasure, and a reverence from the sight.
Thy mighty Masters Embleme, in whose face
Sate meekness, heightned with Majestick Grace

So *Windsor,* humble in it selfe, seemes proud,
To be the Base of that Majesticke load,
Than which no hill a nobler burthen beares,
But *Atlas* onely, that supports the spheres.
Nature this mount so fitly did advance,
We might conclude, that nothing is by chance
So plac't, as if she did on purpose raise
The Hill, to rob the builder of his praise.
For none commends his judgement, that doth chuse
That which a blind man onely could refuse;
Such are the Towers which th' hoary Temples grac'd
Of *Cibele,* when all her heavenly race

1642
MS.H.367 66: Must owe the glory . . .
MS.H.837

MS.H.367 69: Those amonge us noe lesse contest did move

Such seems thy gentle height, made only proud
To be the basis of that pompous load,   50
Than which, a nobler weight no Mountain bears,
But *Atlas* only that supports the Sphears.
When Natures hand this ground did thus advance,
'Twas guided by a wiser power than Chance;
Mark't out for such a use, as if 'twere meant
T' invite the builder, and his choice prevent.
Nor can we call it choice, when what we chuse,
Folly, or blindness only could refuse.
A Crown of such Majestick towrs doth Grace
The Gods great Mother,[3] when her heavenly race   60
Do homage to her, yet she cannot boast
Amongst that numerous, and Celestial host,
More *Hero's* than can *Windsor,* nor doth Fames
Immortal book record more noble names.
Not to look back so far, to whom this Isle
Owes the first Glory of so brave a pile,
Whether to *Cæsar, Albanact,*[4] or *Brute,*[5]
The Brittish *Arthur,* or the Danish *Knute,*
(Though this of old no less contest did move,
Then when for *Homers* birth seven Cities strove)   70
(Like him in birth, thou should'st be like in fame,
As thine his fate, if mine had been his Flame)[6]
But whosoere it was, Nature design'd
First a brave place, and then as brave a mind.
Not to recount those several Kings, to whom

[3] Cybele, a goddess native to Asia Minor, known to the **Romans** as the Great Mother of the Gods, or Great Idaean Mother.

[4] Albanact was the son of Brutus (see below), who, after his father's death, took Scotland as his share of the kingdom, his two brothers, Locrin and Kamber, taking England and Wales.

[5] Brute, or Brut, was the son of Ascanius, and grandson of Aeneas. Expelled from Italy for accidentally killing his father, he came to Britain, and founded London, eventually becoming king of the entire country.

[6]   "These, were my breast inspired with equal flame,
            Like them in beauty, should be like in fame,"
                                        Pope, *Windsor Forest,* ll. 9-10.

1642 78-82: He that the Lyllies wore, and he that wonne,
MS.H.367 And thy *Bellona* who deserves her share
MS.H.837 In all thy glories, Of that royall paire
        Which waited on thy triumph, she brought one,
        Thy sonne the other brought, and she that sonne
        Nor of lesse hopes could her great off-spring prove,
        A Royall Eagle cannot breed a Dove.
1642
MS.H.367 85-86: Each was a Noble cause, nor was it lesse
MS.H.837 I' th institution, then the great successe,
doth strive Whilst every part *conspires* to give it grace,
MS.H.837 The King, the Cause, the Patron, and the Place,

MS.H.837 90: To knowe, as power to actuate her will,

It gave a Cradle, or to whom a Tombe,
But thee (great *Edward*) and thy greater son,[7]
(The lillies which his Father wore, he won)
And thy *Bellona,* who the Consort came
Not only to thy Bed, but to thy Fame,[8]   80
She to thy Triumph led one Captive King,[9]
And brought that son, which did the second[10] bring.[11]
Then didst thou found that Order[12] (whither love
Or victory thy Royal thoughts did move)
Each was a noble cause, and nothing less,
Than the design, has been the great success:
Which forraign Kings, and Emperors esteem
The second honour to their Diadem.
Had thy great Destiny but given thee skill,
To know as well, as power to act her will,   90
That from those Kings, who then thy captives were,
In after-times should spring a Royal pair[13]
Who should possess all that thy mighty power,
Or thy desires more mighty, did devour;
To whom their better Fate reserves what ere
The Victor hopes for, or the Vanquisht fear;

---

[7] *1668, Marginal note, Edward* the Third and the *Black Prince.*
[8] *1668, Marginal note,* Queen *Phillip*[pa].
[9] King David II of Scotland, captured at the battle of Neville's Cross, 1346.
[10] King John II of France, captured at the battle of Poitiers, 1356.

[11]   "Oh would'st thou sing what heroes Windsor bore,
         What kings first breathed upon her winding shore,
         Or raise old warriors, whose adored remains
         In weeping vaults her hallowed earth contains!
         With Edward's acts adorn the shining page,
         Stretch his long triumphs down through ev'ry age,
         Draw monarchs chained, and Crecy's glorious field,
         The lilies blazing on the regal shield."
                         Pope, *Windsor Forest,* ll. 299-306.
[12] The Order of the Garter.
[13] Charles I and Henrietta Maria. The allusion is not strictly accurate, as
the direct line of descent from David II and John II fails in both cases.
Charles I is, however, the direct descendant of Robert II, nephew of David II;
Henrietta Maria the direct descendant of Robert, Duc de Vendome, sixth son
of Louis IX. John II descends from Phillipe III, second son of Louis IX.

1655   109: He, who needs not that Embleme which we paint,

1642   101-113: Thou hadst extended through the conquer'd East,
MS.H.367   Thine and the Christian name, and made them blest
MS.H.837   To serve thee, while that losse this gaine would bring,
Christ for their God, and *Edward* for their King;
When thou that Saint thy Patron didst designe,
In whom the Martyr, and the Souldier joyne;
And when thou didst within the Azure round,
(Who evill thinks may evill him confound)
The English Armes encircle, thou didst seeme
But to foretell, and Prophecie of him,
Who has within that Azure round confin'd
These Realmes, which Nature for their bound design'd.
That bound which to the worlds extreamest ends,
Endlesse her selfe, her liquid armes extends;
In whose Heroicke face I see the Saint
Better exprest then in the liveliest paint,
That fortitude which made him famous here,
That heavenly piety, which Saints him there,
Who when this Order he forsakes, may he
Companion of that sacred Order be.
Here could I fix my wonder, but our eyes,
Nice as our tastes, affect varieties;
And though one please him most, the hungry guest
Tasts every dish, and runs through all the feast;
So having tasted *Windsor*, casting round
My wandring eye, an emulous Hill doth bound,
My more contracted sight, whose top of late

1642
MS.H.367   115: The neighbouring Abbey fell, . . .
MS.H.837

1642
MS.H.367   122: But they, alas, were rich, and he was poor;
MS.H.837

MS.H.367   123: And having . . .
MS.H.837

That bloud, which thou and thy great Grandsire shed,
And all that since these sister Nations bled,
Had been unspilt, had happy *Edward* known
That all the bloud he spilt, had been his own.   100
When he that Patron chose,[14] in whom are joyn'd
Souldier and Martyr, and his arms confin'd
Within the Azure Circle,[15] he did seem
But to foretell, and prophesie of him,[16]
Who to his Realms that Azure round hath joyn'd,
Which Nature for their bound at first design'd.
That bound, which to the Worlds extreamest ends,
Endless it self, its liquid arms extends;
Nor doth he need those Emblemes which we paint,
But is himself the Souldier and the Saint.   110
Here should my wonder dwell, & here my praise,
But my fixt thoughts my wandring eye betrays,
Viewing a neighbouring hill,[17] whose top of late
A Chappel crown'd, till in the Common Fate,
The adjoyning Abby[18] fell: (may no such storm
Fall on our times, where ruine must reform.)
Tell me (my Muse) what monstrous dire offence,
What crime could any Christian King incense
To such a rage? Was't Luxury, or Lust?
Was he so temperate, so chast, so just?   120
Were these their crimes? They were his own much more:
But wealth is Crime enough to him that's poor,
Who having spent the Treasures of his Crown,
Condemns their Luxury to feed his own.
And yet this Act, to varnish o're the shame
Of sacriledge, must bear devotions name.

[14] St. George.
[15] This is probably the silver star, worn by knights of the order, which has in the middle the red cross of St. George encircled by the blue garter. It was not, however, part of the original insignia.
[16] Charles I.
[17] St. Anne's Hill.
[18] Chertsey Abbey.

1642 127-133: And he might think it just, the cause and time
MS.H.367 Considered well, for none commits a crime
MS.H.837 Appearing such, but as 'tis understood
    A reall or at least a seeming good.
    While for the church his learned pen disputes,
    His much more learned sword his pen confutes;
    Thus to the ages past he makes amends

1642
MS.H.367 149-156 omitted.
MS.H.837

No Crime so bold, but would be understood
A real, or at least a seeming good.
Who fears not to do ill, yet fears the Name,
And free from Conscience, is a slave to Fame.   130
Thus he the Church at once protects, & spoils:
But Princes swords are sharper than their stiles.[19]
And thus to th' ages past he makes amends,
Their Charity destroys, their Faith defends.
Then did Religion in a lazy Cell,
In empty, airy contemplations dwell;
And like the block, unmoved lay: but ours,
As much too active, like the stork devours.
Is there no temperate Region can be known,
Betwixt their Frigid, and our Torrid Zone?   140
Could we not wake from that Lethargick dream,
But to be restless in a worse extream?
And for that Lethargy was there no cure,
But to be cast into a Calenture?
Can knowledge have no bound, but must advance
So far, to make us wish for ignorance?
And rather in the dark to grope our way,
Than led by a false guide to erre by day?
Who sees these dismal heaps, but would demand
What barbarous Invader sackt the land?   150
But when he hears, no Goth, no Turk did bring
This desolation, but a Christian King;
When nothing, but the Name of Zeal, appears
'Twixt our best actions and the worst of theirs,
What does he think our Sacriledge would spare,
When such th' effects of our devotions are?
Parting from thence 'twixt anger, shame, & fear,
Those for whats past, & this for whats too near:
My eye descending from the Hill, surveys
Where *Thames* amongst the wanton vallies strays.   160

---

[19] The reference is to Henry VIII's ineffective book, *Assertio septem sacra-
mentorum adversus Martinum Lutherum*, 1521. For writing this Henry re-
ceived from the Pope the title of "Defender of the Faith."

MS. H. 367 161-162: Sweete Thames, the Eldest, and the Noblest Son
MS. H. 837 Of ould Oceanus, doth swiftlye runne

    1642
MS. H. 367 165-166: And though his clearer sand no golden veynes
MS. H. 837 Like Tagus and Pactolus streams containes
  1642
MS. H. 367 171-172 omitted.
MS. H. 837

    1642 173: Nor with a furious and unruly wave
MS. H. 367 Nor with an angry, and unrulye wave
MS. H. 837
    1642 177-186: Then like a lover he forsakes his shores,
MS. H. 837 Whose stay with jealous eyes his spouse implores
            Till with a parting kisse he saves her teares,
            And promising returne, secures her feares;
            As a wise kinge first settles fruitfull peace, etc. (see below)

MS. H. 367 177-186: And as a parting Lover bidds farewell
            To his soules joy seeinge her Eylids swell
            He turnes againe to save her falling teares,
            And with a partinge kisse secures her feares
            So Thames unwillinge yet to be divorc't
            From his lov'd Channell, willingly is forc't
            Backwards against his proper course to swell,
            To take his second though not last farewell:
    1642 As a wise kinge first settles fruitfull peace
MS. H. 367 In his owne realmes, and with their rich increase
MS. H. 837 Seekes warrs abroad, and then in triumph brings
            The spoyles of kingdomes, and the crowns of kings;
            So Thames to London doth at first present
            Those tributes which the neighboring countries sent;
            But as his second visit from the east,
            Spices he brings and treasures from the west;
            Finds wealth where 'tis, and gives it where it wants,
            Cities in deserts, woods in cities plants;
omitted in Rounds the whole globe, and with his flying towers
MS. H. 837 Brings home to us and makes both Indies ours.

Thames, the most lov'd of all the Oceans sons,
By his old Sire to his embraces runs,
Hasting to pay his tribute to the Sea,
Like mortal life to meet Eternity.[20]
Though with those streams he no resemblance hold,
Whose foam is Amber, and their Gravel Gold;
His genuine, and less guilty wealth t' explore,
Search not his bottom, but survey his shore;[21]
Ore which he kindly spreads his spacious wing,
And hatches plenty for th' ensuing Spring.   170
Nor then destroys it with too fond a stay,
Like Mothers which their Infants overlay.
Nor with a sudden and impetuous wave,
Like profuse Kings, resumes the wealth he gave.
No unexpected inundations spoyl
The mowers hopes, nor mock the plowmans toyl:[22]
But God-like his unwearied Bounty flows;
First loves to do, then loves the Good he does.
Nor are his Blessings to his banks confin'd,
But free, and common, as the Sea or Wind;[23]   180
When he to boast, or to disperse his stores
Full of the tributes of his grateful shores,
Visits the world, and in his flying towers
Brings home to us, and makes both *Indies* ours;
Finds wealth where 'tis, bestows it where it wants

20   "And see the rivers how they run . . .
              A various journey to the deep,
              Like human life to endless sleep."
                          Dyer, John, *Grongar Hill*, ll. 93-98.

21   "O'er golden sand let rich Pactolus flow,
              And trees weep amber on the banks of Po;
              Bright Thames's shores the brightest beauties yield;
              Feed here, my lambs, I'll seek no distant field."
                          Pope, *Pastorals, Spring*, ll. 61-64.

22 *Cf. Destruction of Troy*, ll. 294-295.

23   "The time shall come, when, free as seas or wind,
              Unbounded Thames shall flow for all mankind."
                          Pope, *Windsor Forest*, ll. 397-398.

MS. H. 837 Between 188-189: And on the Theames, as many Nations floate
As when Mankinde all soujurn'd in a Boate

1642 189-196: O could my verse freely and smoothly flow
As thy pure flood, heaven should no longer know
Her old Eridanus; thy purer streame
Should bathe the gods, and be the poet's theame

MS. H. 367 189-196: O could my Lynes fullye and smoothlye flowe
MS. H. 837 As thy pure flood, etc. (as in 1642 variant above)

1655 193-196 omitted.

Cities in deserts, woods in Cities plants.
So that to us no thing, no place is strange,
While his fair bosom is the worlds exchange.
O could I flow like thee, and make thy stream[24]
My great example, as it is my theme!   190
Though deep, yet clear, though gentle, yet not dull,
Strong without rage, without ore-flowing full.[25]
Heaven her *Eridanus* no more shall boast,
Whose Fame in thine, like lesser Currents lost,
Thy Nobler streams shall visit *Jove's* aboads,
To shine amongst the Stars, and bath the Gods.[26]
Here Nature, whether more intent to please
Us or her self, with strange varieties,
(For things of wonder give no less delight
To the wise Maker's, than beholders sight.   200
Though these delights from several causes move

[24] For references to lines 189-192 see Appendix E.

[25]   "In Thames, the ocean's darling, England's pride,
            The pleasing emblem of his reign does glide:
            Thames the support and glory of our isle,
            Richer than Tagus or Aegyptian Nile.
            Though no rich sand in him, no pearls are found,
            Yet fields rejoice and meadows laugh around;
            Less wealth his bosom holds, less guilty stores,
            For he exhausts himself t' enrich the shores.
            Mild and serene the peaceful current flows,
            No angry foam, no raging surges knows;
            No dreadful wreck upon his banks appears,
            His crystal stream unstain'd by widow's tears,
            His channel strong and easy, deep and clear.
            No arbitrary inundations sweep
            The ploughman's hopes and life into the deep;
            The even waters the old limits keep."
                        Halifax, Charles Montague, Earl of, *On the
                                Death of . . . Charles II*, ll. 127-143.

[26]   "No seas so rich, so gay no banks appear,
        No lake so gentle, and no spring so clear.
        Nor Po so swells the fabling poet's lays
        While led along the skies his current strays,
        As thine, which visits Windsor's famed abodes,
        To grace the mansion of our earthly gods."
                        Pope, *Windsor Forest*, ll. 225-230.

MS. H. 837 211-212 omitted.

1642
MS. H. 367   217-233: And such the roughnesse of the Hill, on which
MS. H. 837   *Dyana* her toyles, and *Mars* his tents might pitch.

MS. H. 367
angry   And as our *surly* supercilious Lords,
MS. H. 837

Bigge in their frownes, and haughty in their words,
Looke downe on those, whose humble fruitfull paine
Their proud, and barren greatnesse must susteine:
So lookes the Hill upon the streame, betweene
There lies a spatious, and a fertile Greene,
Where from the woods, the *Dryades* oft meet
The *Nayades,* and with their nimble feet,
Soft dances lead, although their airie shape

For so our children, thus our friends we love)
Wisely she knew, the harmony of things,
As well as that of sounds, from discords springs.
Such was the discord, which did first disperse
Form, order, beauty through the Universe;
While driness moysture, coldness heat resists,
All that we have, and that we are, subsists.
While the steep horrid roughness of the Wood
Strives with the gentle calmness of the flood.   210
Such huge extreams when Nature doth unite,
Wonder from thence results, from thence delight.
The stream is so transparent, pure, and clear,
That had the self-enamour'd youth gaz'd here,
So fatally deceiv'd he had not been,
While he the bottom, not his face had seen.
But his proud head the aery Mountain hides
Among the Clouds; his shoulders, and his sides
A shady mantle cloaths; his curled brows
Frown on the gentle stream, which calmly flows,   220
While winds and storms his lofty forehead beat:
The common fate of all that's high or great.
Low at his foot a spacious plain is plac't,
Between the mountain and the stream embrac't:
Which shade and shelter from the Hill derives,
While the kind river wealth and beauty gives;
And in the mixture of all these appears
Variety, which all the rest indears.
This scene had some bold Greek, or Brittish Bard
Beheld of old, what stories had we heard,   230
Of Fairies, Satyrs, and the Nymphs their Dames,
Their feasts, their revels, & their amorous flames:
'Tis still the same, although their aery shape
All but a quick Poetick sight escape.[27]

[27]   "Though marked by none but quick, poetic eyes."
                    Pope, *Rape of the Lock,* Canto V, l. 124.

1642   236: . . . the horrid hoast resorts.

1642   Between 236-237:
MS. H. 367   (When like the Elixar, with his evening beames,
MS. H. 837   The Sunne has turn'd to gold the silver streames)

1642
MS. H. 367   240: . . . but sooner much undone.
MS. H. 837

1642
MS. H. 367   241: Here have I seene our *Charles* . . .
MS. H. 837

1642   243-271: Chacing the royall Stagge, the gallant beast,
MS. H. 367   Rowz'd with the noyse 'twixt hope and feare distrest,
MS. H. 837   Resolv's 'tis better to avoyd, then meet
His danger, trusting to his winged feet:
But when he sees the dogs, now by the view
Now by the scent his speed with speed pursue,
He tries his friends, amongst the lesser Heard,

There *Faunus* and *Sylvanus* keep their Courts,
And thither all the horned hoast resorts,
To graze the ranker mead, that noble heard
On whose sublime and shady fronts is rear'd
Natures great Master-piece; to shew how soon
Great things are made, but sooner are undone.   240
Here have I seen the King, when great affairs
Give leave to slacken, and unbend his cares,
Attended to the Chase by all the flower
Of youth, whose hopes a Nobler prey devour:
Pleasure with Praise, & danger, they would buy,
And wish a foe that would not only fly.
The stagg now conscious of his fatal Growth,
At once indulgent to his fear and sloth,
To some dark covert his retreat had made,
Where nor mans eye, nor heavens should invade   250
His soft repose; when th' unexpected sound
Of dogs, and men, his wakeful ear doth wound.
Rouz'd with the noise, he scarce believes his ear,
Willing to think th' illusions of his fear
Had given this false Alarm, but straight his view
Confirms, that more than all he fears is true.
Betray'd in all his strengths, the wood beset,
All instruments, all Arts of ruine met;
He calls to mind his strength, and then his speed,
His winged heels, and then his armed head;   260
With these t' avoid, with that his Fate to meet:
But fear prevails, and bids him trust his feet.
So fast he flyes, that his reviewing eye
Has lost the chasers, and his ear the cry;
Exulting, till he finds, their Nobler sense
Their disproportion'd speed does recompense.
Then curses his conspiring feet, whose scent
Betrays that safety which their swiftness lent.
Then tries his friends, among the baser herd,

Where he but lately was obey'd, and feard,
Safety he seekes, the heard unkindly wise,

1642
MS. H. *367*   275-288 omitted.
MS. H. *837*

MS. H. *367*   292: . . . when tis in vayne to feare.
MS. H. *837*

1642
MS. H. *367*   293-294 omitted.
MS. H. *837*

1642   297-303: When neither speed, nor art, nor friends, nor force

Where he so lately was obey'd, and fear'd,[28]   270
His safety seeks: the herd, unkindly wise,
Or chases him from thence, or from him flies.
Like a declining States-man, left forlorn
To his friends pity, and pursuers scorn,
With shame remembers, while himself was one
Of the same herd, himself the same had done.
Thence to the coverts, & the conscious Groves,
The scenes of his past triumphs, and his loves;
Sadly surveying where he rang'd alone
Prince of the soyl, and all the herd his own;   280
And like a bold Knight Errant did proclaim
Combat to all, and bore away the Dame;
And taught the woods to eccho to the stream
His dreadful challenge, and his clashing beam.
Yet faintly now declines the fatal strife;
So much his love was dearer than his life.
Now every leaf, and every moving breath
Presents a foe, and every foe a death.
Wearied, forsaken, and pursu'd, at last
All safety in despair of safety plac'd,   290
Courage he thence resumes, resolv'd to bear
All their assaults, since 'tis in vain to fear.
And now too late he wishes for the fight
That strength he wasted in Ignoble flight:
But when he sees the eager chase renew'd,
Himself by dogs, the dogs by men pursu'd:
He straight revokes his bold resolve, and more
Repents his courage, than his fear before;
Finds that uncertain waies unsafest are,
And Doubt a greater mischief than Despair.   300
Then to the stream, when neither friends, nor force,

28   "In Windsor Forest before war destroy'd
        The harmless pleasures which soft peace injoy'd
        A mighty stagg grew monarch of the heard,
        By all his savage slaves obey'd and fear'd."
                Howard, Sir Robert, *The Duell of the Stags,* ll. 1-4.

MS.H.367   Could helpe him towards the streame he bends his course.
MS.H.837   Hoping those lesser beasts would not assay

MS.H.367   307-322: As, in a calme, the oare-fin'de Gallyes creepe
MS.H.837   About a wyndbound, and unweildye Shippe
            Which lyes unmov'd, butt those that come to neare
            Strykes with her thunder, and the rest with feare,
            Tyll through her many Leakes the Sea she drinks,
            Nor yeildes att last; Butt still resistinge sinks,
            Soe standes the Stagg amoungst the lesser Houndes
            Repells their force, and woundes returnes for woundes
            Till Charles from his unerringe hand letts flye
            A Mortall shaft, then glad, and proude to dye
            By such a wounde he falls, the christall floode
            Dyinge he dyes, and purples with his bloode.
            (lines 313-318 omitted)

1642   307-312 omitted.

1642   313: As some brave *Hero*, . . .

1642   316: By vulgar hands, . . .

1642   319-322: So the tall Stagge, amids the lesser hounds
            Repels their force, and wounds returne for wounds,
            Till *Charles* from his unerring hand lets flie
            A mortall shaft, then glad, and proud to dye
            By such a wound he fals, the Chrystall flood
            Dying he dyes, and purples with his blood:

1642
MS.H.367   326: To tyranny, . . .
MS.H.837

1642   Between 328-329: For armed subjects can have no pretence
MS.H.367   Against their Princes, but their just defence,
MS.H.837   And whether then, or no, I leave to them
            To justifie, who else themselves condemne:
            Yet might the fact be just, if we may guesse
            The justnesse of an action from successe

MS.H.367
MS.H.837   333-334 omitted.

Nor speed, nor Art avail, he shapes his course;
Thinks not their rage so desperate t' assay
An Element more merciless than they.
But fearless they pursue, nor can the floud
Quench their dire thirst; alas, they thirst for bloud.
So towards a Ship the oarefin'd Gallies ply,
Which wanting Sea to ride, or wind to fly,
Stands but to fall reveng'd on those that dare
Tempt the last fury of extream despair.   310
So fares the Stagg among th' enraged Hounds,
Repels their force, and wounds returns for wounds.
And as a Hero, whom his baser foes
In troops surround, now these assails, now those,
Though prodigal of life, disdains to die
By common hands; but if he can descry
Some nobler foes approach, to him he calls,
And begs his Fate, and then contented falls.
So when the King a mortal shaft lets fly
From his unerring hand, then glad to dy,   320
Proud of the wound, to it resigns his bloud,
And stains the Crystal with a Purple floud.
This a more Innocent, and happy chase,
Than when of old, but in the self-same place,[29]
Fair liberty pursu'd, and meant a Prey
To lawless power, here turn'd, and stood at bay.
When in that remedy all hope was plac't
Which was, or should have been at least, the last.
Here was that Charter seal'd,[30] wherein the Crown
All marks of Arbitrary power lays down: 330
Tyrant and slave, those names of hate and fear,
The happier stile of King and Subject bear:
Happy, when both to the same Center move,
When Kings give liberty, and Subjects love.

[29] *1668, Marginal note,* Runnymede.
[30] *1668, Marginal note,* Magna Charta.

MS. H. 367 335-336: And yett not longe in force this charter stoode
MS. H. 837 The counterparte was often seal'd in Blood

1642
MS. H. 367 338: But this advantage tooke, . . .
MS. H. 837

MS. H. 367 339 to end: And as by gyvenge the kinges power growes lesse,
MS. H. 837 Soe by reneywing, their demaundes increase,
To lymitt royall greatnes, all conspire,
While each forgetts to lymitt his desire,
Till kinges, lyke ould Anteus, by their fall,
Reenforc't, their courage, from despayre recall,
When a calme river, etc. as in 1642 variant following.

1642 343 to end: And they, whom no denyall can withstand,
Seeme but to aske, while they indeed command.
Thus all to limit Royalty conspire,
While each forgets to limit his desire.
Till Kings like old *Antaeus* by their fall,

1642 Being forc't, their courage from despaire recall.
MS. H. 367 When a calme River rais'd with sudden raines,
MS. H. 837 Or Snowes dissolv'd o'reflowes th' adjoyning Plaines
The Husbandmen with high rais'd bankes secure
Their greedy hopes, and this he can endure,

MS. H. 367
bayes But if with *Bogs,* and Dammes they strive to force,
MS. H. 837

current
MS. H. 367 His *channell* to a new, or narrow course.

No longer then within his bankes he dwels,
First to a Torrent, then a Deluge swels
Stronger, and fiercer by restraint he roares,

MS. H. 367
boundes And knowes no *bound,* but makes his powers his shores:

MS. H. 367
could Thus Kings by grasping more then they *can* hold,
First made their Subjects by oppressions bold,
And popular sway by forcing Kings to give
More, then was fit for Subjects to receive,

Therefore not long in force this Charter stood;
Wanting that seal, it must be seal'd in bloud.
The Subjects arm'd, the more their Princes gave,
Th' advantage only took the more to crave.
Till Kings by giving, give themselves away,
And even that power, that should deny, betray.   340
"Who gives constrain'd, but his own fear reviles
"Not thank't, but scorn'd; nor are they gifts, but spoils.[31]
Thus Kings, by grasping more than they could hold,
First made their Subjects by oppression bold:
And popular sway, by forcing Kings to give
More than was fit for Subjects to receive,

[31] This quotation, if it is one, I have not been able to locate.

Ranne to the same extreame, and one excesse
Made both by stirring to be greater, lesse,
Nor any way, but seeking to have more
Makes either loose, what each possest before.
Therefore their boundlesse power tell Princes draw
Within the Channell, and the shores of Law,
And may that Law, which teaches Kings to sway
Their Scepters, teach their Subjects to obey.

Ran to the same extreams; and one excess
Made both, by striving to be greater, less.
When a calm River rais'd with sudden rains,
Or Snows dissolv'd, oreflows th' adjoyning Plains,   350
The Husbandmen with high-rais'd banks secure
Their greedy hopes, and this he can endure.
But if with Bays and Dams they strive to force
His channel to a new, or narrow course;
No longer then within his banks he dwells,
First to a Torrent, then a Deluge swells:
Stronger, and fiercer by restraint he roars,
And knows no bound, but makes his power his shores.[32]

[32] Cf. *The Destruction of Troy*, ll. 482-485.

A SONG[1]

Morpheus[2] the humble God, that dwells
In cottages and smoaky cells,
Hates gilded roofs and beds of down;
And though he fears no Princes frown,
Flies from the circle of a Crown.[3]

Come, I say, thou powerful God,
And thy Leaden charming Rod,
Dipt in the Lethæan Lake,
Ore his wakeful temples shake,
Lest he should sleep and never wake.

Nature (alas) why art thou so
Obliged to thy greatest Foe?
Sleep that is thy best repast,
Yet of death it bears a taste,
And both are the same thing at last.

[1] From *The Sophy,* first printed in 1642, see p. 296. Printed also as a separate
poem in the 1668 collected edition.

[2] *1668, Somnus.* This was corrected in the errata.
1671, as above.
1684, as above.

[3]   "Why rather, sleep, liest thou in smoky cribs,
        Upon uneasy pallets stretching thee
        And hush'd with buzzing night-flies to thy slumber.
        Than in the perfumed chambers of the great,
        Under the canopies of costly state,
        And lull'd with sound of greatest melody."
                        Henry IV, part II: Act III, Sc. i, ll. 9-14.

NEWS FROM COLCHESTER[1]

OR, A PROPER NEW BALLAD OF CERTAIN CARNAL PASSAGES BETWIXT A QUAKER AND A COLT, AT HORSLY NEAR COLCHESTER IN ESSEX

To the Tune of, Tom of Bedlam.

All in the Land of *Essex,*[2]
Near *Colchester* the Zealous,
  On the side of a bank,
  Was play'd such a Prank,
As would make a Stone-horse[3] jealous.

Help *Woodcock,*[4] *Fox*[5] and *Nailor,*[6]
For Brother *Green's* a Stallion,
  Now alas what hope
  Of converting the Pope,
When a Quaker turns *Italian?*

---

[1] An imitation of this poem, entitled *A Ballad,* by H. Hall of Hereford, which begins "Twas in the land of cyder," appears in *The Grove,* etc., 1721, and *The Nightingale,* etc., 1738.

[2]   " 'All in the land of Essex' next he chaunts,
    How to sleek mares starch Quakers turn gallants;
    How the grave brother stood on bank so green.
    Happy for him if mares had never been!"
                 Gay, *The Shepherd's Week, Saturday,* ll. 109-112.

There is an allusion to "The Essex Quaker" in a letter of Lady Mary Wortley Montagu. Swift, *Works* (ed. Bohn), VIII, 20.

[3] Stallion.

[4] Francis Woodcock was a graduate of Brazen Nose College, Oxford. He was a Parliamentarian, and a member of the Assembly of Divines. Neal, Daniel, *History of the Puritans,* 1844, II, 129.

[5] George Fox was the founder of the sect of Quakers. He thought that it had been revealed to him that all education was useless, and that everything depended on spiritual enlightenment. He first began to teach in 1647 the doctrine of the inner light.

[6] James Naylor was an extravagant, fanatical Quaker who had a considerable following who looked upon him as Christ incarnate. He was pilloried, branded, and tortured by Parliament for blasphemy. Neal, Daniel, *History of the Puritans,* 1844, II, 164-166, 491 ff.

Even to our whole profession
A scandal 'twill be counted,
  When 'tis talkt with disdain
  Amongst the Profane,
How brother *Green* was mounted.

And in the Good time of Christmas,
Which though our Saints have damn'd all,[7]
  Yet when did they hear
  That a damn'd Cavalier
Ere play'd such a Christmas gambal?

Had thy flesh, O *Green,* been pamper'd
With any Cates unhallow'd,
  Hadst thou sweetned thy Gums
  With Pottage of Plums,
Or prophane minc'd Pie hadst swallow'd,

Roll'd up in wanton Swine's-flesh,
The Fiend might have crept into thee;
  Then fullness of gut
  Might have caus'd thee to rut,
And the Devil have so rid through thee.

But alas he had been feasted
With a Spiritual Collation,
  By our frugal Mayor,[8]
  Who can dine on a Prayer,
And sup on an Exhortation.

'Twas meer impulse of Spirit,
Though he us'd the weapon carnal:
  Filly Foal, quoth he,
  My Bride thou shalt be:
And how this is lawful, learn all.

[7] On December 19, 1644, Parliament passed an ordinance that "monthly fasts should be continued, especially on Christmas, in remembrance of our sins, instead of having a sensual feast."

[8] This may be a reference to Sir Isaac Penington, Lord Mayor of London. See p. 132 n.

For if no respect of Persons
Be due 'mongst Sons of *Adam*,[9]
   In a large extent,
   Thereby may be meant
That a *Mare's* as good as a *Madam*.

Then without more Ceremony,
Not Bonnet vail'd, nor kist her,
   But took her by force,
   For better or worse,
And us'd her like a Sister.

Now when in such a Saddle
A Saint will needs be riding,
   Though we dare not say
   'Tis a falling away,
May there not be some back-sliding?

No surely, quoth *James Naylor*,
'Twas but an insurrection
   Of the Carnal part,
   For a Quaker in heart
Can never lose perfection.

For (as our Masters[10] teach us)
The intent being well directed,
   Though the Devil trepan
   The Adamical man,
The Saint stands un-infected.

But alas a Pagan Jury
Ne're judges what's intended,

---

[9] *1668*, " 'mongst the sons . . ." This was corrected in the errata.
1671, as above.
1684, as above.
[10] *1668*, *Marginal note*, the Jesuits. "The news had got abroad, moreover, that 'subtle and dangerous heads,' Jesuits and others had begun to 'creep in among them' to turn Quakerism to political account, and 'drive on designs of disturbance.' " Masson, *Life of Milton*, V, 69.

Then say what we can,
Brother *Green's* outward man
I fear will be suspended.

And our Adopted Sister
Will find no better quarter,[11]
    But when him we inroul
    For a Saint, Filly Foal
Shall pass her self for a Martyr.

Rome that Spiritual *Sodom,*
No longer is thy debter,
    O *Colchester,* now
    Who's *Sodom* but thou,
Even according to the Letter?

THE PROLOGUE TO HIS MAJESTY[1]

Greatest of Monarchs, welcome to this place
Which *Majesty* so oft was wont to grace
Before our Exile, to divert the Court,
And ballance weighty Cares with harmless sport.
This truth we can to our advantage say,
They that would have no *KING*, would have no Play:
The *Laurel* and the *Crown* together went,
Had the same *Foes*, and the same *Banishment:*
The Ghosts of their[2] great Ancestors they fear'd,
Who by the art of conjuring Poets rear'd,
Our *HARRIES* and our *EDWARDS* long since dead
Still on the Stage a march of Glory tread:

[11] "And if a man lie with a beast, he shall surely be put to death; and ye shall slay the beast." (Leviticus, 20:15.) This principle was incorporated into English law.
  [1] Assigned to Denham by Wood (*Athenae Oxoniensis*, 1721, II, 424). The evidence of style supports Wood. First printed in 1660.
  [2] The British Museum copy has a MS. correction to *your.*

Those Monuments of Fame (they thought) would stain
And teach the People to despise their Reign:
Nor durst they look into the Muses Well,
Least the cleer Spring their ugliness should tell;
Affrighted with the shadow of their Rage,
They broke the Mirror of the times, the Stage;
The Stage against them still maintain'd the War,
When they debauch'd the *Pulpit* and the *Bar*.
Though to be *Hypocrites,* be our Praise alone,
'Tis our peculiar boast that we were none.
Whatere they taught, we practis'd what was true,
And something we had learn'd of honor too,
When by Your Danger, and our Duty prest,
We acted in the Field, and not in Jest;
Then for the *Cause* our Tyring-house they sack't,
And silenc't us that they alone might act;
And (to our shame) most dext'rously they do it,
Out-act the Players, and out-ly the Poet;
But all the other Arts appear'd so scarce,
Ours were the *Moral Lectures,* theirs the *Farse:*
This spacious Land their Theater became,
And they *Grave Counsellors,* and *Lords* in Name;
Which these Mechanicks Personate so ill
That ev'n the Oppressed with contempt they fill,
But when the Lyons dreadful skin they took,
They roar'd so loud that the whole Forrest shook;
The noise kept all the Neighborhood in awe,
Who thought 'twas the true Lyon by his Pawe.
If feigned Vertue could such Wonders do,
What may we not expect from this that's true!
But this Great Theme must serve another Age,
To fill our Story, and adorne our Stage.

FRIENDSHIP AND SINGLE LIFE AGAINST LOVE AND MARRIAGE[1]

Love! in what poyson is thy Dart
Dipt, when it makes a bleeding heart?
None know, but they who feel the smart.

It is not thou, but we are blind,
And our corporeal eyes (we find)
Dazle the Opticks of our Mind.

Love to our Cittadel resorts,
Through those deceitful Sally-ports,
Our Sentinels betray our Forts.

What subtle Witchcraft man constrains,
To change his Pleasures into Pains,
And all his freedom into Chains?

May not a Prison, or a Grave
Like Wedlock, Honour's title have?
That word makes Free-born man a Slave.

How happy he that loves not, lives!
Him neither Hope nor Fear deceives,
To Fortune who no Hostage gives.

How unconcern'd in things to come!
If here uneasie, finds at *Rome*,
At *Paris*, or *Madrid* his Home.

Secure from low, and private Ends,
His Life, his Zeal, his Wealth attends
His Prince, his Country, and his Friends.

[1] First printed in the 1668 collected edition.

Danger, and Honour are his Joy;
But a fond Wife, or wanton Boy,
May all those Generous Thoughts destroy.

Then he lays by the publick Care,
Thinks of providing for an Heir;.
Learns how to get, and how to spare.

Nor fire, nor foe, nor fate, nor night,
The Trojan Hero did affright,[2]
Who bravely twice renew'd the fight.

Though still his foes in number grew,
Thicker their Darts, and Arrows flew,
Yet left alone, no fear he knew.

But Death in all her forms appears,
From every thing he sees and hears,
For whom he leads, and whom he bears.[3]

Love making all things else his Foes,
Like a fierce torrent overflows
Whatever doth his course oppose.

This was the cause the Poets sung,
Thy Mother from the Sea was sprung;
But they were mad to make thee young.

Her Father, not her Son, art thou:
From our desires our actions grow;
And from the Cause the Effect must flow.

Love is as old as place or time;
'Twas he the fatal Tree did climb,
Grandsire of Father *Adam's* crime.

Well mayst thou keep this world in awe,
Religion, Wisdom, Honour, Law,
The tyrant in his triumph draw.

[2] Aeneas.
[3] *1668, Marginal note,* His Father and Son.

'Tis he commands the Powers above;
Phœbus resigns his Darts, and *Jove*
His Thunder to the God of Love.

To him doth his feign'd Mother yield,
Nor *Mars* (her Champions) flaming shield
Guards him, when *Cupid* takes the Field.

He clips hopes wings, whose aery bliss
Much higher than fruition is;
But less than nothing, if it miss.

When matches Love alone projects,
The Cause transcending the Effects,
That wild-fire's quencht in cold neglects.

Whilst those Conjunctions prove the best,
Where Love's of blindness dispossest,
By perspectives of Interest.

Though *Solomon* with a thousand wives,
To get a wise Successor strives,
But one (and he a Fool) survives.

Old *Rome* of Children took no care,
They with their Friends their beds did share,
Secure, t'adopt a hopeful Heir.

Love drowsie days, and stormy nights
Makes, and breaks Friendship, whose delights
Feed, but not glut our Appetites.

Well chosen Friendship, the most noble
Of Vertues, all our joys makes double,
And into halves divides our trouble.

But when the unlucky knot we tye,
Care, Avarice, Fear, and Jealousie
Make Friendship languish till it dye.

The Wolf, the Lyon, and the Bear
When they their prey in pieces tear,
To quarrel with themselves forbear.

Yet timerous Deer, and harmless Sheep
When Love into their veins doth creep,
That law of Nature cease to keep.

Who then can blame the Amorous Boy,
Who the Fair *Helen* to enjoy,
To quench his own, set fire on *Troy?*

Such is the worlds preposterous fate,
Amongst all Creatures, mortal hate
Love (though immortal) doth Create.

But Love may Beasts excuse, for they
Their actions not by Reason sway,
But their brute appetites obey.

But Man's that Savage Beast, whose mind
From Reason to self-Love declin'd,
Delights to prey upon his Kind.

TO SIR JOHN MENNIS BEING INVITED FROM CALICE TO BOLOGNE TO EAT A PIG[1]

All on a weeping *Monday*,
 With a fat *Bulgarian* Sloven,
 Little Admiral *John*
 To *Bologne* is gone
Whom I think they call old *Loven.*[2]

Hadst thou not thy fill of Carting
 Will. Aubrey Count of *Oxon!*[3]
 When Nose lay in Breech
 And Breech made a Speech,
So often cry'd a Pox on.[4]

A Knight by Land and Water
 Esteem'd at such a high rate,
 When 'tis told in *Kent*,
 In a Cart that he went,
They'll say now hang him Pirate.

Thou might'st have ta'ne example,
 From what thou read'st in story;

---

[1] "Sir John Denham's poems are going to be all printed together; and among others, some new things; and among them he [Herringman] showed me a copy of verses of his upon Sir John Minnes going heretofore to Bullogne to eat a pig." Pepys, *Diary*, August 10, 1667.

Sir John Mennis (1598-1670) was a graduate of Oxford, "a great traveller, a most noted sea-man, and as well skill'd in marine affairs, in building of ships, and all belonging thereunto, as any man of his time." He was in the navy office under James I, and was Comptroller under Charles I. In 1641 he was knighted, and served at sea as Vice-Admiral. He was with Charles II in exile. At the Restoration he was made Chief Comptroller of the navy. He "was always poetically given, and therefore his company was delightful to all ingenious and witty men." Wood, *Athenae Oxoniensis*, 1721, II, 481.

[2] I have been unable to trace this allusion. Does it mean "loving"?

[3] Perhaps this is William Aubrey, younger brother of John Aubrey, the author of *Brief Lives*. The title here given to him is, of course, jocular.

[4] *1668, Marginal note*, We three riding in a Cart from *Dunkirk* to *Calice* with a fat Dutch Woman who broke wind all along.

Being as worthy to sit
On an ambling Tit,
As thy Predecessor *Dory.*[5]

But Oh! the roof of Linnen,
  Intended for a shelter!
  But the Rain made an Ass
  Of Tilt of Canvas;
And the Snow which you know is a Melter.

But with thee to inveigle,
  That tender stripling, *Astcot*[6]
  Who was soak'd to the skin,
  Through Drugget so thin,
Having neither Coat, nor Wastcoat;

He being proudly mounted,
  Y-clad[7] in Cloak of *Plymouth,*
  Defy'd Cart so base,
  For Thief without Grace,
That goes to make a wry-mouth.

Nor did he like the Omen,
  For fear it might be his doom,

[5] *John Dory* was the name of a popular song of the seventeenth century. The first stanza is as follows:

> "As it fell upon a holyday
>   And upon a holy-tide-a.,
>   John Dory bought him an ambling nag
>   To Paris for to ride-a."

It may be found in collections of songs and ballads of the period.

[6] This may possibly refer to Charles Dormer (1632-1709), who succeeded his father as Earl of Carnarvon, Viscount Ascott, and Baron Dormer of Wyng in 1643. Cokayne, G. E., *Complete Peerage,* 1889, II, 158.

[7] *1668,* Clad. This was corrected in the errata.
1671, as above.
1684, as above.

One day for to sing,
With Gullet in string,
A Hymne of *Robert Wisdom.*[8]

But what was all this business?
For sure it was important:
For who rides i' th' wet,
When affairs are not great,
The neighbors make but a sport on 't.

To a goodly fat Sow's Baby,
O *John,* thou had'st a malice,
The old driver of Swine
That day sure was thine,
Or thou hadst not quitted *Calice.*

---

[8] The only allusions to Wisdom that I have been able to find are the following:

"Thence with *short meal* and *tedious* Grace,
In a loud tone and Publick place,
Sing *Wisdoms hymnes,* that *trot* and pace,
As if *Goliah* scan'd 'um."
                    The Reformation, *Rump,* I, 275.

"That it may please thee to embalm
The Saints in *Robin Wisdom's Psalm,*
And make them musical and calm,"
                    A Lenten Litany, *Rump,* I, 165.

From these it would appear that Wisdom was some obscure religious scribbler.

A *DIALOGUE BETWEEN SIR* JOHN POOLEY *AND MR.* THOMAS KILLIGREW[1]

P. To thee, Dear *Thom.* my self addressing,
Most queremoniously confessing,[2]
That I of late have been compressing.

Destitute of my wonted Gravity,
I perpetrated Arts of Pravity,
In a contagious Concavity.[3]

Making efforts with all my Puissance,
For some Venereal Reiouissance,
I got (as one may say) a nuysance.[4]

K. Come leave this[5] fooling Cousin *Pooley,*
And in plain English tell us truely
Why under th' eyes you look so blewly?

---

[1] First printed in the 1668 collected edition. There is a MS. copy among the papers of the Marquis of Ormonde.

John Pooley (1603-1664), a royalist, was the third son of Sir William Pooley, Knight of Bury. He married in 1653 Catharine Despotine of Bury. Apparently he was once a clergyman. (See below, stanza 6.) He was of the Boxstead branch of this old Suffolk family. Harvey, William, *The Visitation of Suffolke* (ed. J. J. Howard), 1866, I, 269 ff. *Journal of the Lords,* Aug. 8, 15, 18, 1648.

Thomas Killigrew (1617-1638), the dramatist. He was arrested at the outbreak of the war for taking up arms for the King. On being released in 1644, he joined the King at Oxford. In 1647 he went abroad to Prince Charles. He was appointed resident at Venice in 1651, but was recalled the following year for corruption and general debauchery. After the Restoration, he was made Groom of the Bedchamber, Chamberlain to the Queen, and given a patent to erect a new playhouse and raise a company of players.

[2] *MS. Ormonde,* I needs must make my moane, confessing.

[3] *MS. Ormonde,*
> And having layd aside my gravity
> Have bin committing acts of pravity
> In an obnoxious concavity.

[4] *MS. Ormonde,* omits this stanza.

[5] *MS. Ormonde,* your.

'Tis not your hard words will avail you,
Your Latin and your Greek will fail you,
Till you speak plainly what doth ail you.[6]

When young, you led a life Monastick,
And wore a Vest Ecclesiastick;
Now in your Age you grow Fantastick.[7]

P. Without more Preface or Formality,
A Female of Malignant Quality
Set fire on Label of Mortality.[8]

The Fæces of which Ulceration,
Brought o're the Helm a Distillation,
Through the Instrument of Propagation.[9]

K. Then Cousin, (as I guess the matter)
You have been an old Fornicater,
And now[10] are shot 'twixt wind and Water.

Your style has such an ill complexion,
That from your breath I fear infection,
That even your mouth needs an injection.

You that were once so œconomick,
Quitting the thrifty style Laconick,
Turn Prodigal in Makeronick.[11]

[6] *MS. Ormonde,*
> Your hard words will not availe you,
> Your Greek and Latin too will fayle you,
> Till in plaine termes you tell what ayle[s] you.

[7] *MS. Ormonde,* omits this stanza.

[8] *MS. Ormonde,*
> To say the truth without formality
> A woeman of an evil quality
> Has burnt my labell of mortality.

[9] *MS. Ormonde,* omits this stanza.

[10] *MS. Ormonde,* omits "now."

[11] *MS. Ormonde,* omits last two stanzas.

Yet be of comfort, I shall send a
Person of knowledge who can mend a
Disaster in your nether end-a.[12]

Whether it *Pullen* be or *Shanker*,[13]
Corded and crooked like[14] an Anchor,
Your cure too costs[15] you but a spanker.

Or though your Piss[16] be sharp as Razor,
Do but confer[17] with Dr. *Frazer*,[18]
Hee'l make your Running Nag a Pacer.

Nor shall you need[19] your Silver quick Sir,
Take *Mongo Murry's Black Elixir*,
And in a week it Cures your P—— Sir.

But you that are a Man of Learning,
So read in *Virgil*, so discerning,
Methinks towards fifty should take warning.

Once in a Pit you did miscarry,
That danger might have made one wary;
This Pit is deeper then the Quarry.[20]

[12] *MS. Ormonde,*

> But be of comfort for I'll send
> One of condition that shall mend
> The disease in your nether end.

[13] *MS. Ormonde,* Be it poulin, chaudpis or shanker.
[14] *MS. Ormonde,* as.
[15] *MS. Ormonde,* shall cost.
[16] *MS. Ormonde,* Let you piss as.
[17] *MS. Ormonde,* advise.
[18] Dr. Frazer was the physician of Charles II. Clarendon, *History of the Rebellion*, V, 170.
[19] *MS. Ormonde,* You need not use.
[20] *MS. Ormonde,*

> In a stone-pitt once you did mis-carry,
> That danger might have made you wary;
> This pitt was worse than was the quarry.

1668, Marginal note, Hunting near *Paris* he and his Horse fell into a quarry.

P. Give me not such disconsolation,
   Having now cur'd my Inflamation,
   To Ulcerate my Reputation.[21]

Though it may gain the Ladies[22] favour,
Yet it may raise[23] an evil savour
Upon all grave and staid behaviour.

And I will rub my Mater Pia,
To find a Rhyme to Gonorrheia,
And put it in my Letania.[24]

NATURA NATURATA[1]

What gives us that Fantastick Fit,
That all our Judgment and our Wit
To vulgar custom we submit?

Treason, Theft, Murther, all the rest
Of that foul Legion we so detest,
Are in their proper names exprest.

Why is it then taught[2] sin or shame,
Those necessary parts to name,
From whence we went, and whence we came?

---

[21] *MS. Ormonde,*
> Deare Thom! give me this consolation,
> That having cure[d] my inflamation,
> You will not wound my reputation.

[22] *MS. Ormonde,* woman's.
[23] *MS. Ormonde,* I[t] will breed.
[24] *1671,* litania.
1684, litania.
  [1] Apparently written in 1650. (See below, note 3.) It was first printed in the 1668 collected edition.
  [2] *1668,* sought. This was corrected in the errata.
1671, thought.
1684, as above.

Nature, what ere she wants, requires;
With Love enflaming our desires,
Finds Engines fit to quench those fires:

Death she abhors; yet when men die,
We are present; but no stander by
Looks on when we that loss supply:

Forbidden Wares sell twice as dear;
Even Sack prohibited last year,
A most abominable rate did bear.[3]

'Tis plain our eyes and ears are nice,
Only to raise by that device,
Of those Commodities the price.

Thus Reason's shadows us betray
By Tropes and Figures led astray,
From Nature, both her Guide and way.

ON MY LORD CROFT'S AND MY JOURNEY INTO POLAND, FROM WHENCE WE BROUGHT 10000 L. FOR HIS MAJESTY BY THE DECIMATION OF HIS SCOTTISH SUBJECTS THERE[1]

Tole, tole,
Gentle Bell, for the Soul
Of the pure ones in *Pole,*
Which are damned in our Scroul;

[3] An Act Prohibiting the Importing of any wines, ·Wooll or Silk from the Kingdom of France into the Commonwealth of England or Ireland, or any of the Dominions thereunto belonging. 28 August, 1649. *Bibliotheca Lindesiana, Catalogue of Tudor & Stuart Proclamations,* No. 2867, I, 347.

[1] First printed in the 1668 collected edition. William, Lord Crofts. He was brought up at court, being master of the horse to James, Duke of York, captain

Who having felt a touch
Of *Cockram's* greedy Clutch,[2]
Which though it was not much,
Yet their stubbornness was such,

That when we did arrive,
'Gainst the stream we did strive;
They would neither lead, nor drive:

Nor lend
An Ear to a Friend,
Nor an answer would send
To our Letter so well penn'd.

of the guards to the Queen Mother, and gentleman of the bedchamber to Charles
II. He was created Baron Crofts of Saxham in 1658. He had charge of the Duke
of Monmouth after his mother's death. In 1660 he was sent on an embassy to
Poland to announce the King's accession. He died in 1677. Cokayne, G. E., *Complete Peerage*, 1889, II, 426; Dugdale, William, *Baronage*, 1676, II, 476.

He was sent with Denham in 1650 to Poland to raise money for Charles II.
Poland was in sympathy with Charles, and Crofts was an eloquent ambassador.
He made a rhetorical appeal to the Diet which moved the Polish magnates to
tears, and the Diet unanimously voted in December, 1650, a ". . . Subsidium
for H.M. the King of England. In gratitude for the good will of the grandfather
of H.M. the King of England, which he showed to the [Polish] Republic
tempore necessitatis belli Turcici, wishing, to requite it to him in some fashion,
opem ferre in hac ipsius calamitate, we ordain for all the merchants of the
English and Scottish nations who are within the Crown [Poland proper], the
Grand Duchy of Lithuania, and in all the provinces of the Republic, that each
of them *sub juramento* . . . should pay from every hundred zloty [florins] of
his substance ten zloty . . . within eight weeks, *sub poena peculatus.* And the
[manorial] lords and the city officials are to send this money to . . . our Lord
Treasurers for the Crown and for Lithuania, by March 13th, and the latter
must deliver it to the envoy of H.M. the King of England in return for his
receipt." Rudawski, *Historiarum Poloniae* . . . libri IX, 67-68; Prawa,
Konstytucye y przywileie Krolestwa Polskiego y W. X. Litewskiego, IV, 337.
(Constitutions and Resolutions of the Polish Diet.)

There were difficulties to be overcome before Crofts succeeded. The Scottish
and English subjects had already contributed to the King's cause, and were
unwilling to do so again, and the activities of "John Molleson" were troublesome. See notes on the following pages.

[2] Sir John Cockram (Cockran, Cockeram) was sent in 1649 as ambassador
to Denmark, and then to various German Princes in an endeavor to raise
money for Charles. He had preceded Crofts and Denham to Poland. Carte,
Tho., *A Collection of Original Letters,* 1739, I, 347; *A Perfect Diurnal of some
Passages and Proceedings in relation to the armies.* No. 19, p. 205.

Nor assist our affairs,
With their Monies nor their Wares,
As their answer now declares,
But only with their Prayers.

Thus they did persist,
Did and said what they list,
Till the Dyet was dismist;
But then our Breech they kist.

For when
It was mov'd there and then
They should pay one in ten,
The Dyet said Amen.

And because they are loth
To discover the troth,
They must give word and Oath,
Though they will forfeit both.

Thus the Constitution[3]
Condemns them every one,
From the Father to the Son.

But *John*
(Our Friend) *Mollesson,*
Thought us to have out-gone
With a quaint Invention.[4]

Like the Prophets of yore,
He complain'd long before,
Of the Mischiefs in store,
I, and thrice as much more.

[3] The "Constitution" was the name of the general act passed at the end of each session of the Polish Diet.

[4] This and the following stanzas are obscure. I have been unable to find any other reference to John Molleson or his activities. I imagine, however, that he was one of the Parliamentary agents or ambassadors sent to the various Continental powers to offset such Royalist missions as that of Crofts. The "quaint invention" of the letter was, perhaps, a forged letter from Charles II relieving the English and Scottish subjects in Poland from any further contributions. Had

And with that wicked Lye
A Letter they came by,
From our Kings Majesty.

But Fate
Brought the Letter too late,
'Twas of too old a date,
To relieve their damned State.

The Letter's to be seen,
With seal of Wax so green,
At *Dantzige,* where t' as been
Turn'd into good Latin.

But he that gave the hint,
This Letter for to Print,
Must also pay his stint.

That trick,
Had it come in the Nick,
Had touch'd us to the quick,
But the Messenger fell sick.

Had it later been wrought,
And sooner been brought,
They had got what they sought,
But now it serves for nought.

On *Sandys*[5] they ran aground,
And our return was crown'd
With full ten thousand pound.

it been "wrought" later, *i.e.,* later than the instructions given to Crofts and Denham, so as to supersede them, and brought sooner, *i.e.,* before the passing of the decimation law by the Diet, it would have been awkward for the ambassadors of Charles.

[5] *1668, Marginal note,* Mr. *W.*

In a letter of Daniel O'Neile to the Marquis of Ormonde, June 20, 1651, he says: "I have moved his Majesty to allow you £1,000 out of what money Mr. Crofts gets in Poland: he with great cheerfulness told me he would send by Mr. Sands, who goes to him, to let you have that sum, if he could spare it." Carte, Tho., *A Collection of Original Letters,* 1739, II, 31-32.

ON MR. *THO. KILLIGREW'S* RETURN FROM HIS EMBASSIE FROM *VENICE,* AND MR. *WILLIAM MURRAY'S* FROM SCOTLAND[1]

Our Resident *Tom,*
From *Venice* is come,
And[2] hath left the Statesman behind him;
   Talks at the same[3] pitch,
   Is as wise,[4] is as rich,
And just where you left him, you find him.[5]

But who says[6] he was not,
A man of much Plot,
May repent that[7] false Accusation;
   Having plotted and penn'd
   Six plays to attend
The Farce of his Negotiation.

Before you were told
How *Satan* the old[8]
Came here with a Beard to his middle;

---

1 First printed in the 1668 collected edition. There is a MS. copy in the Bodleian Library (*Calendar Clarendon Papers,* II, 143).

For Thomas Killigrew, see *A Dialogue between Sir John Pooley and Mr. Thomas Killigrew,* p. 103, n. 1.

William Murray (1600?-1652) was First Earl of Dysart. As a boy he was educated at court with Prince Charles, and was made gentleman of the bedchamber in 1626. He was closely related to some of the leading Covenanters, and was often used by them as a medium in the negotiations with Charles I. After the King's capture by the army, he retired to the Continent. He was sent to Scotland by the Queen in 1648, and again in 1649 by Charles II. He was created Lord Dysart in 1651, and died not long after.

2 *Clarendon MS.,* But.
3 *Clarendon MS.,* old.
4 *Clarendon MS.,* grave.
5 *Clarendon MS.,* And just where you left you may find him.
6 *Clarendon MS.,* said.
7 *Clarendon MS.,* his.
8 *1668, Marginal note,* Mr. W. Murrey.

Though he chang'd face and name,[9]
Old *Will* was the same,
At the noise[10] of a Can and a Fiddle.

These Statesmen you[11] believe
Send straight for the Sheriffe,[12]
For he is one too, or would be;
  But he drinks no Wine,
  Which is a shrewd[13] sign
That all's not so well[14] as it should be.[15]

These three[16] when they drink,
How little do[17] they think
Of Banishment, Debts, or dying?
  Not old with their years,
  Nor cold with their fears;
But their angry Stars still defying.

Mirth makes them not mad,
Nor Sobriety sad;
But of that they are seldom in danger:
  At *Paris*,[18] at *Rome*,
  At the *Hague* they are[19] at home;
The good Fellow is no where a stranger.

[9] He changed his name by his assumption of the title of Lord Dysart.
[10] *Clarendon MS.*, sight.
[11] *Clarendon MS.*, you'll.
[12] *Clarendon MS.*, shreefe.
[13] *Clarendon MS.*, fowle.
[14] *Clarendon MS.*, sound.
[15] The "sheriffe" is Denham himself, who was appointed High Sheriff of Surrey in 1642 by Charles I. The third line of the stanza refers to his mission to Poland with Lord Crofts (see p. 107) from which he had recently returned; and the last three lines probably refer to the venereal disease from which he suffered when abroad.
[16] *Clarendon MS.*, lads.
[17] *Clarendon MS.*, omits do.
[18] *Clarendon MS.*, Venice.
[19] *Clarendon MS.*, they're.

AN OCCASIONAL IMITATION OF A MODERN AUTHOR UPON THE GAME OF CHESS[1]

A Tablet stood of that abstersive Tree,
Where Æthiops swarthy Bird did build her nest,[2]
Inlaid it was with *Lybian* Ivory,
Drawn from the Jaws of *Africks* prudent beast.

Two Kings like *Saul*, much Taller then the rest,
Their equal Armies draw into the Field;
   Till one take th' other Prisoner they contest;
Courage and Fortune must to Conduct yield.

This game the *Persian Magi* did invent,
The force of Eastern Wisdom to express;
   From thence to busie *Europæans* sent,
And styl'd by *Modern Lombards* pensive Chess.[3]

Yet some that fled from *Troy* to *Rome* report,
Penthesilea Priam did oblige;
   Her *Amazons,* his *Trojans* taught this sport,
To pass the tedious hours of ten years Siege.

---

[1] First printed in the 1668 collected edition.

This poem does not appear to have been influenced by Vida's *The Game of Chess*. It is a burlesque of the style of Sir William D'Avenant's *Gondibert*.

D'Avenant wrote and published the first two books of *Gondibert* in Paris in 1650. They were prefaced by a long letter of the author to Hobbes, setting forth his view of the epic, and by a complimentary letter from Hobbes himself. D'Avenant then left Paris on a voyage to Virginia, but was captured by a Parliamentary ship, and thrown into prison. He wrote part of a third book during this imprisonment, but then abandoned the poem, and never completed it. In his 1650 preface, he took the poem and his theories so seriously that he became the object of much ridicule. See Appendix A.

[2]   "The Seats were made of Ethiops swarthy wood,
   Abstersive ebony, but thinly fill'd."
                     Gondibert, Bk. II, Canto vi, stanza 22.

The word "abstersive" was singled out for special ridicule. It occurs several times in the satirical poems in Appendix A.

[3] Lombardy is the scene of *Gondibert*.

There she presents her self, whilst King and Peers
Look gravely on whilst fierce *Bellona* fights;
Yet Maiden modesty her Motions steers,
Nor rudely skips o're *Bishops* heads like *Knights*.

THE PROGRESS OF LEARNING[1]

THE PREFACE

My early Mistress, now my Antient Muse,
That strong Circæan *liquor cease to infuse,*
Wherewith thou didst Intoxicate my youth,
Now stoop with dis-inchanted wings to Truth;[2]
As the Doves flight did guide Æneas, *now*
May thine conduct me to the Golden Bough;[3]
Tell (like a Tall Old Oake) how Learning shoots
To Heaven Her Branches, and to Hell her Roots.

When God from Earth form'd *Adam* in the East,
He his own Image on the Clay imprest;
As Subjects then the whole Creation came,
And from their Natures *Adam* them did Name,
Not from experience, (for the world was new)
He only from their Cause their Natures knew.
Had Memory been lost with Innocence,
We had not known the Sentence nor th' Offence;
'Twas his chief Punishment to keep in store
The sad remembrance what he was before;   10
And though th' offending part felt mortal pain,
Th' immortal part, its Knowledg did retain.
After the Flood, Arts to *Chaldæa* fell,

[1] First printed in the 1668 collected edition.

[2]   "But stooped to truth, and moralized his song."
                                    Pope, *Epistle to Dr. Arbuthnot,* l. 341.

[3]   "Vix ea fatus˜ erat, geminae quum forte columbae," etc.
                                    Virgil, *Aeneis,* VI, ll. 190 ff.

The Father of the faithful there did dwell,[4]
Who both their Parent and Instructer was;
From thence did Learning into *Ægypt* pass;
Moses in all th' *Ægyptian* Arts was skill'd,
When Heavenly power that chosen Vessel fill'd,
And we to his High Inspiration owe,
That what was done before the Flood, we know.   20
From *Ægypt* Arts their Progress made to *Greece*,
Wrapt in the Fable of the Golden Fleece.
Musæus first, then *Orpheus* civilize
Mankind, and gave the world their Deities;
To many Gods they taught Devotion,
Which were the distinct faculties of one;
The eternal cause, in their immortal lines
Was taught, and Poets were the first Divines:
God *Moses* first, then *David* did inspire,
To compose Anthems for his Heavenly Quire;   30
To th' one the style of Friend he did impart,
On th' other stampt the likeness of his heart:
And *Moses*, in the Old Original,
Even God the Poet of the world doth call.
Next those old *Greeks*, *Pythagoras* did rise,
Then *Socrates*, whom th' Oracle call'd Wise;
The Divine *Plato* Moral Vertue shows,
Then his Disciple *Aristotle* rose,
Who Natures secrets to the world did teach,
Yet that great Soul our Novelists impeach;   40
Too much manuring fill'd that field with weeds,
Whilst Sects, like Locusts, did destroy the seeds;
The tree of Knowledg blasted by disputes,
Produces sapless leaves instead of Fruits;
Proud *Greece*, all Nations else, *Barbarians* held,
Boasting her learning all the world excell'd.
Flying from thence, to *Italy* it came,[5]

[4] Abraham, who lived in Chaldea before his departure into the land of Canaan. Genesis, 11:31.
[5] *1668, Marginal note,* Græcia Major.

And to the Realm of *Naples* gave the Name,
Till both their Nation and their Arts did come
A welcom Trophy to Triumphant *Rome;*   50
Then wheresoe're her Conquering Eagles fled,
Arts, Learning, and Civility were spread;
And as in this our *Microcosm,* the heart
Heat, Spirit, Motion gives to every part;
So *Rome's* Victorious influence did disperse
All her own Vertues through the Universe.
Here some digression I must make t'accuse
Thee my forgetful, and ingrateful Muse:
Could'st thou from *Greece* to *Latium* take thy flight,
And not to thy great Ancestor do Right?   60
I can no more believe Old *Homer* blind
Then those, who say the Sun hath never shin'd;
The age wherein he liv'd, was dark, but he
Could not want sight, who taught the world to see:
They who *Minerva* from *Joves* head derive,
Might make Old *Homers* Skull the Muses Hive;
And from his Brain, that *Helicon* distil,
Whose Racy Liqour did his off-spring fill.
Nor old *Anacreon, Hesiod, Theocrite*
Must we forget; nor *Pindar's* lofty Flight.   70
Old *Homer's* soul at last from *Greece* retir'd;
In *Italy* the *Mantuan* Swain inspir'd.
When Great *Augustus* made wars Tempests cease
His *Halcion* days brought forth the arts of Peace;
He still in his Tryumphant Chariot shines,
By *Horace* drawn, and *Virgil's* mighty lines.
'Twas certainly mysterious, that the Name[6]
Of Prophets and of Poets is the same;
What the *Tragedian* wrote, the late success[7]
Declares was Inspiration, and not Guess: 80
As dark a truth that Author did unfold,

[6] *1668, Marginal note,* Vates.
[7] *1668, Marginal note,* Seneca.

As Oracles, or Prophets e're fore-told:
At last the Ocean shall unlock the Bound[8]
Of things, and a New World by Typhis *found,*
Then Ages, far remote shall understand
The Isle *of* Thule *is not the farthest Land.*[9]
Sure God, by these Discoveries, did design
That his clear Light through all the World should shine,
But the Obstruction from that Discord springs
The Prince of Darkness makes 'twixt Christian Kings;   90
That peaceful age, with happiness to Crown,
From Heaven the Prince of Peace himself came down.
Then, the true Sun of Knowledg first appear'd,
And the old dark mysterious Clouds were clear'd,
The heavy Cause of th' old accursed Flood
Sunk in the sacred Deluge of his Blood.
His Passion, Man from his first fall, redeem'd;
Once more to Paradise restor'd we seem'd;
Satan himself was bound, till th' Iron chain
Our Pride did break, and him let loose again,   100
Still the Old Sting remain'd, and Man began
To tempt the Serpent, as He tempted Man;
Then Hell sends forth her Furies, Avarice, Pride,
Fraud, Discord, Force, Hypocrisie their Guide;
Though the Foundation on a Rock were laid,
The Church was undermin'd, and then betray'd;
Though the *Apostles*, these events fore-told,
Yet, even the Shepherd did devour the Fold:
The Fisher to convert the world began,
The Pride convincing of vain-glorious Man;   110
But soon, his Follower grew a Soveraign Lord,
And *Peter's* Keys exchang'd for *Peter's* Sword,
Which still maintains for his adopted Son
Vast Patrimonies, though himself had none;
Wresting the Text, to the old Gyants sense,

[8] *1668, Marginal note,* The Prophecy.
[9] Seneca, *Medea,* ll. 375 ff.

That Heaven, once more, must suffer violence.
Then subtle Doctors, Scriptures, made their prize,
Casuists, like Cocks, struck out each others Eyes;
Then dark distinctions, Reasons light disguis'd,
And into Attoms, Truth anatomiz'd.   120
Then *Mahomets* Crescent by our fewds encreast,
Blasted the learn'd Remainders of the East:
That project, when from *Greece* to *Rome* it came,
Made Mother Ignorance Devotions Dame;
Then, He, whom *Lucifer's* own Pride did swell,
His faithful Emissary, rose from Hell
To possess *Peter's* Chair, that *Hildebrand*
Whose foot on Miters, then on Crowns did stand,
And before that exalted Idol, all
(Whom we call Gods on Earth) did prostrate fall.   130
Then Darkness, *Europe's* face did over-spread
From lazy Cells, where superstition bred,
Which, link'd with blind Obedience, so encreast
That the whole world, some ages they opprest;
Till through those Clouds, the Sun of Knowledg brake,
And *Europe* from her Lethargy did wake:
Then, first our Monarchs were acknowledg'd here
That they, their Churches Nursing-Fathers were.
When *Lucifer* no longer could advance
His works on the false ground of Ignorance,   140
New Arts he tries, and new designs he laies,
Then, his well-study'd Master-piece he plays;
Loyola, Luther, Calvin he inspires
And kindles, with infernal Flames, their fires,
Sends their fore-runner (conscious of th' event)
Printing, his most pernicious Instrument:
Wild Controversie then, which long had slept,
Into the Press from ruin'd Cloysters leapt;
No longer by Implicite faith we erre,
Whilst every Man's his own Interpreter;   150
No more conducted now by *Aarons* Rod,

Lay-Elders, from their Ends, create their God.
But seven wise men, the ancient world did know,
We scarce know seven, who think themselves not so.
When Man learn'd undefil'd Religion,
We were commanded to be all as one;
Fiery disputes, that Union have calcin'd,
Almost as many minds as men we find,
And when that flame finds combustible Earth,
Thence Fatuus fires and Meteors take their birth,   160
Legions of Sects, and Insects come in throngs;
To name them all, would tire a hundred tongues.
Such were the Centaures of *Ixions* race
Who, a bright Cloud, for *Juno,* did embrace,
And such the Monsters of *Chymæra's* kind,
Lyons before, and Dragons were behind.
Then, from the clashes between Popes and Kings,
Debate, like sparks from Flints collision, springs:
As *Joves* loud Thunderbolts were forg'd by heat,
The like, our Cyclops, on their Anvils, beat;   170
All the rich Mines of Learning, ransackt are
To furnish Ammunition for this War:
Uncharitable Zeal our Reason whets,
And double Edges on our Passion sets;
'Tis the most certain sign, the world's accurst,
That the best things corrupted, are the worst;[10]
'Twas the corrupted Light of knowledg, hurl'd
Sin, Death, and Ignorance o're all the world;
That Sun like this, (from which our sight we have)
Gaz'd on too long, resumes the light he gave;   180
And when thick mists of doubts obscure his beams,
Our Guide is Errour, and our Visions, Dreams;
'Twas no false Heraldry, when madness drew
Her Pedigree from those, who too much knew;

[10]   "For sweetest things turn sourest by their deeds.
         Lillies that fester smell far worse than weeds."
                                    Shakespeare, *Sonnet* XCIV.

Who in deep Mines, for hidden Knowledg, toyls,
Like Guns o're-charg'd, breaks, misses, or recoyls;
When subtle Wits have spun their thred too fine,
'Tis weak and fragile like *Arachnes* line:
True Piety, without cessation tost
By *Theories,* the practick part is lost,   190
And like a Ball bandy'd 'twixt Pride and Wit,
Rather then yield, both sides the Prize will quit,
Then whilst his Foe, each Gladiator foyls,
The Atheist looking on, enjoys the spoyls.
Through Seas of knowledg, we our course advance,
Discovering still new worlds of Ignorance;
And these Discoveries make us all confess
That sublunary Science is but guess,
Matters of fact, to man are only known,
And what seems more, is meer opinion;   200
The standers by, see clearly this event,
All parties say they're sure, yet all dissent,
With their new Light our bold Inspectors press
Like *Cham,* to shew their Fathers Nakedness,[11]
By whose Example, after-ages may
Discover, we more naked are then they;
All humane wisdom to divine, is folly,
This Truth, the wisest man made melancholy,[12]
Hope, or belief, or guess gives some relief,
But to be sure we are deceiv'd, brings grief;   210
Who thinks his Wife is Vertuous, though not so,
Is pleas'd, and patient, till the truth he know.
Our God, when Heaven and Earth he did Create,
Form'd Man, who should of both participate,
If our Lives Motions their's must imitate,
Our knowledge, like our blood, must circulate.

[11] Ham, son of Noah. Genesis, 9: 20 ff.
[12] "And I gave my heart to know wisdom, and to know madness and folly; I perceived that this also is vexation of spirit.
"For in much wisdom is much grief; and he that increaseth knowledge increaseth sorrow." Ecclesiastes, 1: 17, 18.

When like a Bride-groom from the East, the Sun[13]
Sets forth, he thither, whence he came doth run;
Into Earth's Spungy Veins, the Ocean sinks
Those Rivers to replenish which he drinks;   220
So Learning which from Reasons Fountain springs,
Back to the sourse, some secret Channel brings.
'Tis happy when our Streams of Knowledge flow
To fill their banks, but not to overthrow.

Ut metit Autumnus fruges quas parturit Æstas,
Sic Ortum Natura, dedit Deus his quoq; Finem.[14]

TO HIS MISTRESS[1]

Go, Love-born Accents of my dying Heart,
Steal into hers, and sweetly there impart
The boundless Love, with which my Soul does swell,
And all my sighs there in soft Echoes tell:
But if her Heart does yet repugnant prove
To all the Blessings that attend my Love;
Tell her the Flames that animate my Soul,
Are pure, and bright, as those *Prometheus* stole;
From Heav'n, tho' not like his by theft, they come,
But a free Gift, by the eternal Doom.   10
How partial, cruel Fair one, are your Laws,
To reward th' Effect, and yet condemn the Cause?
Condemn my Love, and yet commend my Lays,
That merits love more than these merit praise.
Yet I to you my Love and Verse submit,

[13] *Cf.* Psalms, 19:5.
[14] I have been unable to trace this quotation.
[1] Printed under Denham's name in *Chorus Poetarum or Poems on Several Occasions,* 1694.

This is the sole appearance of this poem, but there is little doubt of its authenticity, as the movement and antithetical expression of lines 11-16 are highly characteristic of Denham.

Without your Smile, that Hope, and these want Wit.
For as some hold no colours are in deed,
But from Reflection of the Light proceed;
So as you shine, my Verse and I must live,
You can Salvation and Damnation give.   20

A SPEECH AGAINST PEACE AT THE CLOSE COMMITTEE[1]

To the Tune of, *I went from* England.

But will you now to Peace incline,
And languish in the main design,
    And leave us in the lurch?
I would not Monarchy destroy,
But as the only way to enjoy[2]
    The ruine of the Church.

---

[1] First printed in 1643. Reprinted in *Rump*, 1662, without change.
Mr. Hampdens speech occasioned upon the Londoners Petition for Peace.
[broadside] the British Museum's copy is dated by Thomason, March 23, 1643.
    Hampden, who is evidently intended as the speaker, was one of the most eminent Parliamentary opponents of Charles I. The close committee was probably the Committee of Safety appointed by Parliament July 4, 1642, composed of five members of the House of Lords and ten of the Commons, among whom were Pym, Hampden, and Holles.
    The poem is a Royalist satire of the motives and ideals that animated the Parliamentary party in the early stages of its struggle with the King. Hampden was one of the five members whom Charles sought to apprehend in person in the Commons on the charge of high treason. He is here represented as being willing to overthrow monarchy in order to accomplish the destruction of the episcopal system of worship, as having been instrumental in bringing in the Scotch army which invaded England in August, 1640, as endeavoring to cast the blame for the rebellion of the Irish Catholics, which broke out in Ireland in 1641, upon the King, and as advocating a policy of destruction in order to retain selfish power as long as possible.
    [2] *Rump*, But only as the way to enjoy . . .
    1668, But only as the way to enjoy . . . This was corrected in the errata.
    1671, as above.
    1684, as above.

Is not the Bishops Bill deny'd,[3]
And we still threatned to be try'd?
   You see the Kings embraces.
Those Councels he approv'd before:
Nor doth he promise, which is more,
   That we shall have their Places.

Did I for this bring in the *Scot?*
(For 'tis no Secret now) the Plot
   Was *Sayes*[4] and mine together:
Did I for this return again,
And spend a Winter there in vain,
   Once more to invite them hither?[5]

Though more our Money than our Cause
Their Brotherly assistance draws,[6]
   My labour was not lost.
At my return I brought you thence
Necessity, their strong Pretence,
   And these shall quit the cost.

[3] This was the bill for the exclusion of the clergy from secular offices, specifically of the bishops from the House of Lords. On June 8, 1641, the Lords threw out the bill on the third reading. This bill was a direct attack on the existing episcopal system, which was vigorously supported by the King.

[4] Saye is William Fiennes (1582-1662), First Viscount Say and Sele. He was a prominent Parliamentarian, and was believed by the Royalists to be one of those responsible for the Scots' invasion.

From 1640 the Scots were practically in rebellion against Charles because of his efforts to impose the episcopal system upon them. In August, 1640, they invaded England and occupied the two northern counties. During these proceedings they were undoubtedly in communication with the English Parliamentary leaders; indeed, treasonable intercourse with the Scots was one of the charges in the King's subsequent attempted impeachment of Hampden. This stanza implies that Hampden went to Scotland in 1640. He "returned" in 1641 when he was made one of the four members of Parliament sent to attend Charles on his visit to Scotland in 1641.

[5] *Rump,* I went more to invite . . .

[6] Soon after the Scots' invasion of England, negotiations were opened between them and Charles at Ripon, which were later carried on at London with the newly convened Long Parliament. The Scots' demand of £25,000 a month during their stay in England (until the conclusion of a treaty) was agreed to. On January 12, 1640/1, they presented demands for large sums to Parliament, and

Did I for this my County bring
To help their Knight against their King,
   And raise the first Sedition?[7]
Though I the business did decline,
Yet I contriv'd the whole Design,
   And sent them their Petition.[8]

So many nights spent in the City
In that invisible Committee;
   The Wheel that governs all.
From thence the Change in Church and State,
And all the Mischiefs bear the date
   From *Haberdashers* Hall.[9]

Did we force *Ireland* to despair,
Upon the King to cast the War,
   To make the world abhor him:
Because the Rebells us'd his Name,
Though we ourselves can do the same,
   While both alike were for him?[10]

on February 3 Parliament replied by voting them £300,000 under the name of a "Brotherly Assistance."

[7] Their knight is Sir John Hotham, whose refusal to surrender the town of Hull to the King, who appeared before the walls in person to demand it, precipitated the Civil War.

[8] It is difficult to say just which one of the great flood of petitions of this period Denham refers to. The most probable reference seems to be to the petition of the twelve English peers who pledged assistance to the Scots if they should invade England. The passage would then mean that Hampden instigated the sending of this petition, although his name does not appear on it.

[9] Soon after the outbreak of hostilities, Parliament appointed special committees to sit in various places in London, Goldsmiths' Hall, Grocers' Hall, etc. Haberdashers' Hall was the meeting place of a monetary committee having power to assess the citizens of London, to collect the money for the maintenance of the Parliamentary armies, and to regulate the compounding of the delinquents for their estates.

[10] The terrible rebellion of the Irish Catholics against the English garrisons in Ireland broke out on October 23, 1641, Parliament having for some time sent neither supplies nor reinforcements to the English army there. Parliament spread reports that the King was in sympathy with the Irish rebels and was aiding

Then the same fire we kindled here
With that was given to quench it there,[11]
  And wisely lost that Nation:
To do as crafty Beggars use,
To maim themselves thereby to abuse
  The simple mans compassion.

Have I so often past between
Windsor and *Westminster* unseen,
  And did my self divide:
To keep his Excellence in awe,
And give the Parliament the Law,
  For they knew none beside?

Did I for this take pains to teach
Our zealous Ignorants to Preach,
  And did their Lungs inspire,
Gave them their Text, set them their Parts,[12]
And taught them all their little Arts,
  To fling abroad the Fire?

Sometimes to beg, sometimes to threaten,
And say the Cavaliers are beaten,
  To[13] stroke the Peoples ears;
Then streight when Victory grows cheap,
And will no more advance the heap,
  To raise the price of Fears.

them, and represented the rebels as saying that they acted on the King's authority.

  [11] On July 30, 1642, Parliament resolved to use in their struggle with Charles £100,000 of the money that had been set aside for the Irish war. The reference may also be to the fact that certain troops raised for service in Ireland were used against the King in England.

  [12] *Rump,* Read them their text, shew'd them their Parts.

  1668, Gave them their text, shew'd them their Parts. Was corrected in the errata.

  1671, Gave them their texts, shew'd them their parts.

  1684, Gave them their text, set them their parts.

  [13] *Rump,* And.

And now the Book's and now the Bells,
And now our Acts the Preacher tells,[14]
    To edifie the People;
All our Divinity is News,
And we have made of equal use
    The Pulpit and the Steeple.

And shall we kindle all this Flame
Only to put it out again,
    And must we now give o're,
And only end where we begun?
In vàin this Mischief we have done,
    If we can do no more.

If men in Peace can have their right,
Where's the necessity to fight,
    That breaks both Law, and Oath?[15]
They'l say they fight not for the Cause,
Nor to defend the King and Laws,
    But us against them both.[16]

[14] *Rump, 1668,* our act the preachers tells. "Act" is corrected in the errata,
and although "preachers" remains unchanged, the singular is clearly intended.
    1671, Our act the preacher tells.
    1684, Our acts the preacher tells.
[15] *Rump,* . . . both law, the oath.
    1668, both law, the oath.
    1671, as above.
    1684, as above.
Broadside,

        "If men in peace can have their right,
        Where is this necessity to fight
            And break both law and oath?
        Who say that they fight for the cause,
        And to defend the King and laws,
            But 'tis against them both."

[16] *Rump,* as against them both.
    1668, as against them both. This was corrected in the errata.
    1671, as against them both.
    1684, us against them both.

Either the cause at first was ill,
Or being good it is[17] so still;
   And thence they will infer,
That either now, or at the first
They were deceiv'd; or which is worst,
   That we our selves may erre.

But Plague and Famine will come in,
For they and we are near of kin,
   And cannot go asunder:
But while the wicked starve, indeed
The Saints have ready at their need
   Gods Providence and Plunder.

Princes we are if we prevail,
And Gallant Villains if we fail,
   When to our Fame 'tis told;
It will not be our least of praise,
Sin' a new State we could not raise,
   To have destroy'd the old.

Then let us stay and fight, and vote,
Till *London* is not worth a Groat;
   Oh 'tis a patient Beast!
When we have gall'd and tyr'd the Mule,
And can no longer have the rule,
   We'le have the spoyl at least.

[17] *Rump,* was.

TO THE FIVE MEMBERS OF THE HON-
OURABLE HOUSE OF COMMONS.
THE HUMBLE PETITION OF THE POETS[1]

After so many Concurring Petitions
From all Ages and Sexes, and all conditions,
We come in the rear to present our Follies
To *Pym, Stroude, Haslerig, H.* and *H.*[2]
Though set form of *Prayer* be an *Abomination*,[3]
Set forms of *Petitions* find great Approbation:
Therefore, as others from th' bottom of their souls,
So we from the depth and bottom of our *Bowls*,
According unto the blessed form you have taught us,
We thank you first for the *Ills* you have brought us,   10
For the *Good* we receive we thank him that gave it,
And you for the Confidence only to crave it.
Next in course, we Complain of the great *violation*
Of *Priviledge* (like the rest of our Nation)
But 'tis none of yours of which we have spoken
Which never had being, until they were broken:
But ours is a *Priviledge* Antient and Native,
Hangs not on an *Ordinance*, or power *Legislative*.
And first, 'tis to speak whatever we please
Without fear of a *Prison*, or *Pursuivants* fees.   20
Next, that we only may *lye* by Authority,
But in that also you have got the Priority.
Next, an old Custom, our Fathers did name it

---

[1] First printed in *Rump*, 1662.
On January 4, 1642, Charles appeared in person in the House of Commons
to demand the arrest of five of their leaders on the charge of high treason. The
incident raised a storm of indignation for its violation of the privileges of Parlia-
ment.

[2] John Pym, William Strode, Sir Arthur Haslerig, John Hampden, and Denzil
Holles. They are too well known to need mention here.
Rump reads between lines 4 and 5:

> And we hope for our labour we shall not be shent,
> For this comes from Christendom, and not from Kent.

[3] A reference to the hostility of Parliament to the ritual of the Church of
England.

Poetical license, and alwaies did claim it.
By this we have power to change Age into Youth,
Turn *Non-sence* to[4] Sence, and Falshood to Truth;
In brief, to make good whatsoever is faulty,
This art some *Poet,* or the *Devil* has taught ye:
And this our Property you have invaded,
And a *Priviledge* of both Houses have made it: 30
But that trust above all in Poets reposed,
That *Kings* by them only are made and Deposed,
This though you cannot do, yet you are willing;
But when we undertake Deposing or Killing,
They're *Tyrants* and *Monsters,* and yet then the Poet
Takes full Revenge on the Villains that do it:
And when we resume a *Scepter* or a *Crown,*
We are Modest, and seek not to make it our own.
But is't not presumption to write Verses to you,
Who make the better *Poems* of the two?   40
For all those pretty Knacks you compose,
Alas, what are they but *Poems* in prose?
And between those and ours there's no difference,
But that yours want the rhime, the wit and the sense:
But for lying (the most noble part of a *Poet*)
You have it abundantly, and your selves know it,
And though you are modest, and seem to abhor it,
'T has done you good service, and thank *Hell*[5] for it:
Although the old Maxime remains still in force,
That a Sanctified Cause, must have a Sanctified Course.   50
If poverty be a part of our Trade,
So far the whole Kingdom *Poets* you have made,
Nay even so far as undoing will do it,
You have made *King Charles* himself a Poet:[6]
But provoke not his Muse, for all the world knows,
Already you have had too much of his *Prose.*[7]

[4] *Rump,* into.
[5] *Rump,* Heav'n.
[6] *Rump,* You have made King Charles in manner a Poet.
[7] The whole passage evidently refers to the interchange of communications between Charles I and Parliament in the early stages of their struggle.

A WESTERN WONDER[1]

Do you not know, not a fortnight ago,
    How they brag'd of a Western wonder?
When a hundred and ten, slew five thousand men,[2]
    With the help of Lightning and Thunder.[3]

There *Hopton* was slain, again and again,
    Or else my Author did lye;

[1] First printed in *Rump*, 1662.

This and the following poem, *A Second Western Wonder*, refer to incidents in the fighting in the west of England in 1643.

Sir Ralph Hopton (later made Lord Hopton, and Knight of the Bath) during the first year of the war successfully commanded a small Royalist force in Cornwall. In January, 1643, Parliament appointed Henry Grey, First Earl of Stamford, commander of their forces in the west, with Maj.-Gen. James Chudleigh as second in command. Stamford advanced into Cornwall but was repulsed. On the twenty-fifth of April, however, Chudleigh drove Hopton back from Sourton Down. This is the engagement referred to in the first stanza of this poem. Encouraged by this success Stamford joined Chudleigh, and established himself at Stratton on the northwest border of Cornwall. Here Hopton attacked him, May 16, and won a complete victory. (See above, stanza 3.) At the crisis of the battle the Parliamentary troops broke and fled, and Stamford was rumored to have been one of the foremost among them. In this battle Chudleigh was captured and soon after transferred his allegiance to the King. He was later killed at the siege of Dartmouth in September, 1643.

[2] The title of the pamphlet here referred to runs as follows: *A Most Miraculous and Happy Victory obtained by James Chidleigh Serjeant Major Generall of the forces under the E. of Stamford, against Sir Ralph Hopton and his Forces. Who with 108 Horse did rout and put to flight 5000 Foot and 500 horse, tooke divers prisoners, arms, ensignes, their standard, with a Portmantell of Letters, Warrants and privy Seales, with many remarkable Passages concerning the same. As also a Letter to Sir Ralph Hopton with a command signed C.R. written upon a silken cloth. Printed this 29. Aprill, for R.D. 1643.*

[3] "And they further notifie . . . two remarkable Passages . . . at the late defeat given to the Cornish Cavaliers on Swarton Downe . . . The second . . . was, that during the rout and flight of the *Cornubians*, an extraordinary storme of Lightning and Thunder fell upon them, which lightning singed and burnt the haire of their heads, and fired the Gunpowder in their Musket pans and Bandeliers, which so lamentably scorched & burnt many of their bodies, that they sent for twelve Chirurgians from *Launceton* to cure them." *Certaine Informations from Severall parts of the Kingdom* . . . No. 17, p. 131.

With a new *Thanksgiving,* for the Dead who are living,[4]
  To God, and his Servant *Chidleigh.*[5]

But now on which side was this Miracle try'd,
  I hope we at last are even;
For Sir *Ralph* and his Knaves, are risen from their Graves,
  To Cudgel[6] the Clowns of *Devon.*

And there *Stamford* came,[7] for his Honour was lame
  Of the Gout three months together;
But it prov'd when they fought, but a running Gout,
  For his heels were lighter then ever.

For now he out-runs his Arms and his Guns,
  And leaves all his money behind him;
But they follow after, unless he take water
  At *Plymouth* again, they will find him.

What *Reading* hath cost,[8] and *Stamford* hath lost,
  Goes deep in the Sequestrations;
These wounds will not heal, with your new Great Seal,[9]
  Nor *Jepsons* Declarations.[10]

[4] *Rump* omits, the dead.
[5] *Rump,* Chudleigh.
At each victory for their forces, Parliament ordered a general thanksgiving to be celebrated in the churches.
[6] *Rump,* And cudgel'd . . .
[7] *Rump,* And now St—— came . . .
1668, and now *Stamford* came . . . This was corrected in the errata.
1671, as above.
1684, as above.
[8] This was the successful siege of Reading by the Earl of Essex, April 15-27, 1643. Essex, however, could not follow up his victory because of lack of pay for his men. On May 17 Commons sent him £15,000 borrowed from the city.
[9] Parliament determined to get the power of the Great Seal into their own hands, and to issue a new seal in their own name, rather than in the name of the King. *Journals of the Commons,* May 10, 11, 15, 1643.
[10] "Mr. *Glyn,* Mr. *Jepson* . . . [13 names] This Committee is appointed to prepare a Declaration, to set forth, That the Rebellion in *Ireland,* and this in *England* spring from one head; and are managed with concurrent Counsels to one End; for the utter Overthrow and Extirpation of the Protestant Religion." *Journals of the Commons,* May 18, 1643.

Now *Peters*,[11] and *Case*,[12] in your Prayer and Grace
  Remember the[13] new *Thanksgiving;*
Isaac and his Wife, now dig for your[14] life,
  Or shortly you'l dig for your[15] living.[16]

[11] See p. 59.

[12] Thomas Case was a popular Presbyterian divine. He is several times mentioned by Pepys as a dull preacher. For a paragraph on his life see Neal, Daniel, *History of the Puritans*, 1844, II, 301 and note.

[13] *Rump,* their.

[14] *Rump,* their.

[15] *Rump,* their.

[16] *Rump,* And shortly must do 't for their living.

The reference here is to Sir Isaac Penington, Lord Mayor of London, and to the fortifications that were thrown up around the city in 1643. Penington (1587-1660) succeeded to his father's business as fishmonger. He became alderman of London, and high sheriff in 1638, and was a member of the Short and Long Parliaments. An ardent Puritan, in 1642 he succeeded Sir Richard Gurney as Lord Mayor. He was one of the King's judges, but did not sign the sentence. He was a member of the Council of State 1648-1651. At the Restoration he was accused of treason and committed to the Tower, where he died December 17, 1660.

In 1643 Charles's near approach to the city caused great consternation, and earthworks were hastily erected.

"The worke in the feilds about London to trench the Citty round goes on a maine, many thousands of men, woemen and servants goe out daily to worke, and this day there went a great company of the Common Councill, and divers other chief men of the citty, with the greatest part of the trained bands that layed downe their armes and marched out with spades, shovells, pickaxes and such like tooles on their shoulders into the feilds with their captaines officers and cullors before them to assiste the worke." May 8, 1643. *A Perfect Diurnall of the Passages in Parliament*, No. 48.

> "Has *Isaac* our L. *Maior*, L. *Maior*,
>   With Tradesmen and his Wenches,
> Spent so much time, and Cakes and Beer,
>   To edifie these Trenches!
> All trades did shew their skill in this,
>   Each Wife an Engineer;
> The Mairess took the tool in hand,
>   The maids the stones did bear."

Rump, On the Demolishing the Forts, I, 246.

A SECOND WESTERN WONDER[1]

You heard of that wonder, of the *Lightning* and *Thunder,*
    Which made the lye so much the louder;
Now list to another, that Miracles Brother,
    Which was done with a *Firkin of powder.*

Oh what a damp, it[2] struck through the Camp!
    But as for honest Sir *Ralph,*[3]
It blew him to the *Vies,*[4] without beard, or eyes,
    But at least three heads and a half.[5]

When out came the book, which the *News-Monger* took
    From the *Preaching Ladies* Letter,[6]

[1] First printed in *Rump,* 1662.
The success of Hopton at Stratton (see *A Western Wonder,* note 1) broke
for a time the Parliamentary strength in the west, and Hopton advanced from
Cornwall into Devonshire and the neighboring counties. Then Parliament sent
Sir William Waller, whose successes had brought him the name of William the
Conqueror, to oppose Hopton. Waller made his headquarters at Bath, and after
some skirmishing, the armies met at Lansdown on July 5, 1643. After a stubborn
battle Waller retreated. The Royalists, however, were too shaken to follow up
their success, and the next day began to retire. At this time, Hopton, who had
been wounded in the arm during the battle, was badly injured by the explosion
of a powder wagon. His army retreated to the town of Devizes in Wiltshire.
Waller followed and besieged the city, taking up his position at Roundway
Down. Hopton, for lack of ammunition, was in desperate straits, but Lord Wil-
mot arrived with timely reinforcements, and on July 13 totally defeated Waller.
The whole Parliamentary army was scattered, Waller flying with the rest.

[2] *Rump* omits, it.
1668 omits, it. This was corrected in the errata.
1671, as above.
1684, as above.

[3] See *A Western Wonder,* note 1.

[4] This seems to be a corruption of Devizes. (See above.)

[5] July 12. "On Thursday morning the enemies Magazine was blown up by
accident, and two Captains blown up therewith, and about 20 more wounded,
whereof Prince *Maurice* was one, and Sir *Ralph Hopton* made a miserable spec-
tacle, his head swoln as big as two heads, and his eyes neer burnt out." *A Perfect
Diurnall of some passages in Parliament,* No. 3.

[6] The various Diurnals and Relations of the time were known as newsbooks.
At their best, they consisted of two sheets, and whatever their size, were in-
variably called "books."
"In Denham's *Second Western Wonder* . . . *Mercurius Civicus* is the 'book'
referred to, Lady Waller the preaching lady, and the 'Conqueror' Sir William
Waller himself. . . . *Mercurius Civicus* was the first illustrated journal, and

Where in the first place, stood the *Conquerours* face,
   Which made it shew much[7] the better.

But now without lying, you may paint him flying,
   At *Bristol* they say you may find him[8]
Great *William* the *Con* so fast he did run,
   That he left half his name behind him.[9]

And now came the Post, saves all that was lost,
   But alas, we are past deceiving,
By a trick so stale, or else such a tale
   Might amount to a new *Thanksgiving*.[10]

This made Mr. *Case*,[11] with a pitiful face,
   In the Pulpit to fall a weeping,
Though his mouth utter'd *lyes*, *truth* fell from his eyes,
   Which kept the Lord *Maior* from sleeping.

Now shut up shops, and spend your last drops,
   For the Laws not your Cause,[12] you that loath 'um,
Lest *Essex* should start, and play the *Second part*,
   Of *Worshipful* Sir *John Hotham*.[13]

usually appeared with some political or military leader's portrait on its title page." *Cambridge History of English Literature*, VII, 397.

[7] *Rump,* so much.

[8] *Rump* omits, him.

[9] *Rump* omits, him.

[10] *Rump,* Might mount for . . .

1668, Might mount for. This was corrected in the errata.

1671, as above.

1684, as above.

For the meaning of Thanksgiving, see p. 131, note 5.

[11] See *A Western Wonder,* stanza 7.

[12] *Rump,* For the laws of your cause . . .

1668, For the laws of your cause . . . This was corrected in the errata.

1671, For the laws, nor your cause . . .

1684, as above.

[13] Sir John Hotham was originally a Royalist, but because of his enmity for the Earl of Strafford sided with Parliament at the opening of hostilities. He was in command of Hull, and refused to surrender the town to the King in April, 1642, although Charles appeared in person before the walls to demand it. By April, 1643, however, he was corresponding with the Royalists. He was discovered and captured when attempting to escape, June 29, 1643. He was imprisoned in the Tower, and executed January 2, 1645.

VERSES ON THE CAVALIERS IM-PRISONED IN 1655[1]

Though the goveringe part cannot finde in their heart
  To free the Imprisoned throng,
Yett I dare affirme, next Michaelmas terme
  Wee'l sett them all out in a Song.

Then Marshall draw neare lett the Prisoners appeare
  And read us theyre treasons at large,
For men thinke itt hard to lye under a Guard
  Without any probable Chardge.

[1] The present text follows the original manuscript in the Bodleian Library *Clarendon State Papers, April-December, 1655*, p. 290. The poem was first printed in *Notes and Queries* (7th Series, X, 41) by C. H. Firth.

Firth ascribed the poem to Denham for the following reasons: "1) John Denham was arrested with the persons mentioned here early in June 1655. An order of the Council dated June 9, 1655 runs as follows: 'Order, on Lambert's report of the names of some persons apprehended last night in and about London, that Lord Newport, Andrew Newport, his brother, Jeffrey Palmer, Francis Lord Willoughby of Perham, and Henry Seymour be committed to the Tower. That Sir Frederick Cornwallis, Ed. Progers, Thos. Panton, and Maj. Gen. Ayres be committed to the Serjeant at Arms, and that John Denham be confined to a place chosen by himself not within 20 miles of London.' [*Calendar State Papers, 1655*, p. 204.]

"2) In the second place, it is exactly in the style of those occasional poems which Denham was fond of writing—full of the personal references in which he was accustomed to indulge. Compare the poems on 'Lord Croft's Journey to Poland,' on 'Killigrew's Return from his Embassy to Venice,' and on 'Sir John Mennis going from Calais to Boulogne to eat Roast Pig' . . . The metre of this poem—not a very common metre—is the same as that of the poem on Killigrew. [Quotes "Our Resident Tom," etc.]

"3) This poem is from a copy in the Clarendon MSS. in the Bodleian. . . . It is remarkable that a copy of Denham's poem on Killigrew is also to be found amongst Clarendon's papers. . . .

"4) If it was not written by Denham the absence of any allusion to so prominent a Cavalier as Denham is difficult to understand."

This reasoning seems to me conclusive, and has led me to accept the poem as one of Denham's.

We gain little definite information from the poem about the persons mentioned, but the reason for their imprisonment, though Denham protests his ignorance of it, is clear. The year 1655 was marked by a renewal of Royalist activities. A general uprising throughout England was planned for April, and, in March, actually broke out at Salisbury. Cromwell acted vigorously to prevent the occurrence of any others of like character. His policy was one of general

Lord Peter[2] wee wonder, what Crime hee fals under,
    Unless it bee Legem pone;[3]
Hee has ended the Strife, betwixt hym and his wife,[4]
But now the State wants Alimonie.

Since the whip's in the hand of an other Command,
    Lord Maynard[5] must have a smart jerke,
For the love that hee beares to the new Cavaliers,
    The Presbetrye, and the Kirke.

intimidation. Royalists appear to have been rounded up in many countries, and sent prisoners to London merely because they were Royalists. *Mercurius Politicus*, No. 262; Masson, *Life of Milton*, V, 50.

The Cavaliers here mentioned were caught in this drag-net, and imprisoned on general suspicion of being concerned in the plotting. *Nicholas Papers* (*Camden Society Publications*), III, 28; *Diary of Henry Townshend* (*Worcestershire Historical Society Publications*), I, 29.

[2] William, Fourth Baron Petre of Writtle, who succeeded to the peerage in 1638. He was later impeached on a charge of high treason for being implicated in a Popish plot, and died in the Tower in 1684. Cokayne, G. E., *Complete Peerage*, 1889, VI, 247.

[3] I have been unable to locate this reference.

[4] His wife was Lady Elizabeth Petre. Pepys says, under April 3, 1664: ". . . called up by W. Joyce . . . his business was to ask advice of me, he being summonsed to the House of Lords tomorrow for endeavouring to arrest my Lady Peters for a debt"; under April 4: "There in the House of Lords saw my Lady Peters, an impudent jade, soliciting all the Lords on her behalf. And at last W. Joyce was called in; and by the consequences, and what my Lord Peterborough told me, I find that he did speak all he said to his disadvantage, and so was committed to the Black Rod, which is very hard, he doing what he did by the advice of my Lord Peters own steward"; and under April 5: "It was a sad sight, methought, to-day to see my Lord Peters coming out of the House fall out with his lady (from whom he is parted) about this business, saying that she disgraced him. But she hath been a handsome woman, and is, it seems, not only a lewd woman, but very high-spirited."

[5] William, First Lord Maynard, died in 1639 and was succeeded by his son William, who after the Restoration held high offices. The reference here seems to be not to Lord Maynard, but to Sir John Maynard, younger brother to the First Lord Maynard. Sir John was a member of the Long Parliament, but in 1647 he was expelled and imprisoned for his hostility toward the army. He was a zealous Covenanter and a sharp antagonist of the Independents. He died in 1658. Collins, A., *Peerage*, 1812, VI, 284 ff.

In the episode treated by this poem, he was arrested June 26, 1655. *Mercurius Politicus*, No. 263.

This Sir John Maynard should not be confused with the Parliamentary lawyer of the same name.

Lord Coventry's[6] in, but for what Loyall Synne,
  His fellows can hardly gather,
Yett hee ought to disburse, for the Seale and the Purse
  Which were soe long kept by his father.[7]

Lord Biron[8] wee know was accus'd of a Bow
  Or of some other dangerous Plott
But hee's noe such foole, for then (by the rule)
  His Bolt had bynne sooner shott.

Lord Lucas[9] is fast, and will bee the Last
  Because hee's soe learned a Peere.
His Law will not doe't nor his Logicke to boot,
  Though hee make the cause never so cleare.

Lord St Johns[10] indeed was presently freed
  For which hee may thanke his wife,
Shee did promise and vow hee was innocent now
  And would be soe all his life.

[6] Sir William Coventry (1628?-1686). He was of Royalist sympathies, but was too young to take an active part in the war. After the Restoration he was appointed a commissioner of the Navy, and became an influential member of Parliament. In 1668 he lost the favor of Charles II, and retired to Oxfordshire for the remainder of his life. He is frequently mentioned with admiration by Pepys. In this instance, he was under arrest by June 26, 1655. *Mercurius Politicus,* No 263.

[7] Thomas, Lord Coventry. He was Lord Keeper of the Great Seal from 1625 to his death in 1640.

[8] Richard, Second Lord Byron, who succeeded his brother in 1652. He was an ardent Royalist, fought as colonel at Edgehill, was governor of Appulby Castle, Westmorland, and later governor of Newark. On May 24, 1655, he was sent prisoner with his eldest son, William, aged nineteen, to St. James. Collins, A., *Peerage,* 1812, VII, 107; *Mercurius Politicus,* No. 259.

[9] Sir John Lucas was a man eminent for his learning, and his accomplishments in many languages. Active in the Royalist cause in the war, he was created Baron Lucas of Shenfield in 1645. He was among the persons whose removal from the King's councils Parliament demanded during the negotiations for the Treaty of Newport in 1648. He was here arrested on June 26, 1655. Collins, A., *Peerage,* 1812, VII, 114; Dugdale, W., *Baronage,* 1676, II, 473; *Journal of Lords,* Oct. 17, 1648; *Mercurius Politicus,* No. 263.

[10] It is not entirely clear which of the several persons of the name of St. Johns or St. John is referred to here. It seems to have been Charles Powlett or Paulet (1625-1699), First Duke of Bolton. He was the eldest son of John, Fifth

There's dainty Jack Russell,[11] that makes a great bustle
    And bledd three tymes in a day;
But a Caulier[12] swore that hee was to bleed more
    Before hee gott cleare away.

Sir Fredericke Cornwallis,[13] without any malice
    Who carryes more gutts then crimes,
Has the fortune to hitt, and bee counted a witt,
    Which hee could not in former tymes.

Ned Progers[14] looks pale, but what does hee ayle?
    (For hee dyetts with that fatt Drolle.)
Hee must dwindle at length, that spends all his strength
    Att the grill and the litle hole.

Marquis of Winchester, "the loyal Marquis," famous for his defense of Basing
House. It seems to have been customary for the heir to this marquisate to take
the title of Lord St. John. Charles, Lord St. John, married (for the second
time) in February, 1654/5, Mary, the illegitimate daughter of the Earl of
Sunderland. Nothing more is known of him until the Restoration, when he
began a long career as a statesman. He succeeded his father as Marquis of
Winchester in 1675, and was created Duke of Bolton in 1689. He became noted
for his eccentricity. Cokayne, G. E., *Complete Peerage*, 1889, I, under Bolton.
Dictionary of National Biography, under Paulet.

[11] John, younger son of Francis, Fourth Earl of Bedford, and brother of
William, Fifth Earl. He was a colonel in the army of Charles I, and at the
Restoration was made colonel of the first regiment of Foot Guards, which post
he held until his death in 1681. Collins, A., *Peerage*, 1812, I, 284.

[12] I have been unable to discover to whom this refers.

[13] He was created a baronet in 1627. At the outbreak of the war he accom-
panied the King to Oxford, and later distinguished himself in the fighting. After
the death of Charles I he followed Charles II into exile. At the Restoration he
was created Baron Cornwallis of Eye. Cokayne, G. E., *Complete Baronetage*,
1900, II, 13.

By June 5, 1655, he was a prisoner at St. James. *Mercurius Politicus*, No. 261;
Calendar State Papers, 1655, p. 588.

[14] Edward Progers was the younger son of Colonel Philip Progers, equerry to
James I. He was page to Charles I, and later a groom of the bedchamber to the
Prince of Wales. In 1650 he was banished from Charles II's presence by the
Estates of Scotland as "an evil instrument and bad counsellor of the King." He
died on January 1, 1713/4. There is a tradition that he died at the age of
ninety-six from inflammation of the gums resulting from the cutting of four
new teeth. *Suffolk Institute of Archaeology*, II, 149.

By June 5, 1655, he was a prisoner at St. James. *Mercurius Politicus*, No. 261;
Calendar State Papers, 1655, p. 588.

Wee prisoners all pray, that brave Shirley[15] may
  Bee gently assest in your books,
Cause under the line, hee has payd a good fine
  To the poore Common-wealth of the Rooks.

Dicke Nicols[16] (they say) and Littleton[17] stay
  For the Governour's owne delight;
One serves hym with play, att Tennis by day,
  And the other with smoaking at night.

Jacke Paston[18] was quitt, by his hand underwritt,
  But his freedome hee hardly enjoyed,
For as it is sayd, hee drunke hymselfe dead
  On purpose to make his bond voyde.

Tom Panton[19] wee thinke, is ready to sinke
  If his friends doe not lend theyr hands;

[15] Sir Robert Shirley. He succeeded to his title in 1646, under the wardship of his uncle, the Earl of Essex. On the Earl's death in the same year he joined the King's cause. He was committed to the Tower in May, 1650, but was released on finding security. He continued, however, to engage in conspiracies, and died in the Tower, November, 1656. Thurloe, John, *A Collection of State Papers*, 1742, IV, 224; *Calendar State Papers, 1650, passim*; *Nicholas Papers (Camden Society Publications)*, II, 218; Colvile, F. L., *The Worthies of Warwickshire*, 1870, p. 686.

[16] Richard Nicolls was granted the degree of Doctor of Laws at Oxford in 1663. He was a groom of the bedchamber to James, Duke of York. Wood, *Athenae Oxoniensis*, 1721, fasti, p. 156.

[17] Sir Charles Lyttelton of Hughley Park, County Worcester. He was an active Royalist, and took part in the siege of Colchester. He was captured, but escaped to France, where in 1650 he was cupbearer to Charles II. He was knighted about 1662. He won rapid promotion in the army, but resigned his places at the Revolution. He succeeded to his brother's baronetcy in 1693, and died in 1716. He was in the Tower until Jan. 16, 1655/6, when he was sent to Lambeth Gate-house. Cokayne, G. E., *Complete Baronetage*, 1900, I, 117; *Calendar State Papers, 1655*, p. 575; *Calendar State Papers, passim*.

[18] Colonel John Paston was the fifth son of Edward Paston, of the younger branch of an old Norfolk family. By June 12, 1655, he was a prisoner at St. James, and was still in confinement on October 3. *Calendar State Papers, 1655*, p. 368; *Norfolk Archaeology*, 1847, IV, 45.

[19] Colonel Thomas Panton. On March 13, 1664, he was granted (with Bernard Grenville) the office of keeper of the lodge and walk at Petersham in Richmond Park.
By June 12, 1655, he was a prisoner at St. James. *Calendar State Papers, 1663-1664*, p. 75; *Mercurius Politicus*, No. 261.

Still lower hee goes, and all men suppose
   Bee[20] swallow'd up in the quicke sands.

For the rest nott here nam'd I would not bee blam'd,
   As if they were scorn'd by our Lyricke,
For Waller intends to use them as ends
   To patch up his next Panegyrick.[21]

And now to conclude, I would not bee rude,
   Nor presse into Reason of State,
But surely some cause besydes the knowne laws
   Has brought us unto this sad fate.

Must wee pay the faults, of our Argonauts,
   And suffer for other men's synns?
Cause like sylly Geese they have mist of the fleece
   Poor Prisoners are shorne to their skyns.[22]

Jaymaica relations[23] soe tickle the nations,
   And Venables[24] looks soe sullen
That everyone cryes the designe was as wise
   As those that are fram'd att Cullen.[25]

Lett them turne but our Taxe into paper and waxe
   (As some able men have endeavour'd)
And wee shall not stand for notes of our hand;
   They're sealed, and wee are delivered.

[20] *MS.,* Hee.

[21] Two editions of Waller's poem, *Panegyrick to my Lord Protector,* appeared in 1655.

[22] In 1655 the fleet of the Commonwealth, under the command of Penn and Venables, set out to attack the Spanish possessions in the West Indies. The whole expedition was rather badly managed. In April, Venables made an unsuccessful attack on Santo Domingo, in which he lost over 600 men. On May 10, however, Jamaica was captured.

[23] See above.

[24] See above.

[25] Cullen or Culin is the spelling in general use in the seventeenth-century periodicals for Cologne (Köln). Charles II resided there from 1654 to 1656. The designs referred to here are evidently the futile Royalist plots of this period, specifically, perhaps, the rising planned for April 18 throughout England, which actually broke out in Salisbury March 12, and which was quickly suppressed.

Yett the Bonds they exact, destroy their own Act
  Of pardon, which all men extoll.[26]
Wee thought wee should bee, good subjects and free,
  But now wee are Bondmen to Noll.

ON MR. JOHN FLETCHERS *WORKS*[1]

So shall we joy, when all whom Beasts and Worms
Had turn'd to their own substances and forms,
Whom Earth to Earth, or Fire hath chang'd to Fire,
We shall behold more then at first entire;
As now we do, to see all thine thy own
In this thy Muses Resurrection,
Whose scatter'd parts, from thy own race, more wounds
Hath suffer'd then *Acteon* from his Hounds;
Which first their Brains, and then their Bellies fed,
And from their excrements new Poets bred.   10
But now thy Muse enraged from her Urn
Like Ghosts of Murdered bodies does return
T'accuse the Murderers, to right the Stage,
And undeceive the long abused Age,
Which casts thy praise on them, to whom thy wit
Gives not more Gold then they give dross to it:
Who not content like Felons to Purloyn,
Adde treason to it, and debase thy Coyn.
But whither am I straid? I need not raise
Trophies to thee from other mens dispraise;   20
Nor is thy Fame on lesser ruines built,
Nor needs thy juster Title the foul guilt
Of Eastern Kings, who to secure their reign,

[26] An Act of Oblivion was passed at Cromwell's instigation, February 24, 1652, declaring a pardon for all treasons and felonies committed before September 3, 1651, the date of the battle of Worcester. Owing to the many exceptions in the act, the Cavaliers did not escape as lightly as they had hoped.

[1] First printed among the prefatory poems in the collected edition of Beaumont and Fletcher's *Comedies and Tragedies*, etc., 1647.

Must have their Brothers, Sons, and Kindred slain.[2]
Then was wits Empire at the Fatal height,
When labouring and sinking with its weight,
From thence a Thousand lesser Poets sprung
Like petty Princes from the fall of *Rome;*
When *Johnson, Shakespear,* and thy self did sit,
And sway'd in the triumvirate of wit—   30
Yet what from *Johnson's* oyl and sweat did flow,
Or what more easie Nature did bestow
On *Shakespear's* gentler Muse, in thee full grown
Their graces both appear, yet so, that none
Can say here Nature ends, and Art begins,
But mixt like th' Elements and born like twins,
So interweav'd, so like, so much the same,
None, this meer Nature, that meer Art can name:
'Twas this the Antients mean't; Nature and Skill
Are the two tops of their *Parnassus* Hill.

[2] " 'Tis the wits nature, or at best, their fate
    Others to scorn, and one another hate.
    They would be sultans if they had their will;
    For each of them would all his brothers kill."
                Orrery, Roger Boyle, Earl of (the Dramatic Works of,
                    1739), *Prologue to Tryphon,* I, 132.

"In our own country a man seldom sets up for a poet without attacking the reputation of all of his brothers in the art. . . . But how much more noble is the fame that is built on candour and ingenuity, according to those beautiful lines of Sir John Denham in his poem on Fletcher's works." Addison, *The Spectator,* No. 253.

    "Should such a man, too fond to rule alone,
      Bear, like a Turk, no brother near the throne,"
            Pope, *Epistle to Dr. Arbuthnot,* ll. 197-198.

TO SIR RICHARD FANSHAW UPON HIS
TRANSLATION OF PASTOR FIDO[1]

Such is our Pride, our Folly, or our Fate,
That few but such as cannot write, Translate.
But what in them is want of Art, or voice,[2]
In thee is either Modesty or Choice.
Whiles this great piece, restor'd by thee doth stand
Free from the blemish of an Artless hand.[3]
Secure of Fame, thou justly dost esteem
Less honour to create, than to redeem.
Nor ought a Genius less than his that writ,
Attempt Translation; for transplanted wit,   10
All the defects of air and soil doth share,
And colder brains like colder Climates are:
In vain they toil, since nothing can beget
A vital spirit, but a vital heat.
That servile path thou nobly dost decline
Of tracing word by word, and[4] line by line.
Those are the labour'd births of slavish brains,
Not the effects of Poetry, but pains;
Cheap vulgar arts, whose narrowness affords
No flight for thoughts, but poorly sticks[5] at words.   20

---

[1] This poem seems to have been written about 1643 or 1644 (see *Epistle Dedicatory*, p. 59). It was first printed in 1648, and reprinted with *Cooper's Hill*, in 1650.

Fanshawe, *Il Pastor Fido; the Faithful Shepheard, with . . . divers other poems*, 1648.

Sir Richard Fanshawe (1608-1666) was a graduate of Jesus College, Cambridge. He joined Charles I at Oxford at the outbreak of the war, and remained a zealous adherent of the King's cause, following Charles II abroad. He was captured at the battle of Worcester in 1651, but was later freed on bail. He remained in England until 1658, when he rejoined the King. After the Restoration he was sent as ambassador to Portugal, and later to Spain.

[2] *1650*, . . . wit, or voice.

[3] *1650*, Whiles this restored work at thy command
      Casts off the blemish of an artlesse hand.

[4] *1650*, or.

[5] *1648*, sticks.
1650, strikes.

A new and nobler way thou dost pursue
To make Translations and Translators too.
They but preserve the Ashes, thou the Flame,
True to his sense, but truer to his fame.
Foording his current, where thou find'st it low
Let'st in thine own to make it rise and flow;
Wisely restoring whatsoever grace
It lost by change of Times, or Tongues, or Place.
Nor fetter'd to his Numbers, and his Times,
Betray'st his Musick to unhappy Rimes,   30
Nor are the nerves of his compacted strength
Stretch'd and dissolv'd into unsinnewed length:
Yet after all, (lest we should think it thine)
Thy spirit to his circle dost confine.
New names, new dressings, and the modern cast,
Some Scenes some persons alter'd, had out-fac'd
The world, it were thy work; for we have known
Some thank't and prais'd for what was less their own.
That Masters hand[6] which to the life can trace
The airs, the lines, and features of a face,   40
May with a free and bolder stroke express
A varyed posture, or a flatt'ring Dress;
He could have made those like, who made the rest,
But that he knew his own design was best.

AN ELEGIE UPON THE DEATH OF THE LORD HASTINGS[1]

Reader, preserve thy peace: those busie eyes
Will weep at their own sad Discoveries;
When every line they adde, improves thy loss,

[6] *1650,* That curious hand . . .
[1] First printed in *Lachrymae Musarum: or the Tears of the Muses,* 1650.
It was not included in the 1668 edition.
Henry, Lord Hastings (1630-1649) was the eldest son of Ferdinando, Sixth
Earl of Huntington. "He was a nobleman of great learning, and of so sweet a

Till, having view'd the whole, they sum a Cross,
Such as derides thy Passions best relief,
And scorns the succours of thy easie Grief.
Yet lest thy Ignorance betray thy name
Of Man and Pious; read, and mourn: the shame
Of an exemption from just sense, doth show
Irrational, beyond excessive Wo.   10
Since Reason then can priviledge a Tear,
Manhood, uncensur'd, pay that Tribute here
Upon this Noble Urn. Here, here remains
Dust far more precious then in *India's* veins:
Within these cold embraces ravisht lies
That which compleats the Ages Tyrannies;
Who weak to such another Ill appear:
For, what destroys our Hope, secures our Fear.
What Sin unexpiated in this Land
Of Groans, hath guided so severe a hand?   20
The late Great Victim that your Altars knew,[2]
You angry gods, might have excus'd this new
Oblation; and have spar'd one lofty Light
Of Vertue, to inform our steps aright:
By whose Example good, condemned we
Might have run on to kinder Destiny.
But as the Leader of the Herd fell first,
A Sacrifice to quench the raging thirst
Of inflam'd Vengeance for past Crimes: so none
But this white fatted Youngling could atone,   30
By his untimely Fate, that impious Stroke[3]
That sullied Earth, and did Heaven's pity choke.[4]

disposition that no less than ninety-eight elegies were made on him." Collins, A.,
Peerage, 1812, VI, 660.
   Denham's elegy compares favorably with that of Dryden (one of the ninety-
eight), which is his first published work, and is in the metaphysical style. From
Dryden we learn a few more facts about Hastings: that he was a skillful
linguist, and that he died, on the eve of his wedding, of smallpox.
   [2] Charles I.
   [3] *Lachrymae Musarum*, Smoke.
   [4] The execution of Charles I.

Let it suffice for us, that we have lost,
In Him, more then the widow'd World can boast
In any lump of her remaining Clay.
Fair as the grey-ey'd Morn, He was: the Day,
Youthful, and climbing upwards still, imparts
No haste like that of his increasing Parts:
Like the Meridian-beam, his Vertues light
Was seen; as full of comfort, and as bright.   40
Ah that that Noon had been as fix'd as clear! But He,
That onely wanted Immortality
To make him perfect, now submits to night;
In the black bosom of whose sable Spight,
He leaves a cloud of Flesh behinde, and flies,
Refin'd, all Ray and Glory, to the Skies.
Great *saint* shine there in an eternal Sphere,
And tell those Powers to whom thou now drawst neer,
That, by our trembling Sense, in *Hastings* dead,
Their Anger, and our ugly Faults, are read: 50
The short lines of whose Life did to our eyes,
Their Love and Majestie epitomize.
Tell them whose stern Decrees impose our Laws,
The feasted Grave may close her hollow Jaws.
Though Sin search Nature, to provide her here
A second Entertainment half so dear;
She'll never meet a Plenty like this Herse,
Till Time present her with the Universe.

A PANEGYRICK *ON* HIS EXCELLENCY, THE LORD GENERAL GEORGE MONCK[1]

If *England's* bleeding story may transmit
One Renown'd Name to Time, Yours must be it:
Who with such Art dost heal, that we resound,
Next to our Cure, the glory of our Wound.
Thou sav'st three shatter'd KINGDOMS gasping Life,
Yet from our desperate Gangrene keep'st thy Knife.
And though each searching Weapon rallied stand,
And all Fates keen Artilery wait at hand:

[1] First printed in 1659 as a broadside. Wood says, "Tho' the name of John Denham is not set to it, yet the frequent report was then among the Academians that he was the author of it." *Athenae Oxoniensis*, 1721, II, 423.

Evidence of style supports Wood's statement, and makes it almost certain the poem is by Denham. It is not included in the 1668 edition.

George Monk, or Monck (1608-1670), was eminent as a soldier. He entered upon this career early in life, and served with distinction in many campaigns on the continent. In 1642 he returned from Ireland, where he commanded a regiment, and fought for Charles until captured in 1644. After remaining in prison two years, he was released on condition of his serving for Parliament against the Irish. He remained in Ireland until driven out by Ormonde in 1649. He accompanied Cromwell to Scotland in 1651, and remained there as commander-in-chief in 1652. In 1652 and 1653 he was made a general of the fleet, and won several important victories over the Dutch. He then returned to Scotland as commander-in-chief, where he remained until 1659. After the Restoration he was made Duke of Albermarle. He again fought the Dutch in 1665-1666. He retired in 1668.

In May, 1659, Lambert, Ludlow, and other army chiefs compelled Richard Cromwell to abdicate the Protectorship. Public opinion forced them to restore the Rump Parliament, dissolved by Oliver in 1653, but in August Lambert dissolved the Rump, and vested the authority in a council of officers. Monk, in Scotland, took the part of Parliament. Lambert marched north, and the two armies faced each other near the border. Civil war seemed inescapable. Monk, however, by delaying and parleying, waited until public opinion swung again to the Rump, and Lambert's army disintegrated. Monk then marched to London. Before his arrival riots had occurred between the city of London and the Rump. As Monk had given no hint of his real intentions, though doubtless from the first they had been to restore Charles II, there was great anxiety to know whether he would side with the city, whose sympathies were Royalist, or Rump, the stronghold of Republicanism. After first obeying Parliament's command to break down the gates of the city and suppress any disorders, Monk reversed his position, espoused the cause of the city, and demanded the election of a new Parliament, which meant the inevitable recall of Charles.

Thou curb'st those Terrors from inflicting harms;
Swords are Thy Instruments, but not Thy Armes. 10
Thou with Thy Pause and Treaty rout'st Thy Foes;
And Thy tame Conference a Conquest growes.
With the Great *Fabius* then advance Thy Bayes,
Who sinking *Rome* restor'd by wise Delayes.
Let other Victors count their Dead, and lay
Sad Wreaths of conscious Lawrel, where they slay,
Whilest thou alone Dry Trophies dost assume;
They know to Kill, but Thou to Overcome.
Hence, though some foming spleens and working hates
Make Thee the *Sampson* to our Citie Gates; 20
At length Thou introducest cooler Votes,
To be the temper to impetuous Throats.
Choosing that safe Sobriety of thy way,
Not to Eject their fury, but Allay.
With like inspired Prudence didst Thou guide
Thy doubtful Answers, when their fears apply'd
Their subt'lest Emissaries to disclose,
Which strugling Cause thy Courage would oppose.
When though Thy innocent brest resolved stood
The steady Bulwark of the General Good; 30
Thy then unripe Affairs left them such scope,
That who deserv'd no help, might still have hope.
The Superstitious thus return'd of old
From their consulted Oracles, that unfold
Two-handed Fates, which when they false appear,
Delphos spoke true, false the Interpreter.
Apollo's awful Tripos would not lye,
Yet the Receivers sense might mis-apply.
So thy Consultors from their proud hopes fell:
They gave Delusion, Thou gav'st Oracle. 40
Hence secret trains and snares Thy steps pursue;
So dangerous 'mongst the False 'tis to be True.
Return, Return! and shroud Thy envy'd Name,
In those glad Roofs thy sole Arme skreen'd from flame.

Thus threatned *TROY* no stronger Fortress seeks
Than her *Palladium*, 'gainst the trecherous *Greeks*.
And that *Palladium* ne're was seen no more,
When once by Rapine from the Temple tore.
What she to *Troy*, *Troy* did to her become,
And was the *Pallas* to *Palladium*.   50
Thence did their mutual Protections start;
Together both, neither were safe apart.
So Thou without Us safe canst hardly be,
And we despise all safety without Thee.
Return, Return! Enshrine Thy Glories here;
Thou, whom both Seas and Shore do love and fear.
'Midst Triumphs great, like those, Thy Valor stood,
Whilst *Hollands* faithless Gore did stain the Floud:
When Thy bold Shot made their proud Vessels creep,
And cleanse their guilty Navie in the Deep.   60
Let Land and Waters yet thy Deeds proclaime,
Till Nature mints more Elements for Thy FAME.

ON MR ABRAHAM COWLEY

HIS DEATH AND BURIAL AMONGST THE ANCIENT POETS[1]

Old *Chaucer*, like the morning Star,
To us discovers day from far,
His light those Mists and Clouds dissolv'd,
Which our dark Nation long involv'd;
But he descending to the shades,
Darkness again the Age invades.
Next (like *Aurora*) *Spencer* rose,
Whose purple blush the day foreshows;
The other three, with his own fires,
Phœbus, the Poets God, inspires;   10

---

[1] First printed in 1667.

By *Shakespear's, Johnson's, Fletcher's* lines,
Our Stages lustre *Rome's* outshines:
These Poets neer our Princes sleep,
And in one Grave their Mansion keep;
They liv'd to see so many days,
Till time had blasted all their Bays:
But cursed be the fatal hour
That pluckt the fairest, sweetest flower
That in the Muses Garden grew,
And amongst wither'd Lawrels threw.   20
Time, which made them their Fame outlive,
To *Cowly* scarce did ripeness give.
Old Mother Wit, and Nature gave
Shakespear and *Fletcher* all they have;
In *Spencer,* and in *Johnson,* Art,
Of slower Nature got the start;
But both in him so equal are,
None knows which bears the happy'st share;
To him no Author was unknown,
Yet what he wrote was all his own;[2]   30
He melted not the ancient Gold,
Nor with *Ben Johnson* did make bold
To plunder all the *Roman* stores
Of Poets, and of Orators:
Horace his wit, and *Virgil's* state,
He did not steal, but emulate,
And when he would like them appear,
Their Garb, but not their Cloaths, did wear:
He not from *Rome* alone, but *Greece,*
Like *Jason* brought the Golden Fleece;   40
To him that Language (though to none
Of th' others) as his own was known.

[2]
"To steal a hint was never known,
But what he writ was all his own."
Swift, *On the Death of Dr. Swift,* ll. 334-335.

On a stiff gale (as *Flaccus* sings)[3]
The *Theban* Swan extends his wings,
When through th' ætherial Clouds he flies,
To the same pitch our Swan doth rise;
Old *Pindar's* flights by him are reacht,
When on that gale his wings are stretcht;
His fancy and his judgment such,
Each to the other seem'd too much,   50
His severe judgment (giving Law)
His modest fancy kept in awe:
As rigid Husbands jealous are,
When they believe their Wives too fair.
His English stream so pure did flow,
As all that saw, and tasted, know.
But for his Latin vein, so clear,
Strong, full, and high it doth appear,[4]
That were immortal *Virgil* here,
Him, for his judge, he would not fear;   60
Of that great Portraicture, so true
A Copy Pencil never drew.
My Muse her Song had ended here,
But both their Genii strait appear,
Joy and amazement her did strike,
Two Twins she never saw so like.
'Twas taught by wise *Pythagoras*,
One Soul might through more Bodies pass;
Seeing such Transmigration here,
She thought it not a Fable there.[5]   70
Such a resemblance of all parts,
Life, Death, Age, Fortune, Nature, Arts,

[3] *1668, Marginal note,* His pindarics.
           "Multa Dircaeum levat aura cycnum
           Tendit, Antoni, quotiens in altos
           Nubium tractus."
                        Horace, *Odes*, Bk. IV, ode ii, ll. 25-27.

[4] *1668, Marginal note,* His last work.
[5] *1667,* omits lines 67-70.

Then lights her Torch at theirs, to tell,
And shew the world this Parallel,
Fixt and contemplative their looks,
Still turning over Natures Books:
Their works chast, moral, and divine,
Where profit and delight combine;
They guilding dirt, in noble verse
Rustick Philosophy rehearse;   80
When Heroes, Gods, or God-like Kings
They praise, on their exalted wings,
To the Celestial orbs they climb,
And with the Harmonious sphears keep time; [6]
Nor did their actions fall behind
Their words, but with like candour shin'd,
Each drew fair Characters, yet none
Of these they feign'd, excels their own; [7]
Both by two generous Princes lov'd,
Who knew, and judg'd what they approv'd: 90
Yet having each the same desire,
Both from the busie throng retire,
Their Bodies to their Minds resign'd,
Car'd not to propagate their Kind:
Yet though both fell before their hour,
Time on their off-spring hath no power,
Nor fire, nor fate their Bays shall blast,
Nor Death's dark vail their day o'recast.

[6] *1667*, omits lines 81-84.
[7] *1667*, omits lines 87-88.

ON THE EARL OF STRAFFORD'S *TRYAL AND DEATH*[1]

Great *Strafford!* worthy of that Name, though all
Of thee could be forgotten, but thy fall,
Crusht by Imaginary Treasons weight,
Which too much Merit did accumulate:
As Chymists Gold from Brass by fire would draw,
Pretexts are into Treason forg'd by Law.
His Wisdom such, at once it did appear
Three Kingdoms wonder, and three Kingdoms fear;

---

[1] First printed in the 1668 collected edition.

Thomas Wentworth, Earl of Strafford, counsellor of Charles I, was impeached for high treason, and beheaded May 12, 1641.

There are two manuscripts of this poem in the British Museum: Stowe 970, which is an imperfect copy of the 1668 text, lacking lines 3-10, and 21-26; and Egerton 2421, which is a shorter and quite different text.

The Egerton manuscript evidently is an early state of the poem, probably written not long after the execution of the Earl. The 1668 text, on the other hand, is a late revision done not earlier than 1662, as lines 25 and 26 allude to the reversal of his attainder, in February, 1661/2.

Egerton manuscript 2421:

> "Great Straford, worthy of that name tho' all
> Of thee could be forgotten but thy fall.
> How greate thy ruine when no lesse a weight
> Could serve to crush thee then three kingdoms hate;
> Yet single they accounted thee (although
> Each had an army) as an equall foe.
> Thy wisdome such, at once it did appeare
> Three kingdomes wonder, and three kingdomes feare,
> Joyned with an eloquence so greate to make
> Us heere with greater passion then he spake;
> That we forced him to pitty us whilst he
> Seemed more unmov'd and unconcern'd then we.
> And mad[e] them wish who had his death decreed
> Him rather then their owne discreation freede.
> So powerfull[y] it wrought, at once they greive
> That he should dye, yet feared to let him live.
> Farwell greate soule, the glory of thy fall
> Outeweighes the cause, whom we at once may call
> The enimy and martire of the state,
> *Our nations glory and our nations hate."

> "Our nation's glory and our nation's crime."
> Waller, *Upon his Majesty's Repairing of Paul's*, l. 4.

Whilst single he stood forth, and seem'd, although
Each had an Army, as an equal Foe.   10
Such was his force of Eloquence, to make
The Hearers more concern'd than he that spake;
Each seem'd to act that part, he came to see,
And none was more a looker on than he:
So did he move our passion, some were known
To wish for the defence, the Crime their own.
Now private pity strove with publick hate,
Reason with Rage, and Eloquence with Fate:
Now they could him, if he could them forgive;
He's not too guilty, but too wise to live;   20
Less seem those Facts which Treasons Nick-name bore,
Than such a fear'd ability for more.
They after death their fears of him express.
His Innocence, and their own guilt confess.
Their Legislative Frenzy they repent;
Enacting it should make no President.[2]
This Fate he could have scap'd, but would not lose
Honour for Life, but rather nobly chose
Death from their fears, then safety from his own,
That his last Action all the rest might crown.   30

[2] "At the Restoration of King Charles II his [Strafford's] attainder was re-
versed, and the articles of accumulative treason declared null, because what is
not treason in the several parts cannot amount to treason in the whole." Nal-
son, John, *An Impartial Collection of the Great Affairs of State*, 1683, II, 203.
  The bill for this purpose passed the third reading in the House of Lords
February 17, 1661/2, and the House of Commons February 27.

TO THE HONOURABLE *EDWARD HOWARD ESQ;* UPON HIS POEM OF THE BRITISH PRINCES[1]

What mighty Gale hath rais'd a flight so strong?
So high above all vulgar eyes? so long?
One single rapture, scarce it self confines,
Within the limits, of four thousand lines,
And yet I hope to see this noble heat
Continue, till it makes the piece compleat,
That to the latter Age it may descend,
And to the end of time, its beams extend,
When Poesie joyns profit, with delight,
Her Images, should be most exquisite,   10
Since man to that perfection cannot rise,
Of always virt'ous, fortunate, and wise:
Therefore, the patterns man should imitate,
Above the life our Masters should create.
Herein, if we consult with *Greece,* and *Rome,*
Greece (as in warre) by *Rome* was overcome,
Though mighty raptures, we in *Homer* find,
Yet like himself, his Characters were blind:
Virgil's sublimed eyes not only gaz'd,
But his sublimed thoughts to heaven were rais'd.   20
Who reads the Honors, which he paid the Gods
Would think he had beheld their bless'd abodes,
And that his Hero, might accomplish'd be,
From divine blood, he draws his Pedigree,
From that great Judge your Judgment takes its law,
And by the best Original, does draw
Bonduca's Honor, with those Heroes time
Had in oblivion wrapt, his sawcy crime,
To them and to your Nation you are just,

[1] First printed as a prefatory poem to Howard's *British Princes,* 1669.
    Howard was the fifth son of Thomas, First Earl of Berkshire. Both as a poet and as a dramatist he was ridiculed by his contemporaries, and it is more than likely that this eulogy of Denham's is not to be taken seriously.

In raising up their glories from the dust,   30
And to Old *England* you that right have done,
To shew, no story nobler, than her own.

ELEGY ON THE DEATH OF JUDGE
CROOKE[1]

This was the Man! the Glory of the Gown
Just to Himself, his Country and the[2] Crown!

[1] There are two manuscripts of this poem in the British Museum: Egerton
2421, entitled *Upon Judge Crooke;* and Harleian 6933, entitled *An Elegy on
the Death of Judge Crooke by Mr. John Denham MS. not printed in his
Poems.* Evidence of style makes it certain that it is correctly ascribed to Denham.
The present text follows MS. Harleian. The poem was first printed in *The
Topographer for the year 1790,* London, 1790 (II, 177 ff.).
   Sir George Croke (1559-1641) was a graduate of University College, Oxford.
After studying at Inner Temple, he became a justice of Common Pleas, and
later one of the twelve judges of the King's Bench. He was noted for his up-
rightness and learning, and his reports were long held in high repute. He became
famous largely because of his decision in the ship-money case.
   The dispute about ship-money was one of the underlying causes of the civil
war. Charles, anxious to rule without Parliament, was confronted with the
problem of raising money for the support of the fleet without following the
regular course of having a subsidy for this purpose voted by Parliament. He
adopted the expedient of following an old precedent, and issued writs calling
upon the coast towns to furnish the monetary equivalent of certain ships,
manned and equipped. The first writs were issued in 1634, and in the following
year were extended to include all the towns of England, inland as well as
coastal. By the time that the third writs were issued in 1636, hostility to
them had become widespread. Objectors argued that the writs were illegal.
The original writs were issued in times of sudden emergency, but these of
Charles, issued yearly in times of peace, constituted a tax without the consent
of Parliament, and hence violated the "fundamental laws" of the kingdom.
John Hampden, by refusing payment, brought a test case before the King's
Bench, where the legality of the writs was argued. As the fundamental issue was
whether the King could raise money without the consent of Parliament, and was,
in fact, above the law, the case became very famous, and the decisions of the
judges momentous. Seven upheld the legality of ship-money. Of the five who
dissented, Croke was the most outspoken in his condemnation.
   It is of considerable interest to find that Denham's father, who was one of
the judges, supported Croke, for the poet doubtless got from his father his
admiration for Croke, and perhaps also his views on the King's prerogative.
   [2] *Egerton 2421,* his.

The Atlas of our Liberty; as high
In this own Fame as others Infamy.
Great by his vertues, greate by others Crimes,
The best of Judges in the Worst of Times.
He was the first who happily did sound
Unfathomd Royalty and felt the Ground;
Yet happier to behold that dawning Ray,
Shot from himself, become a perfect Day;   10
To hear his Judgment so authentic grown,
The Kingdoms voice the Eccho to his own.
Nor did he speak, but live[3] the Laws; altho
From his sage Mouth grave oracles did flow,
Who knew his Life Maxims might thence derive
Such as the Law to Law itself might give.
Who saw him on the Bench would think the name
Of Friendship or Affection never came
Within his[4] thoughts: who saw him thence might know
He never had nor could deserve a Foe;   20
Only assuming Rigor with his Gown,
And with his Purple laid his Rigor down.
Him nor Respect nor Disrespect could move;
He knew no Anger, nor[5] his Place no Love.
So mixd the Stream of all his Actions ran,
So much a Judge so much a Gentleman;
Who durst be just when justice was a crime,
Yet durst no more even in too[6] just a Time;
Not hurried by the highest Movers force
Against his proper and resolved course;[7]   30
But when our World did turn, so kept his Ground
He seemd the Axe on which the Wheel went[8] round.
Whose Zeal was warm when all to Ice did turn,

[3] *Egerton 2421*, lived.
[4] *Egerton 2421*, omits, his.
[5] *Egerton 2421*, and.
[6] *Egerton 2421*, so.
[7] A certain amount of royal pressure was exerted on the judges in the ship-money case.
[8] *Egerton 2421*, turned.

Yet was but warm when all the World did burn.
No ague in Religion eer inclin'd
To this or that Extream his fixed Mind.[9]
Rest, happy Soul, till the Worlds last assize,
When calld by thy Creator thou shalt rise,
With thy Redeemer in Commission joynd
To sit upon the Clouds and judge Mankind.   40

[9] *Egerton 2421*, transposes these two couplets.

TRANSLATIONS

THE DESTRUCTION OF TROY[1]
THE PREFACE

THERE are so few Translations which deserve praise, that I scarce ever saw any which deserv'd pardon; those who travel in that kind, being for the most part so unhappy, as to rob others, without enriching themselves, pulling down the fame of good Authors, without raising their own: Neither hath any Author been more hardly dealt withal than this our Master; and the reason is evident, for, what is most excellent, is most inimitable; and if even the worst Authors are yet made worse by their Translators, how impossible is it not to do great injury to the best? And therefore I have not the vanity to think my Copy equal to the Original, nor (consequently) my self altogether guiltless of what I accuse others; but if I can do *Virgil* less injury than others have done, it will be, in some degree to do him right; and indeed, the hope of doing him more right, is the only scope of this Essay, by opening this new way of translating this Author, to those whom youth, leisure, and better fortune makes fitter for such undertakings.

I conceive it a vulgar error in translating Poets, to affect being *Fidus Interpres;* let that care be with them who deal in matters of Fact, or matters of Faith: but whosoever aims at it in Poetry, as he attempts what is not required, so he shall never perform what he attempts; for it is not his busines alone to translate Language into Language, but Poesie into Poesie; & Poesie is of so subtile a spirit, that in pouring out of one Language into another, it will all evaporate; and if a new spirit be not added in the transfusion, there will remain nothing but a *Caput mortuum*, there being certain Graces and Happinesses peculiar to every Language, which gives life and energy to the words; and whosoever offers at Verbal Translation, shall have the

---

[1] Announced as newly published in *Mercurius Politicus*, April 17-24, 1656, No. 306.

For a discussion of the relation of this to Denham's translation of Books II to VI of the *Aeneid*, in the unprinted Hutchinson MS., see p. 41.

misfortune of that young Traveller, who lost his own language abroad, and brought home no other instead of it: for the grace of the Latine will be lost by being turned into English words; and the grace of the English, by being turned into the Latine Phrase. And as speech is the apparel of our thoughts, so are there certain Garbs 'and Modes of speaking, which vary with the times; the fashion of our clothes being not more subject to alteration, than that of our speech: and this I think *Tacitus* means, by that which he calls *Sermonem temporis istius auribus accommodatum;* the delight of change being as due to the curiosity of the ear, as of the eye; and therefore if *Virgil* must needs speak English, it were fit he should speak not only as a man of this Nation, but as a man of this age; and if this disguise I have put upon him (I wish I could give it a better name) fit not naturally and easily on so grave a person, yet it may become him better than that Fools-Coat wherein the French and Italian have of late presented him; at least, I hope, it will not make him appear deformed, by making any part enormously bigger or less than the life, (I having made it my principal care to follow him, as he made it his to follow Nature in all his proportions) Neither have I any where offered such violence to his sense, as to make it seem mine, and not his. Where my expressions are not so full as his, either our Language, or my Art were defective (but I rather suspect my self;) but where mine are fuller than his, they are but the impressions which the often reading of him, hath left upon my thoughts; so that if they are not his own Conceptions, they are at least the results of them; and if (being conscious of making him speak worse than he did almost in every line) I erre in endeavouring sometimes to make him speak better; I hope it will be judged an error on the right hand, and such an one as may deserve pardon, if not imitation.

ARGUMENT

The first Book speaking of Æneas his voyage by Sea, and how being cast by tempest upon the coast of Carthage, *he was received by Queen* Dido, *who after the Feast, desires him to make the relation of the destruction of* Troy, *which is the Argument of this Book.*

While all with silence & attention wait,
Thus speaks *Æneas* from the bed of State:
Madam, when you command us to review
Our Fate, you make our old wounds bleed anew
And all those sorrows to my sence restore,
Whereof none saw so much, none suffer'd more:
Not the most cruel of Our conqu'ring Foes
So unconcern'dly can relate our woes,
As not to lend a tear, Then how can I
Repress the horror of my thoughts, which fly   10
The sad remembrance? Now th' expiring night
And the declining Stars to rest invite;
Yet since 'tis your command, what you, so well
Are pleas'd to hear, I cannot grieve to tell.
By Fate repell'd, and with repulses tyr'd,
The *Greeks,* so many Lives and years expir'd,
A Fabrick like a moving Mountain frame,
Pretending vows for their return; This, Fame
Divulges, then within the beasts vast womb
The choice and flower of all their Troops intomb,   20
In view the Isle of *Tenedos,* once high
In fame and wealth, while *Troy* remain'd, doth lie,
(Now but an unsecure and open Bay)
Thither by stealth the *Greeks* their Fleet convey:
We gave them gone, and to *Mycenæ* sail'd,
And *Troy* reviv'd, her mourning face unvail'd;
All through th' unguarded Gates with joy resort
To see the slighted Camp, the vacant Port;
Here lay *Ulysses,* there *Achilles,* here
The Battels joyn'd, the Grecian Fleet rode there;   30

But the vast Pile th' amazed vulgar views
Till they their Reason in their wonder lose;
And first *Tymœtes* moves, (urg'd by the Power
Of Fate, or Fraud) to place it in the Tower,
But *Capis* and the graver sort thought fit,
The *Greeks* suspected Present to commit
To Seas or Flames, at least to search and bore
The sides, and what that space contains t' explore;[2]
Th' uncertain Multitude with both engag'd,
Divided stands, till from the Tower, enrag'd   40
Laocoon ran, whom all the crowd attends,
Crying, what desperat Frenzy's this? (oh friends)
To think them gone? Judge rather their retreat
But a design, their gifts but a deceit,
For our Destruction 'twas contriv'd no doubt,
Or from within by fraud, or from without
By force; yet know ye not *Ulysses* shifts?
Their swords less danger carry than their gifts.
(This said) against the Horses side, his spear
He throws, which trembles with inclosed fear,   50
Whilst from the hollows of his womb proceed
Groans, not his own; And had not Fate decreed
Our Ruine, We had fill'd with *Grecian* blood
The Place, Then *Troy* and *Priam's* Throne had stood;
Meanwhile a fetter'd pris'ner to the King
With joyful shouts the *Dardan* Shepherds bring,
Who to betray us did himself betray,
At once the Taker, and at once the Prey,[3]
Firmly prepar'd, of one Event secur'd,
Or of his Death or his Design assur'd.   60
The *Trojan* Youth about the Captive flock,
To wonder, or to pity, or to mock.

---

[2] 37-38   "at least to bore
          The hollow sides, and hidden frauds explore."
                                        Dryden, *Aeneid*, l. 48.

[3] 58   "At once the chaser, and at once the prey."
                                        Pope, *Windsor Forest*, l. 82.

Now hear the *Grecian* fraud, and from this one
Conjecture all the rest.
Disarm'd, disorder'd, casting round his eyes
On all the Troops that guarded him, he cries,
What Land, what Sea, for me what Fate attends?
Caught by my Foes, condemned by my Friends,[4]
Incensed *Troy* a wretched Captive seeks
To sacrifice, a Fugitive, the Greeks.   70
To Pity, This Complaint our former Rage,
Converts, we now enquire his Parentage,
What of their Councils, or affairs he knew,
Then fearless, he replies, Great King to you
All truth I shall relate: Nor first can I
My self to be of *Grecian* birth deny,
And though my outward state, misfortune hath
Deprest thus low, it cannot reach my Faith.
You may by chance have heard the famous name
Of *Palimede,* who from old *Belus* came,   80
Whom, but for voting Peace, the *Greeks* pursue,
Accus'd unjustly, then unjustly slew,
Yet mourn'd his death. My Father was his friend,
And me to his commands did recommend,
While Laws and Councils did his Throne support,
I but a youth, yet some Esteem and Port
We then did bear, till by *Ulysses* craft
(Things known I speak) he was of life bereft:
Since in dark sorrow I my days did spend,
Till now disdaining his unworthy end   90
I could not silence my Complaints, but vow'd
Revenge, if ever fate or chance allow'd
My wisht return to *Greece;* from hence his hate,
From thence my crimes, and all my ills bear date:
Old guilt fresh malice gives; The peoples ears
He fills with rumors, and their hearts with fears,

---

4   "What fate a wretched fugitive attends,
           Scorned by my foes, abandoned by my friends."
                                        Dryden, *Aeneid,* ll. 89-90.

And then[5] the Prophet to his party drew.
But why do I these thankless truths pursue;
Or why defer your Rage? on me, for all
The *Greeks*, let your revenging fury fall.   100
Ulysses this, th' *Atridæ* this desire
At any rate. We streight are set on fire
(Unpractis'd in such Mysteries) to enquire
The manner and the cause, Which thus he told
With gestures humble, as his Tale was bold.
Oft have the *Greeks* (the siege detesting) tyr'd
With tedious war, a stoln retreat desir'd,
And would to heaven they had gone: But still dismay'd
By Seas or Skies, unwillingly they stay'd,
Chiefly when this stupendious Pile was rais'd   110
Strange noises fill'd the Air, we all amaz'd[6]
Dispatch *Eurypilus* to enquire our Fates
Who thus the sentence of the Gods relates,
A Virgins slaughter did the storm appease
When first towards *Troy* the *Grecians* took the Seas,
Their safe retreat another *Grecians* blood
Must purchase; All, at this confounded stood:
Each thinks himself the Man, the fear on all
Of what, the mischief, but on one can fall:
Then *Calchas* (by *Ulysses* first inspir'd)   120
Was urg'd to name whom th' angry Gods requir'd,
Yet was I warn'd (for many were as well
Inspir'd as he) and did my fate foretel.
Ten days the Prophet in suspence remain'd,
Would no mans fate pronounce; at last constrain'd
By *Ithacus*, he solemnly design'd
Me for the Sacrifice; the people joyn'd
In glad consent, and all their common fear
Determine in my fate, the day drew near;

[5] Them?
[6] 110-111 "Portents and prodigies their souls amazed;
          But most, when this stupendous pile was raised."
                                        Dryden, *Aeneid*, ll. 154-155.

The sacred Rites prepar'd, my temples crown'd   130
With holy wreaths, Then I confess I found
The means to my escape, my bonds I brake,
Fled from my Guards, and in a muddy Lake
Amongst the Sedges all the night lay hid,
Till they their Sails had hoist (if so they did)
And now alas no hope remains for me
My home, my father and my sons to see,
Whom, they enrag'd, will kill for my Offence,
And punish for my guilt their Innocence.
Those Gods who know the Truths I now relate,   140
That faith which yet remains inviolate
By mortal men, By these I beg, redress
My causless wrongs, and pity such distress.
And now true Pity in exchange he finds
For his false Tears, his Tongue, his hands unbinds.
Then spake the King, be Ours whoere thou art,
Forget the *Greeks*. But first the truth impart,
Why did they raise, or to what use intend
This Pile? to a Warlike, or Religious end?
Skilful in fraud, (his native Art) his hands   150
Toward heaven he rais'd, deliver'd now from bands.
Ye pure, Æthereal flames, ye Powers ador'd
By mortal men, ye Altars, and the sword
I scap'd; ye sacred Fillets that involv'd
My destin'd head, grant I may stand absolv'd
From all their Laws and Rites, renounce all name
Of faith or love, their secret thoughts proclaim;
Only O *Troy*, preserve thy faith to me,
If what I shall relate preserveth thee.
From *Pallas* favour, all our hopes, and all   160
Counsels, and Actions took Original,
Till *Diomed* (for such attempts made fit
By dire conjunction with *Ulysses* wit)
Assails the sacred Tower, the Guards they slay,
Defile with bloudy hands, and thence convey

The fatal Image; straight with our success
Our hopes fell back, whilst prodigies express
Her just disdain, her flaming eyes did throw
Flashes of lightning, from each part did flow
A briny sweat, thrice brandishing her spear,   170
Her Statue from the ground it self did rear;
Then, that we should our Sacrilege restore
And reconveigh their Gods from *Argos* shore,
Calchas perswades, till then we urge in vain
The fate of *Troy*. To measure back the Main
They all consent, but to return agen,
When re-inforc'd with aids of Gods and men.
Thus *Calchas*, then instead of that, this Pile
To *Pallas* was design'd; to reconcile
Th' offended Power, and expiate our guilt,   180
To this vast height and monstrous stature built,
Lest through your gates receiv'd, it might renew
Your vows to her, and her Defence to you.
But if this sacred gift you dis-esteem,
Then cruel Plagues (which heaven divert on them)
Shall fall on *Priams* State: but if the horse
Your walls ascend, assisted by your force,
A League 'gainst *Greece* all *Asia* shall contract;
Our Sons then suffering what their Sires would act.
Thus by his fraud and our own faith o'recome,   190
A feigned tear destroys us, against whom
Tydides nor *Achilles* could prevail,
Nor ten years conflict, nor a thousand sail.
This seconded by a most sad Portent
Which credit to the first imposture lent;
Laocoon, Neptunes Priest, upon the day
Devoted to that God, a Bull did slay,
When two prodigious serpents were descride,
Whose circling stroaks the Seas smooth face divide;
Above the deep they raise their scaly Crests,   200
And stem the floud with their erected brests,

Their winding tails advance and steer their course,
And 'gainst the shore the breaking Billow force.[7]
Now landing, from their brandisht tongues there came
A dreadful hiss, and from their eyes a flame:
Amaz'd we fly, directly in a line
Laocoon they pursue, and first intwine
(Each preying upon one) his tender sons,
Then him, who armed to their rescue runs,
They seiz'd, and with intangling folds embrac'd   210
His neck twice compassing, and twice his wast,
Their poys'nous knots he strives to break, and tear,
Whilst slime and bloud his sacred wreaths besmear,
Then loudly roars, as when th' enraged Bull
From th' Altar flies, and from his wounded skull
Shakes the huge Ax; the conqu'ring serpents fly
To cruel *Pallas* Altar, and there ly
Under her feet, within her shields extent;
We in our fears conclude this fate was sent
Justly on him, who struck the Sacred Oak   220
With his accursed Lance. Then to invoke
The Goddess, and let in the fatal horse
We all consent:
A spacious breach we make, & *Troys* proud wall
Built by the Gods, by our own hands doth fall;
Thus, all their help to their own ruine give,
Some draw with cords, and some the Monster drive
With Rolls and Leavers, thus our works it climbs,
Big with our fate, the youth with Songs and Rhimes,
Some dance, some hale the Rope; at last let down   230
It enters with a thundering noise the Town.

[7]   "When (dreadful to behold!) from sea we spied
        Two serpents, ranked abreast, the seas divide,
        And smoothly sweep along the swelling tide.
        Their flaming crests above the waves they show;
        Their bellies seem to burn the seas below;
        Their speckled tails advance to steer their course,
        And on the sounding shore the flying billows force."
                          Dryden, *Aeneid*, ll. 269-275.

O *Troy* the seat of Gods, in war renown'd;
Three times it stuck, as oft the clashing sound
Of Arms was heard, yet blinded by the Power
Of Fate, we place it in the sacred Tower.
Cassandra then foretels th' event, but she
Finds no belief (such was the Gods decree.)
The Altars with fresh flowers we crown, & wast
In Feasts that day, which was (alas) our last.[8]
Now by the revolution of the Skies,   240
Nights sable shadows from the Ocean rise,
Which heaven and earth, and the *Greek* frauds involv'd,
The City in secure repose dissolv'd,
When from the Admirals high Poop appears
A light, by which the *Argive* Squadron Steers
Their silent course to *Iliums* well known Shore,
When *Synon* (sav'd by the Gods partial power)
Opens the horse, and through the unlockt doors
To the free Ayr the armed fraight restores:
Ulysses, Stenelus, Tysander slide   250
Down by a Rope, *Machaon* was their guide;[9]
Atrides, Pyrrhus, Thoas, Athamas,
And *Epeus* who the frauds contriver was,
The Gates they seize, the Guards with sleep and wine
Opprest, surprize, and then their forces joyn.
'Twas then, when the first sweets of sleep repair

8   "Four times he struck: as oft the clashing sound
         Of arms was heard, and inward groans rebound.
         Yet, mad with zeal, and blinded with our fate,
         We haul along the horse in solemn state;
         Then place the dire portent within the tower.
         Cassandra cried, and cursed the unhappy hour;
         Foretold our fate; but, by the god's decree,
         All heard, and none believed the prophecy.
         With branches we the fanes adorn, and waste
         In jollity, the day ordained to be the last."
                              Dryden, *Aeneid,* ll. 318-326.

9   "Thessander bold, and Sthenelus their guide,
         And dire Ulysses down the cables slide."
                              Dryden, *Aeneid,* ll. 340-341.

Our bodies spent with toil, our minds with care[10]
(The Gods best gift) When bath'd in tears and blood
Before my face lamenting *Hector* stood,
Such his aspect when soyl'd with bloudy dust   260
Dragg'd by the cords which through his feet were thrust
By his insulting Foe; O how transform'd!
How much unlike that *Hector* who return'd
Clad in *Achilles* spoyls; when he, among
A thousand ships (like *Jove*) his Lightning flung;
His horrid Beard and knotted Tresses stood
Stiff with his gore, & all his wounds ran blood,
Intranc'd I lay, then (weeping) said, The Joy,
The hope and stay of thy declining *Troy;*
What Region held thee, whence, so much desir'd,   270
Art thou restor'd to us consum'd and tir'd
With toyls and deaths; but what sad cause confounds
Thy once fair looks, or why appear those wounds?
Regardless of my words, he no reply
Returns, but with a dreadful groan doth cry,
Fly from the Flame, O Goddess-born, our walls
The *Greeks* possess, and *Troy* confounded falls
From all her Glories;[11] if it might have stood
By any Power, by this right hand it should.
What Man could do, by me for *Troy* was done,   280
Take here her Reliques and her Gods, to run
With them they Fate, with them new Walls expect,
Which, tost on Seas, thou shalt at last erect;
Then brings old *Vesta* from her sacred Quire,

---

10   ". . . their forces join
      To invade the town, oppressed with sleep and wine.
      Those few they find awake, first meet their fate;
      Then to their fellows they unbar the gate.
      'Twas in the dead of night, when sleep repairs
      Our bodies worn with toils, our minds with cares."
                         Dryden, *Aeneid*, ll. 346-351.

11   "The foes already have possessed the wall;
      Troy nods from high, and totters to her fall."
                         Dryden, *Aeneid*, ll. 383-384.

Her holy Wreaths, and her eternal Fire.[12]
Mean while the Walls with doubtful cries resound
From far (for shady coverts did surround
My Fathers house) approaching still more near
The clash of Arms, and voice of men we hear:
Rowz'd from my Bed, I speedily ascend   290
The house's top, and listning there attend,
As flames rowl'd by the winds conspiring force,
Ore full-ear'd Corn, or Torrents raging course
Bears down th' opposing Oaks, the fields destroys
And mocks the Plough-mans toil,[13] th' unlookt for noise
From neighb'ring hills, th' amazed Shepherd hears;
Such my surprise, and such their rage appears,
First fell thy house *Ucalegon,* then thine
Deiphobus, Sigæan Seas did shine
Bright with *Troys* flames, the Trumpets dreadful sound,   300
The louder groans of dying men confound.
Give me my arms, I cry'd, resolv'd to throw
My self 'mongst any that oppos'd the Foe:
Rage, anger, and Despair at once suggest
That of all Deaths, to die in Arms was best.
The first I met was *Panthus, Phœbus* Priest,
Who scaping with his Gods and Reliques fled,
And towards the shore his little Grandchild led;
Panthus, what hope remains? what force? what place
Made good? but sighing, he replies (alas)   310
Trojans we were, and mighty *Ilium* was;
But the last period and fatal hour
Of *Troy* is come: Our Glory and our Power

12   "From their assistance happier walls expect,
        Which, wandering long, at last thou shalt erect.
        He said, and brought me, from their blest abodes,
        The venerable statues of the gods,
        With ancient Vesta from the sacred choir,
        The wreaths and reliques of the immortal fire."
                                        Ibid., ll. 391-396.
13 *Cf. Cooper's Hill,* ll. 175-176.

Incensed *Jove* transfers to Grecian hands,
The foe within, the burning Town commands;
And (like a smother'd fire) an unseen force
Breaks from the bowels of the fatal Horse:
Insulting *Synon* flings about the flame,
And thousands more than e're from *Argos* came[14]
Possess the Gates, the Passes and the Streets,   320
And these the sword oretakes, & those it meets,
The Guard nor fights nor flies, Their fate so near
At once suspends their Courage and their Fear.
Thus by the Gods, and by *Atrides*[15] words
Inspir'd, I make my way through fire, through swords,
Where Noises, Tumults, Out-cries and Alarms
I heard, first *Iphitus* renown'd for Arms
We meet, who knew us (for the Moon did shine)
Then *Ripheus, Hippanis* and *Dymas* joyn
Their force, and young *Choræbus Mygdons* son,   330
Who, by the Love of fair *Cassandra*, won,
Arriv'd but lately in her Fathers Ayd
Unhappy, whom the Threats could not disswade
Of his Prophetick Spouse;
Whom, when I saw, yet daring to maintain
The fight, I said, Brave Spirits (but in vain)
Are you resolv'd to follow one who dares
Tempt all extreams? The state of Our affairs

---

[14]   "Troy is no more and Ilium was a town!
The fatal day, the appointed hour, is come,
When wrathful Jove's irrevocable doom
Transfers the Trojan state to Grecian hands,
The fire consumes the town, the foe commands;
And armed hosts, an unexpected force,
Break from the bowels of the fatal horse.
Within the gates, proud Sinon throws about
The flames; and foes, for entrance, press without,
With thousand others, whom I fear to name,
More than from Argos or Mycenæ came."
                         Dryden, *Aeneid*, ll. 436-446.

[15] *1668*, Otrides.

You see: The Gods have left us, by whose aid
Our Empire stood; nor can the flame be staid: 340
Then let us fall amidst Our Foes; this one
Relief the vanquisht have, to hope for none.
Then re-inforc'd, as in a stormy night
Wolves urged by their raging appetite[16]
Forrage for prey, which their neglected young
With greedy jaws expect, ev'n so among
Foes, Fire and Swords, t' assured death we pass,
Darkness our Guide, Despair our Leader was.[17]
Who can relate that Evenings woes and spoils,
Or can his tears proportion to our Toils!   350
The City, which so long had flourisht, falls;
Death triumphs o're the Houses, Temples, Walls
Nor only on the *Trojans* fell this doom,
Their hearts at last the vanquish'd re-assume;
And now the Victors fall, on all sides, fears,
Groans and pale Death in all her shapes appears:[18]
Androgeus first with his whole Troop was cast
Upon us, with civility misplac't;
Thus greeting us you lose by your delay,
Your share both of the honour and the prey,   360
Others the spoils of burning *Troy* convey
Back to those ships, which you but now forsake.
We making no return; his sad mistake
Too late he finds: As when an unseen Snake
A Travellers unwary foot hath prest,
Who trembling starts, when the Snakes azure Crest,
Swoln with his rising Anger, he espies,

16   "As hungry wolves, with raging appetite,
          Scour through the fields, nor fear the stormy night."
                                        Dryden, *Aeneid,* ll. 479-480.

17   "Night was our friend; our leader was despair."
                                        Dryden, *Aeneid,* ll. 487.

18   "All parts resound with tumults, plaints, and fears;
          And grisly death, in sundry shapes appears."
                                        Dryden, *Aeneid,* ll. 498-499.

So from our view surpriz'd *Androgeus* flies.[19]
But here an easie victory we meet:
Fear binds their hands, and ignorance their feet,   370
Whilst Fortune, our first Enterprize, did aid,
Encourag'd with success, *Chorœbus* said,
O Friends, we now by better Fates are led,
And the fair Path they lead us, let us tread.[20]
First change your Arms, and their distinctions bear;[21]
The same, in foes, Deceit and Vertue are.
Then of his Arms, *Androgeus* he divests,
His Sword, his Shield he takes, and plumed Crests,
Then *Ripheus, Dymas,* and the rest, All glad
Of the occasion, in fresh spoils are clad.   380
Thus mixt, with Greeks, as if their Fortune still
Follow'd their swords, we fight, pursue, and kill.
Some re-ascend the Horse, and he whose sides
Let forth the valiant, now, the Coward hides.
Some, to their safer Guard, their Ships, retire;
But vain's that hope, 'gainst which the Gods conspire:
Behold the Royal Virgin, The Divine
Cassandra, from *Minerva's* fatal shrine
Dragg'd by the hair, casting tow'rds heaven in vain,
Her Eyes; for Cords her tender hands did strain: 390
Chorœbus at the spectacle enrag'd,
Flies in amidst the foes: we thus engag'd,
To second him, amongst the thickest ran;
Here first our ruine from our friends began,
Who from the Temples Battlements a shower
Of Darts and Arrows on our heads did powr:

[19]   "As when some peasant in a bushy brake,
           Has with unwary footing pressed a snake;
           He starts aside, astonished, when he spies
           His rising crest, blue neck, and rolling eyes;
           So, from our arms, surprised Androgeos flies."
                                    Dryden, *Aeneid,* ll. 510-514.
[20] *1668,* dread.

[21]   "Then change we shields, and their devices bear."
                                    Dryden, *Aeneid,* l. 526.

They, us for Greeks, and now the Greeks (who knew
Cassandra's rescue) us for Trojans slew.
Then from all parts *Ulysses, Ajax,* then,
And then th' *Atridæ* rally all their men;   400
As winds, that meet from several Coasts, contest,
Their prisons being broke, the South and West,
And *Eurus* on his winged Coursers born
Triumphing in their speed, the woods are torn,[22]
And chafing *Nereus* with his *Trident* throws
The billows from their bottom; Then all those
Who in the dark our fury did escape,
Returning, know our borrowed Arms and shape
And diff'ring Dialect: Then their numbers swell
And grow upon us; first *Choræbus* fell   410
Before *Minerva's* Altar, next did bleed
Just *Ripheus,* whom no Trojan did exceed
In virtue, yet the Gods his fate decreed.
Then *Hippanis* and *Dymas* wounded by
Their friends; nor thee *Panthus* thy Piety,
Nor consecrated Mitre, from the same
Ill fate could save; My Countreys funeral flame
And *Troys* cold ashes I attest, and call
To witness for my self, That in their fall
No Foes, no Death, nor Danger I declin'd   420
Did, and deserv'd no less, my Fate to find.
Now *Iphitus* with me, and *Pelias*
Slowly retire, the one retarded was
By feeble Age, the other by a wound,
To Court the Cry directs us, where We found
Th' Assault so hot, as if 'twere only there,
And all the rest secure from foes or fear:[23]

---

22   "South, east and west, on airy coursers bourne—
      The whirlwind gathers, and the woods are torn."
                                   Dryden, *Aeneid,* ll. 567-568.

23   "Or as all Ilium else were void of fear,
      And tumult, war, and slaughter, only there."
                                   Dryden, *Aeneid,* ll. 598-599.

The Greeks the Gates approach'd, their Targets cast,
Over their heads, some scaling ladders plac't
Against the walls, the rest the steps ascend, 430
And with their shields on their left Arms defend
Arrows and darts, and with their right hold fast
The Battlement; on them the Trojans cast
Stones, Rafters, Pillars, Beams, such Arms as these,
Now hopeless, for their last defence they seize.
The gilded Roofs, the marks of ancient state
They tumble down,[24] and now against the Gate
Of th' Inner Court their growing force they bring,
Now was Our last effort to save the King.
Relieve the fainting, and succeed the dead. 440
A Private Gallery 'twixt th' appartments led,
Not to the Foe yet known, or not observ'd,
(The way for *Hectors* hapless Wife reserv'd,
When to the aged King, her little son
She would present) Through this we pass and run
Up to the highest Battlement, from whence
The Trojans threw their darts without offence.[25]
A Tower so high, it seem'd to reach the sky,
Stood on the Roof, from whence we could descry
All *Ilium*—both the Camps, the Grecian Fleet; 450
This, where the Beams upon the Columns meet,
We loosen, which like Thunder from the Cloud
Breaks on their heads, as sudden and as loud.
But others still succeed: mean time, nor stones
Nor any kind of weapons cease.
Before the Gate in gilded Armour, shone
Young *Pyrrhus,* like a Snake his skin new grown,
Who fed on poys'nous herbs, all winter lay

[24] "And gilded roofs, come tumbling from on high,
The marks of state, and ancient royalty."
Ibid., ll. 611-612.

[25] "Through this we pass, and mount the tower, from whence
With unavailing arms the Trojans make defence."
Ibid., 625-626.

Under the ground, and now reviews the day
Fresh in his new apparel, proud and young,   450
Rowls up his Back, and brandishes his tongue,
And lifts his scaly breast against the Sun;
With him his Fathers Squire, *Antomedon*
And *Periphas* who drove his winged steeds,
Enter the Court; whom all the youth succeeds
Of *Scyros* Isle, who flaming firebrands flung
Up to the roof, *Pyrrhus* himself among
The formost with an Axe an entrance hews
Through beams of solid Oak, then freely views
The Chambers, Galleries, and Rooms of State,   470
Where *Priam* and the ancient Monarchs sate.
At the first Gate an Armed Guard appears;
But th' Inner Court with horror, noise and tears
Confus'dly fill'd, the womens shrieks and cries
The Arched Vaults re-eccho to the skies;
Sad Matrons wandring through the spacious Rooms
Embrace and kiss the Posts: Then *Pyrrhus* comes
Full of his Father, neither Men nor Walls
His force sustain, the torn Port-cullis falls,
Then from the hinge, their strokes the Gates divorce,   480
And where the way they cannot find, they force:
Not with such rage a Swelling Torrent flows
Above his banks, th' opposing Dams orethrows,
Depopulates the Fields, the Cattel, Sheep,
Shepherds, and folds the foaming Surges sweep.
And now between two sad extreams I stood,
Here *Pyrrhus* and th' *Atridæ* drunk with blood,
There th' hapless Queen amongst an hundred Dames,
And *Priam* quenching from his wounds those flames
Which his own hands had on the Altar laid: 490
Then they the secret Cabinets invade,
Where stood the Fifty Nuptial Beds, the hopes
Of that great Race, the Golden Posts whose tops
Old hostile spoils adorn'd, demolisht lay,
Or to the foe, or to the fire a Prey.

Now *Priams* fate perhaps you may enquire,
Seeing his Empire lost, his *Troy* on fire,[26]
And his own Palace by the Greeks possest,
Arms, long disus'd, his trembling limbs invest;
Thus on his foes he throws himself alone,   500
Not for their Fate, but to provoke his own:
There stood an Altar open to the view
Of Heaven, near which an aged Lawrel grew,
Whose shady arms the houshold Gods embrac'd;
Before whose feet the Queen her self had cast,
With all her daughters, and the Trojan wives,
As Doves whom an approaching tempest drives
And frights into one flock; But having spy'd
Old *Priam* clad in youthful Arms, she cry'd,
Alas my wretched husband, what pretence   510
To bear those Arms, and in them what defence?
Such aid such times require not, when again
If *Hector* were alive, he liv'd in vain;
Or here We shall a Sanctuary find,
Or as in life, we shall in death be joyn'd.
Then weeping, with kind force held & embrac'd
And on the sacred seat the King she plac'd;
Mean while *Polites* one of *Priams* sons
Flying the rage of bloudy *Pyrrhus,* runs
Through foes & swords, & ranges all the Court   520
And empty Galleries, amaz'd and hurt,[27]
Pyrrhus pursues him, now oretakes, now kills,

26   "Perhaps you may of Priam's fate enquire.
          He—when he saw his regal town on fire."
                                 Dryden, *Aeneid,* ll. 691-692.

27   "With us, one common shelter thou shalt find,
          Or in one common fate with us be joined.
          She said, and with a last salute embraced
          The poor old man, and by the laurel placed.
          Behold! Polites, one of Priam's sons,
          Pursued by Pyrrhus, there for safety runs.
          Through swords and foes, amazed and hurt, he flies
          Through empty courts and open galleries."
                                 Dryden, *Aeneid,* ll. 714-721.

And his last blood in *Priams* presence spills.
The King (though him so many deaths inclose)
Nor fear, nor grief, but Indignation shows;
The Gods requite thee (if within the care
Of those above[28] th' affairs of mortals are)
Whose fury on the son but lost had been,
Had not his Parents Eyes his murder seen:
Not That *Achilles* (whom thou feign'st to be   530
Thy Father) so inhumane was to me;
He blusht, when I the rights of Arms implor'd;
To me my *Hector*, me to *Troy* restor'd:
This said, his feeble Arm a Javelin flung,[29]
Which on the sounding shield, scarce entring, rung.
Then *Pyrrhus;* go a messenger to Hell
Of my black deeds, and to my Father tell
The Acts of his degenerate Race. So through
His Sons warm bloud, the trembling King he drew
To th' Altar; in his hair one hand he wreaths;   540
His sword, the other in his bosom sheaths.
Thus fell the King, who yet surviv'd the State,
With such a signal and peculiar Fate.
Under so vast a ruine not a Grave,
Nor in such flames a funeral fire to have:
He, whom such Titles swell'd, such Power made proud
To whom the Scepters of all *Asia* bow'd,
On the cold earth lies th' unregarded King,
A headless Carkass, and a nameless Thing.[30]

[28] *1668,* alone. This was corrected in the errata.
1671, above.
1684, alone.

[29]   "This said, his feeble hand a javelin threw."
                                        Dryden, *Aeneid,* l. 742.

[30]   "Thus Priam fell, and shared one common fate
              With Troy in ashes, and his ruined state—
              He, who the Sceptre of all Asia swayed,
              Whom monarchs like domestic slaves obeyed.
              On the bleak shore now lies the abandoned king,
              A headless carcase, and a nameless thing."
                                        Dryden, *Aeneid,* ll. 757-763.

SARPEDON'S *SPEECH* TO GLAUCUS *IN THE* 12TH *OF* HOMER[1]

Thus to *Glaucus* spake
Divine *Sarpedon,* since he did not find
Others as great in Place, as great in Mind.
Above the rest, why is our Pomp, our Power?
Our flocks, our herds, and our possessions more?
Why all the Tributes Land and Sea affords
Heap'd in great Chargers, load our sumptuous boards?
Our chearful Guests carowse the sparkling tears
Of the rich Grape, whilst Musick charms their ears.
Why as we pass, do those on *Xanthus* shore,   10
As Gods behold us, and as Gods adore?[2]
But that as well in danger, as degree,
We stand the first; that when our *Lycians* see
Our brave examples, they admiring say,
Behold our Gallant Leaders! These are They
Deserve the Greatness; and un-envied stand:
Since what they act, transcends what they command.
Could the declining of this Fate (oh friend)
Our Date to Immortality extend?
Or if Death sought not them, who seek not Death,   20
Would I advance? Or should my vainer breath
With such a Glorious Folly thee inspire?

---

[1] First printed in the 1668 collected edition.
   "I ought not to neglect putting the reader in mind that this speech of Sarpedon is excellently translated by Sir John Denham, and if I have done it with any spirit, it is partly owing to him." Pope, *Iliad* [1763], Bk. XII, l. 387, note.
   "The first translation which he [Pope] gave to the world was 'The Episode of Sarpedon' . . . 'It has,' said the poet, 'been rendered in English by Sir John Denham, after whom the translator had not the vanity to attempt it for any other reason, than that the episode must have been very imperfect without so noble a part of it.'" Pope, *Poetry* (ed. Elwin Courthope), I, 45.

[2]   "Why decked with all that land and sea afford,
         Why angels called and angel-like adored."
                    Pope, *Rape of the Lock,* Canto V, ll. 11-12.

But since with Fortune Nature doth conspire,
Since Age, Disease, or some less noble End,
Though not less certain, doth our days attend;
Since 'tis decreed, and to this period lead,
A thousand ways the noblest path we'll tread;
And bravely on, till they, or we, or all,
A common Sacrifice to Honour fall.

MARTIAL. EPIGRAM[1]

OUT OF AN EPIGRAM OF MARTIAL

Prithee die and set me free,
　Or else be
Kind and brisk, and gay like me;
I pretend not to the wise ones,
　To the grave, to the grave,
Or the precise ones.

'Tis not Cheeks, nor Lips nor Eyes,
　That I prize,
Quick Conceits, or sharp Replies,
If wise thou wilt appear, and knowing,
　Repartie, Repartie
To what I'm doing.

Prithee why the Room so dark?
　Not a Spark
Left to light me to the mark;
I love day-light and a candle,
　And to see, and to see,
As well as handle.

---

[1] First printed in the 1668 collected edition. From Martial, Book XI, 104,
"Uxor vade soras, aut moribus utere nostris."

Why so many Bolts and Locks,
    Coats and Smocks,
And those Drawers with a Pox?
I could wish, could Nature make it,
    Nakedness, Nakedness
It self were naked.

But if a Mistress I must have,
    Wise and grave,
Let her so her self behave
All the day long *Susan* Civil,
    Pap by night, pap by night
Or such a Divel.

THE PASSION OF DIDO *FOR* ÆNEAS[1]

Having at large declar'd *Joves* Ambassy,
Cyllenius from *Æneas* straight doth flye;[2]
He loth to disobey the Gods command,
Nor willing to forsake this pleasant Land,
Asham'd the kind *Eliza* to deceive,
But more afraid to take a solemn leave;
He many waies his labouring thoughts revolves,
But fear o're-coming shame, at last resolves
(Instructed by the God of Thieves)[3] to steal
Himself away, and his escape conceal.   10
He calls his Captains, bids them Rigg the Fleet,
That at the Port they privately should meet;
And some dissembled colour to project,
That *Dido* should not their design suspect;
But all in vain he did his Plot disguise:

---

[1] First printed in the 1668 collected edition. For a discussion of the relation
between this and Denham's translation of Books II to VI of the *Aeneid* in the
unprinted Hutchinson MS., see p. 41.
  For the relation between this and Waller's translation, see p. 39.
[2] *1668, Marginal note,* Mercury.
[3] *1668, Marginal note,* Mercury.

No Art a watchful Lover can surprize.
She the first motion finds; Love though most sure,
Yet always to itself seems unsecure;
That wicked Fame which their first Love proclaim'd,
Fore-tells the end; The Queen with rage inflam'd   20
Thus greets him, thou dissembler would'st thou flye
Out of my arms by stealth perfidiously?
Could not the hand I plighted, nor the Love,
Nor thee the Fate of dying *Dido* move?
And in the depth of Winter in the night,
Dark as thy black designs to take thy flight,
To plow the raging Seas to Coasts unknown,
The Kingdom thou pretend'st to not thine own;
Were *Troy* restor'd, thou shouldst mistrust a wind
False as they Vows, and as thy heart unkind.   30
Fly'st thou from me? by these dear drops of brine
I thee adjure, by that right hand of thine,
By our Espousals, by our Marriage-bed,
If all my kindness ought have merited;
If ever I stood fair in thy esteem,
From ruine, me, and my lost house redeem.
Cannot my Prayers a free acceptance find?
Nor my Tears soften an obdurate mind?
My Fame of Chastity, by which the Skies
I reacht before, by thee extinguisht dies;   40
Into my Borders now *Iarbus* falls,
And my revengeful Brother scales my walls;
The wild *Numidians* will advantage take,
For thee both *Tyre* and *Carthage* me forsake.
Hadst thou before thy flight but left with me
A young *Æneas*, who resembling thee,
Might in my sight have sported, I had then
Not wholly lost, nor quite deserted been;
By thee no more my Husband, but my Guest,
Betray'd to mischiefs, of which death's the least.[4]   50

4 This couplet is not in the original.

With fixed looks he stands, and in his Breast
By *Joves* command his struggling care supprest;
Great Queen, your favours and deserts so great,
Though numberless, I never shall forget;
No time, until my self I have forgot;
Out of my heart *Eliza's* name shall blot:
But my unwilling flight the Gods inforce,
And that must justifie our sad Divorce;
Since I must you forsake, would Fate permit,
To my desires I might my fortune fit;   60
Troy to her Ancient Splendour I would raise,
And where I first began, would end my days;
But since the *Lycian* Lotts, and *Delphick* God
Have destin'd *Italy* for our abode;
Since you proud *Carthage* (fled from *Tyre*) enjoy,
Why should not *Latium* us receive from *Troy?*
As for my Son, my Fathers angry Ghost,
Tells me his hopes by my delays are crost,
And mighty *Joves* Ambassadour appear'd
With the same message, whom I saw and heard;[5]   70
We both are griev'd when you or I complain,
But much the more, when all complaints are vain;
I call to witness all the Gods and thy
Beloved head, the Coast of *Italy*
Against my will I seek.
Whilst thus he speaks, she rowls her sparkling eyes,
Surveys him round, and thus incens'd replies;
Thy Mother was no Goddess, nor thy stock
From *Dardanus*, but in some horrid rock,
Perfidious wretch, rough *Caucasus* thee bred,   80
And with their Milk *Hircanian* Tygers fed.
Dissimulation I shall now forget,
And my reserves of rage in order set;
Could all my Prayers and soft Entreaties force

[5]   "Even now the herald of the Gods appeared—
     Waking I saw him, and his message heard."
                          Dryden, *Aeneid*, ll. 510-511.

Sighs from his Breast, or from his look remorse.
Where shall I first complain? can Mighty *Jove*
Or *Juno* such Impieties approve?
The just *Astræa* sure is fled to Hell,
Nor more in Earth, nor Heaven it self will dwell.
Oh Faith! him on my Coasts by Tempest cast,   90
Receiving madly, on my Throne I plac'd;
His Men from Famine, and his Fleet from Fire
I rescu'd: now the *Lycian Lotts* conspire
With *Phœbus;* now *Joves Envoyé* through the Air
Brings dismal tydings, as if such low care
Could reach their thoughts, or their repose disturb;
Thou art a false Impostor, and a Fourbe;
Go, go, pursue thy Kingdom through the Main,[6]
I hope if Heaven her Justice still retain,
Thou shalt be wrackt, or cast upon some rock,   100
Where thou the name of *Dido* shalt invoke;
I'le follow thee in Funeral flames, when dead
My Ghost shall thee attend at Board and Bed,
And when the Gods on thee their vengeance show,
That welcom news shall comfort me below.
This saying, from his hated sight she fled;
Conducted by her Damsels to her bed;
Yet restless she arose, and looking out,[7]
Beholds the Fleet, and hears the Seamen shout:
When great *Æneas* pass'd before the Guard,   110
To make a view how all things were prepar'd.
Ah cruel Love! to what dost thou inforce
Poor Mortal Breasts? again she hath recourse
To Tears, and Prayers, again she feels the smart
Of a fresh wound from his tyrannick Dart.
That she no ways nor means may leave untry'd,
Thus to her Sister she her self apply'd:

[6]   "Go! seek thy promised kingdom through the main!"
                                              Ibid., l. 549.
[7] About fifteen lines omitted.

Dear Sister, my resentment had not been
So moving, if this Fate I had fore-seen;
Therefore to me this last kind office do,   120
Thou hast some interest in our scornful Foe,
He trusts to thee the Counsels of his mind,
Thou his soft hours, and free access canst find;
Tell him I sent not to the *Ilian* Coast
My Fleet to aid the *Greeks;* his Fathers Ghost
I never did disturb; ask him to lend
To this the last request that I shall send,
A gentle Ear; I wish that he may find
A happy passage, and a prosp'rous wind.
That contract I not plead, which he betray'd,   130
Nor that his promis'd Conquest be delay'd;
All that I ask, is but a short Reprieve,
Till I forget to love, and learn to grieve;
Some pause and respite only I require,
Till with my tears I shall have quencht my fire.
If thy address can but obtain one day
Or two, my Death that service shall repay.
Thus she intreats; such messages with tears
Condoling *Anne* to him, and from him bears;
But him no Prayers, no Arguments can move,   140
The Fates resist, his Ears are stopt by *Jove:*[8]
As when fierce Northern blasts from th' *Alpes* descend,
From his firm roots with struggling gusts to rend
An aged sturdy Oak, the ratling sound
Grows loud, with leaves and scatter'd arms the ground
Is over-layd; yet he stands fixt, as high
As his proud head is raised towards the Sky,

8   "This mournful message pious Anna bears,
         And seconds, with her own, her sister's tears:
         But all her arts are still employed in vain;
         Again she comes, and is refused again.
         His hardened heart nor prayers nor threatenings move;
         Fate, and the God, had stopped his ears to love."
                                    Dryden, *Aeneid*, ll. 632-637.

So low towards Hell his roots descend.[9] With Pray'rs
And Tears the *Hero* thus assail'd, great cares
He smothers in his Breast, yet keeps his Post,   150
All their addresses and their labour lost.
Then she deceives her Sister with a smile,
Anne in the Inner Court erects a Pile;[10]
Thereon his Arms and once lov'd Portraict lay,
Thither our fatal Marriage-bed convey;
All cursed Monuments of him with fire
We must abolish (so the Gods require)[11]
She gives her credit, for no worse effect
Then from *Sichæus* death she did suspect,
And her commands obeys.   160
Aurora now had left *Tithonus* bed,[12]
And o're the world her blushing Raies did spread;[13]
The Queen beheld as soon as day appear'd,
The Navy under Sail, the Haven clear'd;
Thrice with her hand her Naked Breast she knocks,
And from her forehead tears her Golden Locks.
O *Jove*, she cry'd, and shall he thus delude
Me and my Realm! why is he not pursu'd?
Arm, Arm, she cry'd, and let our *Tyrians* board
With ours his Fleet, and carry Fire and Sword;   170
Leave nothing unattempted to destroy
That perjur'd Race, then let us dye with joy;
What if the event of War uncertain were,
Nor death, nor danger, can the desperate fear?
But oh too late! this thing I should have done,

[9] *Cf* the Preface to the *Progress of Learning*.
[10] Forty lines omitted.

[11]   "All relics of the wretch are doomed to fire;
            For so the priestess and her charms require."
                                          Dryden, *Aeneid*, ll. 718-719.
[12] Eighty lines omitted.

[13]   "Aurora now had left her saffron bed,
            And beams of early light the heavens o'erspread,"
                                          Dryden, *Ibid.*, ll. 839-840.

When first I plac'd the Traytor on my Throne.
Behold the Faith of him who sav'd from fire
His honour'd houshold gods, his Aged Sire
His Pious shoulders from *Troy's* Flames did bear;
Why did I not his Carcase piece-meal tear   180
And cast it in the Sea? why not destroy
All his Companions and beloved Boy
Ascanius? and his tender limbs have drest,
And made the Father on the Son to Feast?
Thou Sun, whose lustre all things here below
Surveys; and *Juno* conscious of my woe;
Revengeful Furies, and Queen *Hecate*,
Receive and grant my prayer! if he the Sea
Must needs escape, and reach th' *Ausonian* land,
If *Jove* decree it, *Jove's* decree must stand;   190
When landed, may he be with arms opprest
By his rebelling people, be distrest
By exile from his Country, be divorc'd
From young *Ascanius* sight, and be enforc'd
To implore Forrein aids, and lose his Friends
By violent and undeserved ends:
When to conditions of unequal Peace
He shall submit, then may he not[14] possess
Kingdom nor Life, and find his Funeral
I' th' Sands, when he before his day shall fall: 200
And ye oh *Tyrians* with immortal hate
Pursue his race, this service dedicate
To my deplored ashes; let there be
'Twixt us and them no League nor Amity;
May from my bones a new *Achilles* rise,
That shall infest the *Trojan* Colonies
With Fire, and Sword, and Famine, when at[15] length

[14] *1668,* nor.
1671, as above.
1684, as above.
[15] *1668,* omits at.
1671, as above.
1684, as above.

Time to our great attempts contributes strength;
Our Seas, our Shores, our Armies theirs oppose,
And may our Children be for ever Foes.   210
A ghastly paleness deaths approach portends,[16]
Then trembling she the fatal pile ascends;
Viewing the *Trojan* relicks, she unsheath'd
Æneas Sword, not for that use bequeath'd:
Then on the guilty bed she gently lays
Her self, and softly thus lamenting prays:
Dear Reliques whilst that Gods and Fates gave leave,
Free me from care, and my glad soul receive;
That date which fortune gave I now must end,
And to the shades a noble Ghost descend;   220
Sichœus blood by his false Brother spilt,
I have reveng'd, and a proud City built;
Happy, alas! too happy I had liv'd,
Had not the *Trojan* on my Coast arriv'd;
But shall I dye without revenge? yet dye,
Thus, thus with joy to thy *Sichœus* flye.
My conscious Foe my Funeral fire shall view
From Sea, and may that Omen him pursue.
Her fainting hand let fall the Sword besmear'd
With blood, and then the Mortal wound appear'd;   230
Through all the Court the fright and clamours rise,
Which the whole City fills with fears and cries,
As loud as if her *Carthage,* or old *Tyre*
The Foe had entred, and had set on Fire:[17]
Amazed *Anne* with speed ascends the stairs,
And in her arms her dying Sister rears:
Did you for this, your self, and me beguile
For such an end did I erect this Pile?
Did you so much despise me, in this Fate
My self with you not to associate?   240

[16] Fifteen lines omitted.
[17]   "Not less the clamour, than if—ancient Tyre,
           Or the new Carthage, set by foes on fire—"
                          Dryden, *Aeneid,* ll. 962-963.

Your self and me, alas! this fatal wound
The Senate, and the People, doth confound.
I'le wash her Wound with Tears, and at her Death,
My Lips from hers shall draw her parting Breath.
Then with her Vest the Wound she wipes and dries;
Thrice with her Arm the Queen attempts to rise,
But her strength failing, falls into a swound,
Life's last efforts yet striving with her Wound;
Thrice on her Bed she turns, with wandring sight
Seeking, she groans when she beheld the light;   250
Then *Juno* pitying her disastrous Fate,
Sends *Iris* down, her Pangs to Mitigate,
(Since if we fall before th' appointed day,
Nature and Death continue long their Fray)
Iris Descends; This Fatal lock (says she)
To *Pluto* I bequeath, and set thee free,
Then clips her Hair, cold Numness strait bereaves
Her Corps of sense, and th' Ayr¹⁸ her Soul receives.   258

*OF PRUDENCE. OF JUSTICE*¹

A PREFACE TO THE FOLLOWING TRANSLATION

Going this last Summer to visit the *Wells*,² I took an occasion (by
the way) to wait upon an Ancient and Honourable Friend of mine,
whom I found diverting his (then solitary) retirement with the Latin
Original of this Translation, which (being out of Print) I had never
seen before: when I looked upon it, I saw that it had formerly
passed through two Learned hands, not without approbation; which

---

¹⁸ *1668,* ayrs. This was corrected in the errata.
1671, as above.
1684, as above.
¹ First printed in the 1668 edition. From Dominicus Mancinus, *Libellus de
quattuor virtutibus et omnibus officiis ad bene beateque vivendum. Paris,* 1488.
The British Museum catalogues three sixteenth-century translations.
² "Last summer" is 1667. See p. 190, note 3.
"The Wells" is probably Epsom, but possibly Tunbridge Wells.

were *Ben Johnson,* and *Sir Kenelme Digby*; but I found it, (where I
shall never find my self) in the service of a better Master, the *Earl* of
Bristol,[3] of whom I shall say no more; for I love not to improve
the Honour of the Living, by impairing that of the Dead; and my
own Profession hath taught me, not to erect new Superstructions
upon an old Ruine. He was pleased to recommend it to me for my
companion of the *Wells,* where I lik'd the entertainment it gave me
so well, that I undertook to redeem it from an obsolete English dis-
guise, wherein an old *Monk* had cloathed it, and to make as becom-
ing a new Vest for it, as I could.

The Author was a Person of Quality in *Italy,* his name *Mancini,*
which Family matched since with the Sister of *Cardinal Mazarine*; he
was co-temporary to *Petrarch,* and *Mantuan,* and not long before
Torquato Tasso; which shews, that the Age they lived in, was not so
unlearned, as that which preceded, or that which followed.

The Author writ upon the four Cardinal Vertues, but I have Trans-
lated only the two first, not to turn the kindness I intended to him
into an injury; for the two last are little more then repititions and
recitals of the first; and (to make a just excuse for him) they could
not well be otherwise, since the two last Vertues are but descendants
from the first; Prudence being the true Mother of Temperance, and
true Fortitude the Child of Justice.

OF PRUDENCE

Wisdoms first Progress is to take a View
What's decent or un-decent, false or true.
Hee's truly Prudent, who can separate
Honest from Vile, and still adhere to that;
Their difference to measure, and to reach,
Reason well rectify'd must Nature teach.

[3] The Earl of Bristol was in disgrace for some years after his attack in
1663 on Clarendon. As he was again in Parliament July 30, 1667, Denham
must have visited him early in the summer. This was probably at Wimbledon,
where in 1661 the Earl had bought the palace of Henrietta Maria. Wimbledon
is directly on the road from London to Epsom, and not far out of the way to
Tunbridge Wells.

And these high Scrutinies are subjects fit
For Man's all-searching and enquiring wit;
That search of Knowledge did from *Adam* flow;
Who wants it, yet abhors his wants to show.   10
Wisdom of what her self approves, makes choice,
Nor is led Captive by the Common voice.
Clear-sighted Reason Wisdoms Judgment leads,
And Sense, her Vassal, in her footsteps treads.
That thou to Truth the perfect way may'st know,
To thee all her specifick forms I'le show;
He that the way to Honesty will learn,
First what's to be avoided must discern.
Thy self from flattering self-conceit defend,
Nor what thou dost not know, to know pretend.   20
Some secrets deep in abstruse Darkness lye;
To search them, thou wilt need a piercing Eye.
Not rashly therefore to such things assent,
Which undeceiv'd, thou after may'st repent;
Study and Time in these must thee instruct,
And others old experience may conduct.
Wisdom her self her Ear doth often lend
To Counsel offer'd by a faithful Friend.
In equal Scales two doubtful matters lay,
Thou may'st chuse safely that which most doth weigh;   30
'Tis not secure, this place, or that to guard,
If any other entrance stand unbarr'd;
He that escapes the Serpents Teeth, may fail
If he himself secure not from his Tayl.
Who saith, who could such ill events expect?
With shame on his own Counsels doth reflect;
Most in the World doth self-conceit deceive,
Who just and good, what e're they act, believe;
To their Wills wedded, to their Errours slaves,
No man (like them) they think himself behaves.   40
This stiff-neckt Pride, nor Art, nor Force, can bend,
Nor high-flown hopes to Reasons Lure descend.

Fathers sometimes their Childrens Faults regard
With Pleasure, and their Crimes with gifts reward.
Ill Painters when they draw, and Poets write,
Virgil and *Titian,* (self admiring) slight;
Then all they do, like Gold and Pearl appears,
And others actions are but Dirt to theirs;
They that so highly think themselves above
All other Men, themselves can only Love;   50
Reason and Vertue, all that Man can boast
O're other Creatures, in those Brutes are lost.
Observe (if thee this Fatal Errour touch,
Thou to thy self contributing too much)
Those who are generous, humble, just, and wise,
Who nor their Gold, nor themselves Idolize;
To form thy self by their Example, learn,
(For many Eyes can more then one discern)
But yet beware of Councels when too full,
Number makes long disputes and graveness dull;   60
Though their Advice be good, their Counsel wise,
Yet Length still loses Opportunities:
Debate destroys dispatch; as Fruits we see
Rot, when they hang too long upon the Tree;
In vain that Husbandman his Seed doth sow,
If he his Crop, not in due season mow.
A General sets his Army in Array
In vain, unless he Fight, and win the day.
'Tis Vertuous Action that must Praise bring forth,
Without which, slow advice is little worth.   70
Yet they who give good Counsel, Praise deserve,
Though in the active part they cannot serve:
In action, Learned Counsellours their Age,
Profession, or Disease, forbids t' ingage.
Nor to Philosophers is praise deny'd,
Whose wise Instructions After-ages guide;
Yet vainly most their Age in study spend;
No end of writing Books, and to no end:

Beating their brains for strange and hidden things,
Whose Knowledge, nor Delight, nor Profit brings;   80
Themselves with doubts both day and night perplex,
Nor Gentle Reader please, or teach, but vex.
Books should to one of these four ends conduce,
For Wisdom, Piety, Delight, or Use.
What need we gaze upon the spangled Sky?
Or into Matters hidden Causes pry?
To describe every City, Stream, or Hill
I'th World, our fancy with vain Arts to fill?
What is't to hear a Sophister that pleads,
Who by the Ears the deceiv'd Audience leads?   90
If we were wise, these things we should not mind,
But more delight in easie matters find.
Learn to live well, that thou may'st dye so too;
To live and dye is all we have to do:[4]
The way (if no Digression's made) is even,
And free access, if we but ask, is given.
Then seek to know those things which make us blest,
And having found them, lock them in thy Breast;
Enquiring then the way, go on, nor slack,
But mend thy pace, nor think of going back.   100
Some their whole Age in these enquiries wast,
And dye like Fools before one step they past;
'Tis strange to know the way, and not t' advance,
That Knowledge is far worse then Ignorance.
The Learned teach, but what they teach, not do;
And standing still themselves, make others go.
In vain on Study, time away we throw,
When we forbear to act the things we know.
The Souldier that Philosopher well blam'd,
Who long and loudly in the Schools declaim'd;   110

4   "To read and weep is all they now can do."
                    Pope, *Eloisa to Abelard*, l. 48.

        "Oh let me live my own, and die so too
        (To live and die is all I have to do) !"
                Pope, *Epistle to Dr. Arbuthnot*, ll. 261-262.

Tell (said the Souldier) venerable Sir
Why all these Words, this Clamour, and this stir?
Why do disputes in wrangling spend the day?
Whilst one says only yea, and t' other nay.
Oh, said the Doctor, we for Wisdom toyl'd,
For which none toyls too much: the Souldier smil'd;
Y' are gray and old, and to some pious use
This mass of Treasure you should now reduce:
But you your store have hoarded in some bank,
For which th' Infernal Spirits shall you thank.   120
Let what thou learnest be by practise shown,
'Tis said, that Wisdoms Children make her known.
What's good doth open to th' enquirer stand,
And it self offers to th' accepting hand;
All things by Order and true Measures done,
Wisdom will end, as well as she begun.
Let early care thy main Concerns secure,
Things of less moment may delays endure:
Men do not for their Servants first prepare,
And of their Wives and Children quit the care;   130
Yet when we're sick, the Doctor's fetch't in haste,
Leaving our great concernment to the last.
When we are well, our hearts are only set
(Which way we care not) to be Rich, or Great;
What shall become of all that we have got;
We only know that us it follows not;
And what a trifle is a moments Breath,
Laid in the Scale with everlasting Death?
What's Time, when on Eternity we think?
A thousand Ages in that Sea must sink;   140
Time's nothing but a word, a million
Is full as far from Infinite as one.
To whom thou much dost owe, thou much must pay,
Think on the Debt against th' accompting-day;
God, who to thee, Reason and Knowledge lent,
Will ask how these two Talents have been spent.

Let not low Pleasures thy high Reason blind,
He's mad, that seeks what no man e're could find.
Why should we fondly please our Sense, wherein
Beasts us exceed, nor feel the stings of sin?   150
What thoughts Mans Reason better can become,
Then th' expectation of his welcom home?
Lords of the World have but for Life their Lease,
And that too, (if the Lessor please) must cease.
Death cancels Natures Bonds, but for our Deeds
(That Debt first paid) a strict account succeeds;
If here not clear'd, no Surety-ship can Bail
Condemned Debtors from th' Eternal Goal;
Christ's Blood's our Balsom, if that cures us here,
Him, when our Judge, we shall not find severe;   160
His yoke is easie, when by us embrac'd,
But loads and galls, if on our Necks 'tis cast.
Be just in all thy actions, and if joyn'd
With those that are not, never change thy mind;
If ought obstruct thy course, yet stand not still,
But wind about, till thou have topp'd the Hill;
To the same end Men several Paths may tread,
As many Doors into one Temple lead;
And the same hand into a fist may close,
Which instantly a Palm expanded shows: 170
Justice and Faith never forsake the Wise,
Yet may occasion put him in Disguise;
Not turning like the wind, but if the state
Of things must change, he is not obstinate;
Things past, and future with the present weighs,
Nor credulous of what vain rumour says:
Few things by Wisdom are at first believ'd,
An easie Ear deceives, and is deceiv'd;
For many Truths have often past for Lies,
And Lies as often put on Truths Disguise: 180
As Flattery too oft like Friendship shows,
So them, who speak plain Truth we think our Foes.

No quick reply to dubious questions make,
Suspence and caution still prevent mistake.
When any great design thou dost intend,
Think on the means, the manner, and the end:
All great Concernments must delays endure;
Rashness and haste make all things unsecure:
And if uncertain thy Pretensions be,
Stay till fit time wear out uncertainty;   190
But if to unjust things thou dost pretend,
E're they begin let thy Pretensions end.
Let thy Discourse be such, that thou may'st give
Profit to others, or from them receive:
Instruct the Ignorant, to those that live
Under thy care, good rules and patterns give;
Nor is't the least of Vertues, to relieve
Those whom afflictions or oppressions grieve.
Commend but sparingly whom thou dost love;
But less condemn whom thou dost not approve: 200
Thy Friend, like Flattery, too much Praise doth wrong,
And too sharp censure shews an evil tongue:
But let inviolate Truth be always dear
To thee, even before Friendship, Truth prefer;
Then what thou mean'st to give, still promise less;
Hold fast the Power, thy Promise to increase:
Look forward what's to come, and back what's past,
Thy life will be with Praise and Prudence grac'd:
What loss, or gain may follow thou may'st guess,
Thou then wilt be secure of the success;   210
Yet be not always on affairs intent,
But let thy thoughts be easie, and unbent;
When our Minds Eyes are dis-ingag'd and free,
They clearer, farther, and distinctly see;
They quicken sloth, perplexities untye,
Make roughness smooth, and hardness mollifie;
And though our hands from labour are releast,
Yet our minds find (even when we sleep) no rest.

Search not to find how other Men offend,
But by that Glass thy own offences mend;   220
Still seek to learn, yet care not much from whom,
(So it be Learning) or from whence it come.
Of thy own actions, others judgments learn,
Often by small, great matters we discern:
Youth, what Mans age is like to be doth show;
We may our Ends by our Beginnings know.
Let none direct thee what to do or say,
Till thee thy Judgment of the Matter sway;
Let not the pleasing many, thee Delight,
First judge, if those whom thou dost please, judge right.   230
Search not to find what lies too deeply hid,
Nor to know things, whose knowledge is forbid;
Nor climb on Pyramids, which thy head turns round
Standing, and whence no safe Descent is found:
In vain his Nerves, and Faculties he strains
To rise, whose raising unsecure remains:
They whom Desert and Favour forwards thrust,
Are wise, when they their measures can adjust.
When well at ease, and happy, live content,
And then consider why that life was lent;   240
When Wealthy, shew thy Wisdom not to be
To Wealth a Servant, but make Wealth serve thee.
Though all alone, yet nothing think or do,
Which nor a Witness, nor a Judge might know.
The highest Hill, is the most slippery place,
And Fortune mocks us with a smiling face;
And her unsteady hand hath often plac'd
Men in high Power, but seldom holds them fast;
Against her then her forces Prudence joyns,
And to the Golden Mean her self confines.   250
More in Prosperity is Reason tost,
Then Ships in Storms, their Helms and Anchors lost;
Before fair Gales not all our Sayls we bear,
But with side Winds into safe Harbours steer;

More Ships in Calms on a deceitful Coast,
Or unseen Rocks, then in high Storms are lost.
Who casts out threats and frowns, no man deceives,
Time for resistance, and defence he gives;
But Flattery still in sugar'd words betrays,
And Poyson in high tasted Meats conveys;   260
So, Fortunes smiles unguarded Man surprize,
But when she frowns, he arms, and her defies.

OF JUSTICE

'Tis the first Sanction, Nature gave to Man,
Each other to assist in what they can;
Just or unjust, this Law for ever stands,
All things are good by Law which she commands;
The first step, Man towards Christ must justly live,
Who t' us himself, and all we have did give;
In vain doth man the name of Just expect,
If his Devotions he to God neglect;
So must we reverence God, as first to know
Justice from him, not from our selves doth flow;   10
God those accepts who to Mankind are Friends,
Whose Justice far as their own Power extends;
In that they imitate the Power Divine,
The Sun alike on Good and Bad doth shine;
And he that doth no Good, although no Ill,
Does not the office of the Just fulfil.
Virtue doth Man to virtuous actions steer,
'Tis not enough that he should Vice forbear;
We live not only for our selves to care,
Whilst they that want it are deny'd their share.   20
Wise *Plato* said, the world with men was stor'd,
That succour each to other might afford;
Nor are those succours to one sort confin'd,
But several parts to several men consign'd;
He that of his own stores no part can give,

May with his Counsel or his Hands relieve.
If Fortune make thee powerful, give Defence
'Gainst Fraud, and Force, to naked Innocence:
And when our Justice doth her Tributes pay,
Method and Order must direct the way: 30
First to our God we must with Reverence bow,
The second honour to our Prince we owe;
Next to Wives, Parents, Children, fit respect,
And to our Friends and Kindred we direct:
Then we must those, who groan beneath the weight
Of Age, Disease, or Want, commiserate:
'Mongst those whom honest Lives can recommend,
Our Justice more compassion should extend;
To such, who thee in some distress did aid,
Thy Debt of thanks with Interest should be paid: 40
As *Hesiod* sings, spread waters o're thy field,
And a most just and glad increase 'twill yield;
But yet take heed, lest doing good to one,
Mischief and wrong be to another done;
Such moderation with thy bounty joyn,
That thou may'st nothing give that is not thine;
That Liberality is but cast away,
Which makes us borrow what we cannot pay:
And no access to wealth let Rapine bring;
Do nothing that's not just, to be a King.   50
Justice must be from Violence exempt,
But Fraud's her only Object of Contempt.
Fraud in the Fox, Force in the Lyon dwells;
But Justice both from humane hearts expels;
But he's the greatest Monster (without doubt)
Who is a Wolf within, a Sheep without;
Nor only ill injurious actions are,
But evil words and slanders bear their share.
Truth Justice loves, and Truth Injustice fears,
Truth above all things a Just man reveres: 60
Though not by Oaths we God to witness call,

He sees and hears, and still remembers all;
And yet our attestations we may wrest,
Sometimes to make the Truth more manifest;
If by a Lye a man preserve his Faith,
He Pardon, Leave, and absolution hath;
Or if I break my Promise, which to thee
Would bring no good, but prejudice to me.
All things committed to thy trust, conceal,
Nor what's forbid by any means reveal.   70
Express thy self in plain, not doubtful words,
That, ground for Quarrels or Disputes affords:
Unless thou find occasion, hold thy tongue,
Thy self or others, careless talk may wrong.
When thou art called into publick Power,
And when a crowd of Suiters throng thy Door,
Be sure no great Offenders 'scape their dooms,
Small praise from Lenity and Remissness comes;
Crimes pardoned, others to those Crimes invite,
Whilst Lookers on, severe Examples fright: 80
When by a pardon'd Murderer blood is split,
The Judge that pardon'd, hath the greatest guilt;
Who accuse Rigour, make a gross mistake,
One Criminal pardon'd, may an hundred make;
When Justice on Offenders is not done,
Law, Government, Commerce, are overthrown;
As besieg'd Traytors with the Foe conspire,
T' unlock the Gates, and set the Town on Fire.
Yet let not Punishment th' Offence exceed,
Justice with Weight and Measure must proceed: 90
Yet when pronouncing sentence, seem not glad,
Such Spectacles, though they are just, are sad;
Though what thou dost, thou ought'st not to repent,
Yet Humane Bowels cannot but relent;
Rather then all must suffer, some must dye;
Yet Nature must condole their misery;
And yet if many equal guilt involve,

Thou may'st not these condemn, and those absolve.
Justice when equal Scales she holds, is blind,
Nor Cruelty, nor Mercy, change her mind;   100
When some escape for that which others dye,
Mercy to those, to these is Cruelty.
A fine and slender Net the Spider weaves,
Which little and light Animals receives;
And if she catch a common Bee or Flye,
They with a piteous groan, and murmur dye;
But if a Wasp or Hornet she entrap,
They tear her Cords like *Sampson*, and escape;
So like a Flye the poor Offender dyes;
But like the Wasp, the Rich escapes, and flyes.   110
Do not if one but lightly thee offend,
The punishment beyond the Crime extend;
Or after warning the Offence forget;
So God himself our failings doth remit.
Expect not more from Servants then is just,
Reward them well, if they observe their trust;
Nor them with Cruelty or Pride invade,
Since God and Nature them our Brothers made;
If his Offence be great, let that suffice;
If light, forgive, for no Man's alwaies wise.   120

CATO MAJOR[1]

To the Reader.

I CAN neither call this Piece *Tully's* nor my own, being much altered from the Original, not only by the change of the Style, but by addition and subtraction. I believe you will be better pleas'd, to receive it, as I did, at the first sight; for to me *Cicero* did not so much appear to write, as *Cato* to speak; and to do right to my Author, I believe no Character of any person was ever better drawn to the life than this. Therefore neither consider *Cicero*, nor Me, but *Cato* himself, who being then rais'd from the dead to speak the language of that Age and Place, neither the distance of place or time makes it less possible to raise him now to speak ours.

Though I dare not compare my Copy with the Original, yet you will find it mention'd here, how much fruits are improv'd by Grafting; and here, by grafting Verse upon Prose, some of these severer Arguments may receive a more mild and pleasant taste.

Cato sayes (in another place) of himself, that he learn'd to speak Greek between the seventieth and eightieth year of his Age, beginning that so late, he may not yet be too old to learn English, being now but between his seventeenth and eighteenth hundred year. For these reasons I shall leave to this Piece no other name than what the Author gave it of

CATO MAJOR.

[1] Sir James Ware (*The Whole Works*, vol. II, *The Writers of Ireland*, Bk. I, p. 158) gives 1648 as the date but this seems impossible:
  (1) It is contradicted by
      "Such as your Tully lately dress'd in verse"
   in Samuel Butler's *A Panegyric upon Sir John Denham's recovery from his madness*, l. 17. This poem refers to Denham's recovery from his madness, which occurred about 1667.
  (2) In 1647-1648 Denham was actively engaged in political intrigues, and could hardly have found leisure for such an extended piece of work.
  (3) The versification is in Denham's late, mature style.
It was first printed in 1669, the text of which edition is followed here.

THE PREFACE

That Learned Critick, the younger Scaliger, *comparing the two great Orators, sayes, that nothing can be taken from* Demosthenes, *nor added to* Tully; *and if there be any fault in the last, it is the Resumption, or dwelling too long upon his arguments: for which reason having intended to translate this Piece into Prose, (where Translation ought to be strict) finding the matter very proper for Verse, I took the liberty, to leave out what was only necessary to that Age, and Place, and to take, or add what was proper to this present Age, and occasion; by laying his sense closer, and in fewer words, according to the style and ear of these times. The three first parts I dedicate to my old friends, to take off those melancholy reflections, which the sense of Age, Infirmity, and Death may give them. The last part I think necessary for the Conviction of those many, who believe not, or at least mind not the immortality of the Soul, of which the Scripture speaks only positively, as a Lawgiver, with an* Ipse dixit; *but it may be, they neither believe that (from which they either make doubts, or sport,) nor those, whose business it is to interpret it, supposing they do it only for their own ends: But if a Heathen Philosopher bring such arguments from reason, nature, and Second Causes, which none of our Atheistical Sophisters can confute, if they may stand convinced, that there is an Immortality of the Soul, I hope they will so weigh the consequences, as neither to talk, nor live as if there were no such thing.*

OF OLD-AGE

Cato, Scipio, Lælius.
Scipio to Cato.[2]

Though all the Actions of your Life are crown'd
With Wisdom, nothing makes them more Renown'd,
Then that those years, which others think extreme,
Nor to your self, nor us uneasie seem,
Under which weight, most like th' old Giant's groan,

[2] Denham omits the prefatory remarks of Cicero to Atticus.

When *Ætna* on their backs by *Jove* was thrown.

Cat. What you urge (*Scipio*) from right reason flows,
All parts of Age.seem burthensome to those,
Who Virtue's, and true Wisdom's happiness
Cannot discern, but they who those possess   10
In what's impos'd by Nature, find no grief,
Of which our Age is (next our Death) the chief,
Which though all equally desire to' obtain,
Yet *when they have obtain'd it,* they complain;
Such our inconstancies, and follies are,
We say it steals upon us unaware:
Our want of reas'ning these false measures makes,
Youth runs to Age, as Childhood Youth o'retakes;
How much more grievous would our lives appear
To reach th' eight hundreth, then the eightieth year: 20
Of what, in that long space of time hath past,
To foolish Age will no remembrance last,[3]
My Ages conduct when you seem to' admire,
(Which that it may deserve, I much desire)
'Tis my first rule, on Nature, as my Guide
Appointed by the Gods, I have rely'de,
And Nature, (which all Acts of life designes)
Not like ill Poets, in the last declines;
But some one part must be the last of all,
Which like ripe fruits, must either rot, or fall, 30
And this from Nature must be gently born,
Else her (as Giants did the Gods) we scorn.

Læl. But Sir, 'tis *Scipio's,* and my desire,
Since to long life we gladly would aspire,
That from your grave Instructions we might hear,
How we, like you, might this great burthen bear.

Cat. This I resolv'd before, but now shall do
With great delight, since 'tis requir'd by you.

Læl. If to your self it will not tedious prove,

---

[3] *Praeterita enim aetas quamvis longa cum effluxisset, nulla consolatio permulcere posset stultam senectutem.*

Nothing in us a greater joy can move,   40
That as old Travellers the young instruct,
Your long, our short experience may conduct.
Cat.   'Tis true, (as the old Proverb doth relate)
Equals with equals often congregate.
Two Consuls[4] (who in years my equals were,)
When Senators, lamenting I did hear,
That Age from them had all their pleasures torn,
And them their former suppliants now scorn,
They, what is not to be accus'd, accuse,
Not others, but themselves their age abuse,   50
Else this might me concern, and all my friends,
Whose cheerful Age, with Honour, Youth attends,
Joy'd that from pleasure's slavery they are free,
And all respects due to their age they see,
In its true colours, this complaint appears
The ill effect of Manners, not of years,
For on their life no grievous burthen lies,
Who are well-natur'd, temperate, and wise:
But an inhumane, and ill-temper'd mind
Not any easie part in life can find.   60
Læl.   This I believe, yet others may dispute,
Their age (as yours) can never bear such fruit,
Of Honour, Wealth, and Power, to make them sweet,
Not every one such happiness can meet.
Cat.   Some weight your argument (my *Lælius*) bears,
But not so much, as at first sight appears,
This answer by *Themistocles* was made,
(When a *Seriphian* thus did him upbraid,
You those great Honours to your Country owe,
Not to your self) had I at *Seripho*[5]   70
Been born, such honour I had never seen,
Nor you, if an *Athenian* you had been:
So Age, cloath'd in undecent povertie,

---

[4] *1669, Marginal note,* Caius Salinator. Spurius Albinus.
[5] *1669, Marginal note,* An isle to which condemn'd men were banisht.

To the most prudent cannot easie be,
But to a fool, the greater his estate,
The more uneasie is his Age's weight.
Age's chief arts, and arms, are to grow wise,
Virtue to know, and known to exercise,
All just returns to Age then Virtue makes,
Nor her in her extremity forsakes,   80
The sweetest Cordial we receive at last
Is conscience of our virtuous actions past.
I, (when a youth) with reverence did look
On *Quintus Fabius,* who *Tarentum* took,
Yet in his age such cheerfulness was seen,
As if his years and mine had equal been,
His Gravity was mixt with Gentleness,
Nor had his Age made his good humour less,
Then was he well in years (the same that he
Was Consul, that of my Nativity)   90
(A Stripling then) in his fourth Consulate
On him at *Capua* I in armes did wait,
I five years after at *Tarentum* wan
The Quæstorship, and then our love began,
And four years after, when I Prætor was
He Pleaded, and the *Cincian* Law did pass.[6]
With youthful diligence he us'd to' ingage,
Yet with the temperate Arts of patient Age
He breaks fierce *Hannibal's* insulting heats;
Of which exploit thus our friend *Ennius* treats,   100
He by delay restor'd the Common-wealth,
Nor preferr'd Rumour before publick Health.[7]

[6] *1669, Marginal note,* Against Bribes.

[7] These remarks on Quintus Fabius are but part of an extended eulogy in the original Latin. The remainder, together with a passage on Plato, Isocrates, etc., is transferred to part I, ll. 47-98. A passage condeming Ennius is omitted altogether. This reading is followed in all subsequent editions, but the transposition seems a mere printer's error. See p. 208, note 9.

THE ARGUMENT

When I reflect on Age, I find there are
Four Causes, which its Misery declare.
1. Because our Bodies Strength it much impairs;
2. That it takes off our Minds from great Affairs:
3. Next, That our Sense of Pleasures it deprives:
4. Last, That approaching Death attends our Lives.
Of all these several Causes I'le discourse,
And then of each, in Order, weigh the force.

THE FIRST PART

The Old from such affairs is only freed,
Which vigourous youth, and strength of body need.
But to more high affairs our age is lent,
Most properly when heats of youth are spent.
Did *Fabius,* and your Father *Scipio*
(Whose Daughter my Son married) nothing do?
Fabricii, Coruncani, Curii;
Whose courage, counsel, and authority,
The Roman Common-wealth, restor'd, did boast,
Nor *Appius,* with whose strength his sight was lost,   10
Who when the Senate was to Peace inclin'd
With *Pyrrhus,* shew'd his reason was not blind.
Whither's our Courage and our Wisdom come?
When *Rome* it self conspires the fate of *Rome?*[8]
The rest with ancient gravity and skill
He spake (for his Oration's extant still)
'Tis seventeen years since he had Consul been
The second time, and there were ten between;
Therefore their Argument's of little force,

---

[8] Given, in the original, as a quotation from Ennius:
> *"Quo vobis mentes, rectae quae stare solebant*
> *Antehac, dementis sese flexere viai?"*

This is a good illustration of Denham's rhetorical heightening.

Who Age from great Imployments would divorce. 20
As in a Ship some climb the Shrouds, to' unfold
The Sails, some sweep the Deck, some pump the Hold;
Whil'st he that guides the Helm, imploys his skill,
And gives the Law to them by sitting still.
Great actions less from Courage, strength, and speed,
Then from wise Counsels and Commands proceed;
Those Arts Age wants not, which to Age belong,
Not heat, but cold experience makes us strong,
A Consul, Tribune, General, I have been,
All sorts of war I have past through, and seen 30
And now grown old, I seem to' abandon it,
Yet to the Senate I prescribe what's fit.
I every day 'gainst *Carthage* war proclaim,
(For *Rome's* destruction hath been long her aim)
Nor shall I cease till I her ruine see,
Which Triumph may the Gods designe for thee;
That *Scipio* may revenge his Grandsire's Ghost,
Whose life at *Cannæ* with great Honour lost
Is on Record, nor had he wearied been
With Age, if he an hundred years had seen, 40
He had not us'd Excursions, Spears, or Darts,
But Counsel, Order, and such aged Arts,
Which, if our Ancestors had not retain'd,
The *Senate's* Name, our Council had not gain'd.
The *Spartans* to their highest Magistrate,
The Name of *Elder* did appropriate:
Therefore his fame for ever shall remain,[9]
How gallantly *Tarentum* he did gain,
With vigilant Conduct, when that sharp reply
He gave to *Salinator*, I stood by, 50
Who to the Castle fled, the Town being lost,
Yet he to *Maximus* did vainly boast,
'Twas by my means *Tarentum* you obtain'd;

[9] 47-98 transposed from introduction. (See p. 206, note 7.) The lines are certainly out of place, because to have line 47 follow as a consequence of 46 makes nonsense. On the other hand, line 99 follows 46 logically.

'Tis true, had you not lost, I had not gain'd;
And as much Honour on his Gown did wait,
As on his Arms, in his Fifth Consulate,
When his Colleague *Carvilius* stept aside,
The Tribune of the People would divide
To them the *Gallick,* and the *Picene* Field,
Against the Senate's will, he will not yield,   60
When being angry, boldly he declares
Those things were acted under happy starres,
From which the Commonwealth found good effects,
But othewise, they came from bad Aspects.
Many great things of *Fabius* I could tell,
But his Son's death did all the rest excell;
(His Gallant Son, though young, had Consul been)
His Funeral Oration I have seen
Often, and when on that I turn my eyes,
I all the Old Philosophers dispise,   70
Though he in all the Peoples eyes seem'd great,
Yet greater he appear'd in his retreat;
When feasting with his private friends at home,
Such Counsel, such Discourse from him did come,
Such Science in his Art of Augury,
No Roman ever was more learn'd than he;
Knowledge of all things present, and to come,
Remembring all the Wars of ancient *Rome,*
Nor only these, but all the World's beside;
Dying in extreme age, I prophesi'd   80
That which is come to pass, and did discern
From his Survivors I could nothing learn.
This long discourse was but to let you see,
That his long life could not uneasie be.
Few like the *Fabii* or the *Scipio's* are
Takers of Cities, Conquerors in War,
Yet others to like happy Age arrive,
Who modest, quiet, and with vertue live:
Thus *Plato* writing his Philosophy,

With Honour after ninety years did die.[10]
The *Athenian Story* writ at ninety four
By *Isocrates,* who yet liv'd five years more,
His Master *Gorgias* at the hundredth year
And seventh, not his studies did forbear,
And askt, why he no sooner left the Stage,
Said, he saw nothing to accuse Old Age.
None but the foolish, who their lives abuse
Age, of their own Mistakes and Crimes accuse,
All Commonwealths (as by Record is seen)
As by Age preserv'd, by Youth destroy'd have been.   100
When the Tragedian *Nævius* did demand,
Why did your Common-wealth no longer stand?
'Twas answer'd, that their Senators were new,
Foolish, and young, and such as nothing knew;
Nature to Youth hot rashness doth dispence,
But with cold prudence Age doth recompence;
But Age ('tis said) will memory decay,
So (if it be not exercis'd) it may;
Or, if by Nature it be dull, and slow,
Themistocles (when ag'd) the Names did know   110
Of all th' *Athenians,* and none grow so old,
Not to remember where they hid their Gold.[11]
From Age such Art of Memory we learn,
To forget nothing, which is our concern.
Their interest no Priest, nor Sorcerer
Forgets, nor Lawyer, nor Philosopher;
No understanding, Memory can want,
Where Wisdome studious industry doth plant.
Nor does it only in the active live,
But in the quiet and contemplative;   120
When *Sophocles* (who Plays, when aged wrote)
Was by his Sons before the Judges brought,
Because he pay'd the Muses such respect,

[10] . . . *qualem accepimus Platonis, qui uno et octogesimo anno scribens est mortuus* . . .
[11] 110-112 greatly condensed.

His Fortune, Wife, and Children to neglect,
Almost condemn'd, he mov'd the Judges thus,
Hear, but instead of me, my *Oedipus*,
The Judges hearing with applause, at th' end,
Freed him, and said no Fool such Lines had penn'd.[12]
What Poets, and what Orators can I
Recount? What Princes in Philosophy?[13]   130
Whose constant Studies with their Age did strive,
Nor did they those, though those did them survive.
Old Husbandmen I at *Sabinium* know,
Who for another year dig, plough, and sow.
For never any man was yet so old,
But hop'd his life one Winter more might hold.
Cæcilius vainly said, each day we spend[14]
Discovers something, which must needs offend,
But sometimes Age may pleasant things behold,
And nothing that offends: He should have told   140
This not to Age, but Youth, who oftner see
What not alone offends, but hurts, then wee:
That, I in him, which he in Age condemn'd,
That us it renders odious, and contemn'd.
He knew not vertue, if he thought this, truth;
For Youth delights in Age, and Age in Youth.
What to the Old can greater pleasure be,
Then hopeful, and ingenious Youth to see?
When they with rev'rence follow where we lead,
And in strait paths by our directions tread;   150
And even my conversation here I see,
As well receiv'd by you, as yours by me.
'Tis dis-ingenious to accuse our Age
Of Idleness, who all our pow'rs ingage
In the same Studies, the same Course to hold;
Nor think our reason for new Arts too old.

[12] 121-128 good example of Denham's power of condensation and rhetorical heightening.
[13] Denham omits thirteen specific references to Greek poets and philosophers.
[14] Short passage omitted.

Solon the Sage his Progress never ceast,
But still his Learning with his dayes increast;
And I with the same greediness did seek
As (water when I thirst) to swallow Greek,   160
Which I did only learn, that I might know
Those great Examples, which I follow now:
And I have heard that *Socrates* the wise
Learn'd on the Lute for his last exercise,
Though many of the Antients did the same,
To improve Knowledge was my only aime.   166

THE SECOND PART

Now int' our second grievance I must break,
That loss of strength makes understanding weak.
I grieve no more my youthful strength to want,
Then young, that of a Bull or Elephant;
Then with that force content, which Nature gave,
Nor am I now displeas'd with what I have.
When the young Wrestlers at their sport grew warm,
Old *Milo* wept, to see his naked arm;
And cry'd, 'twas dead, Trifler thine heart, and head,
And all that's in them (not thy arme) are dead;   10
This folly every looker on derides,
To glory only in thy armes and sides.
Our gallant Ancestors[15] let fall no tears,
Their strength decreasing by increasing years;
But they advanc'd in Wisdom ev'ry hour,
And made the Common-wealth advance in power.
But Orators may grieve, for in their sides
Rather than heads, their faculty abides;
Yet I have heard old voices loud and clear,
And still my own sometimes the Senate hear.   20
When th' Old with smooth and gentle voices plead,
They by the ear their well-pleas'd Audience lead:

[15] Substituted for three proper names.

Which, if I had not strength enough to do,
I could (my *Lælius* and my *Scipio*)
What's to be done, or not be done, instruct,
And to the Maximes of good life conduct.
Cneius and *Publius Scipio,* and (that man[16]
Of men) your Grandsire the great Affrican,
Were joyful, when the flower of Noble blood
Crowded their Dwellings, and attending stood,   30
Like Oracles their Counsels to receive,
How in their Progress they should act, and live.
And they whose high examples youth obeys,
Are not despised, though their strength decays.
And those decayes (to speak the naked truth,
Though the defects of Age) were Crimes of Youth.
Intemperate Youth (by sad experience found)
Ends in an Age imperfect, and unsound.
Cyrus, though ag'd (if *Xenophon* say true)
Lucius Metellus (whom when young I knew)   40
Who held (after his Second Consulate)
Twenty two years the high Pontificate;
Neither of those in body, or in mind
Before their death the least decay did find.
I speak not of my self, though none deny
To age (to praise their youth) the liberty:
Such an unwasted strength I cannot boast,[17]
Yet now my years are eighty four almost:
And though from what it was my strength is far,
Both in the first and second *Punick* war,   50
Nor at *Thermopylæ,* under *Glabrio,*
Nor when I Consul into *Spain* did go;
But yet I feel no weakness, nor hath length
Of Winters quite enervated my strength;
And I, my Guest, my Client, or my friend,

[16] Short passage omitted.
[17] Rather long passage omitted, giving an example of Nestor's talking of his own merits.

Still in the Courts of Justice can defend:
Neither must I that Proverb's truth allow,
Who would be Antient, must be early so.
I would be youthful still, and find no need
To appear old, till I was so indeed.   60
And yet you see my hours not idle are,
Though with your strength I cannot mine compare.
Yet this Centurion's doth yours surmount,
Not therefore him the better man I count.
Milo when entring the Olympick Game,
With a huge Oxe upon his shoulder came.
Would you the force of *Milo's* body find?
Rather than of *Pythagoras's* mind?
The force which Nature gives with care retain,
But when decay'd, 'tis folly to complain;   70
In age to wish for youth is full as vain,
As for a youth to turn a child again.
Simple, and certain Nature's wayes appear,
As she sets forth the seasons of the year.
So in all parts of life we find her truth,
Weakness to childhood, rashness to our youth:
To elder years to be discreet and grave,
Then to old age maturity she gave.
(*Scipio*) you know, how *Masinissa* bears
His Kingly Port, at more than ninety years;   80
When marching with his foot, he walks till night;
When with his horse, he never will alight;
Though cold, or wet, his head is alwayes bare;
So hot, so dry, his aged members are.
You see how Exercise and Temperance
Even to old years a youthful strength advance.
Our Law (because from age our strength retires)
No duty which belongs to strength requires.
But age doth many men so feeble make,
That they no great design can undertake;   90
Yet, that to age not singly is appli'd,

But to all man's infirmities beside.
That *Scipio* (who adopted you) did fall
Into such pains, he had no health at all;
Who else had equall'd *Africanus* parts,
Exceeding him in all the Liberal Arts.
Why should those errors then imputed be
To Age alone, from which our youth's not free?
Ev'ry disease of age we may prevent,
Like those of youth, by being diligent.   100
When sick, such moderate exercise we use,
And diet, as our vital heat renues;
And if our bodies thence refreshment finds,
Then must we also exercise our minds.
If with continual Oyl we not supply
Our Lamp, the Light for want of it will die:
Though bodies may be tir'd with exercise,
No weariness the mind could e're surprise.
Cæcilius, the Comedian, when of Age,
He represents the follies on the Stage;   110
They're credulous, forgetful, dissolute,
Neither those Crimes to age he doth impute;
But to old men to whom those Crimes belong.
Lust, petulance, rashness, are in youth more strong
Than age, and yet young men those vices hate,
Who vertuous are, discreet, and temperate:
And so what we call dotage, seldome breeds
In bodies, but where Nature sow'd the seeds.
There are five Daughters and four gallant Sons,
In whom the blood of Noble *Appius* runs,   120
With a most num'rous Family beside;
When he alone though old, and blind did guide.
Yet his clear-sighted mind was still intent,
And to his business like a Bow stood bent:
By Children, Servants, Neighbours so esteem'd,
He not a Master, but a Monarch seem'd.
All his Relations his admirers were,

His Sons paid reverence, and his Servants fear:
The Order and the antient Discipline
Of Romans, did in all his actions shine.   130
Authority (kept up) old age secures,
Whose dignity, as long as life endures.
Something of youth I in old age approve,
But more the marks of age in youth I love.
Who this observes, may in his body find
Decrepit age, but never in his mind.
The seven Volumes of my own Reports,
Wherein are all the Pleadings of our Courts.
All noble Monuments of *Greece* are come
Unto my hands, with those of ancient *Rome*.   140
The Pontificial, and the Civil Law,
I study still, and thence Orations draw.
And to confirm my Memory, at night,
What I hear, see, do, by day, I still recite.
These exercises for my thoughts I find,
These labours are the Chariot of my mind.
To serve my friends, the Senate I frequent,
And there what I before digested, vent.
Which only from my strength of mind proceeds,
Not any outward force of body needs: 150
Which, if I could not do, I should delight
On what I would to ruminate at night.
Who in such practices their minds engage,
Nor fear, nor think of their approaching age;
Which by degrees invisibly doth creep:
Nor do we seem to die, but fall asleep.

THE THIRD PART

Now must I draw my forces 'gainst that Host
Of Pleasures, which i' th' Sea of age are lost.
Oh, thou most high transcendent gift of age!
Youth from its folly thus to disengage.

And now receive from me that most divine
Oration of that noble *Tarentine*,[18]
Which at *Tarentum* I long since did hear;
When I attended the great *Fabius* there.
Yee Gods, was it man's Nature? or his Fate?[19]
Betray'd him with sweet pleasures poyson'd bait?   10
Which he, with all designs of art, or power,
Doth with unbridled appetite devour;
And as all poysons seek the noblest part,
Pleasure possesses first the head and heart;
Intoxicating both, by them, she finds,
And burns the Sacred Temples of our Minds.
Furies, which Reasons divine chains had bound,
(That being broken) all the World confound.
Lust, Murder, Treason, Avarice, and Hell
It self broke loose; in Reason's Pallace dwell,   20
Truth, Honour, Justice, Temperance, are fled,
All her attendants into darkness led.
But why all this discourse? when pleasure's rage
Hath conquer'd reason, we must treat with age.
Age undermines, and will in time surprize
Her strongest Forts, and cut off all supplies.
And joyn'd in league with strong necessity,
Pleasure must flie, or else by famine die.
Flaminius, whom a Consulship had grac'd
(Then Censor) from the Senate I displac'd;   30
When he in *Gaul* a Consul, made a Feast,
A beautious Curtesan did him request,
To see the cutting off a Prisoner's head;
This Crime I could not leave unpunished,
Since by a private villany he stain'd
That Publick Honour, which at *Rome* he gain'd.[20]
Then to our age (when not to pleasures bent)

[18] *1669, Marginal note*, Archytas, much praised by Horace.
[19] 9-29 a free paraphrase. Rather long passage following the speech of
Fabius omitted.
[20] Here follow in the original Latin, III, ll. 89-98. See p. 219.

This seems an honour, not disparagement.
We, not all pleasures like the Stoicks hate;
But love and seek those which are moderate.   40
(Though Divine *Plato* thus of pleasures thought,
They us, with hooks and baits, like fishes caught.)
When Quæstor, to the Gods, in Publick Halls[21]
I was the first, who set up Festivalls.
Not with high tastes our appetites did force,
But fill'd with conversation and discourse;
Which Feasts, *Convivial Meetings* we did name.
Not like the Antient Greeks, who to their shame,
Call'd it a *Compotation,* not a Feast;
Declaring the worst part of it the best.   50
Those Entertainments I did then frequent
Sometimes with youthful heat and merriment:
But now (I thank my age) which gives me ease
From those excesses, yet my self I please
With cheerful talk to entertain my guests,
(Discourses are to age continual feasts)
The love of meat and wine they recompence,
And cheer the mind, as much as those the Sence.
I'm not more pleas'd with gravity among
The ag'd, than to be youthful with the young;   60
Nor 'gainst all pleasures proclaim open war,
To which, in age, some natural motions are.
And still at my *Sabinum* I delight
To treat my Neighbours till the depth of night.
But we the sence and gust of pleasure want,
Which youth at full possesses, this I grant;
But age seeks not the things which youth requires,
And no man needs that, which he not desires.
When *Sophocles* was ask'd if he deny'd
Himself the use of pleasures, he reply'd,   70
I humbly thank th' Immortal Gods, who me
From that fierce Tyrants insolence set free.

[21] 43-50 a free paraphrase. An anecdote of Duilius omitted, and a long passage considerably condensed.

But they whom pressing appetites constrain,
Grieve when they cannot their desires obtain.
Young men the use of pleasure understand,
As of an object new, and neer at hand:
Though this stands more remote from age's sight,
Yet they behold it not without delight:
As ancient souldiers from their duties eas'd,
With sense of Honour and Rewards are pleas'd,   80
So from ambitious hopes, and lusts releast,
Delighted with it self, our age doth rest.[22]
No part of life's more happy, when with bread
Of ancient Knowledge, and new Learning fed;
All youthful pleasures by degrees must cease,
But those of age even with our years increase.[23]
We love not loaded Boards, and Goblets crown'd,
But free from surfets, our repose is sound.
When old *Fabritius* to the Samnites went[24]
Ambassadour from *Rome* to *Pyrrhus* sent,   90
He heard a grave Philosopher maintain,
That all the actions of our life were vain;
Which with our sence of pleasure not conspir'd.
Fabritius the Philosopher desir'd,
That he to *Pyrrhus* would that Maxime teach,
And to the Samnites the same doctrine preach;
Then of their Conquest he should doubt no more,
Whom their own pleasures overcame before.
Now into Rustick matters I must fall,
Which pleasure seems to me the chief of all.   100
Age no impediment to those can give,
Who wisely by the Rules of Nature live.
Earth (though our Mother) cheerfully obeys,

[22] This simile is not suggested by the original, *Ut Turpione Ambivio magis delectatur qui in prima cavea spectat, delectatur tamen etiam qui in ultima, sic adulescentia voluptates propter intuens magis fortasse laetatur, sed delectatur etiam senectus procul eas spectans tantum quantum sat est.*

[23] 83-86 a brief generalization of a long passage, giving many instances of men who pursued intellectual pleasures in old age.

[24] 89-98 transposed from III, ll. 36 ff. See p. 217.

All the commands her race upon her lays.
For whatsoever from our hand she takes,
Greater, or less, a vast return she makes,
Nor am I only pleas'd with that resource,
But with her wayes, her method, and her force,
The seed her bosom (by the plough made fit)
Receives, where kindly she embraces it,   110
Which with her genuine warmth, diffus'd, and spread
Sends forth betimes a green, and tender head,
Then gives it motion, life, and nourishment,
Which from the root through nerves and veins are sent,
Streight in a hollow sheath upright it grows,
And, form receiving, doth it self disclose,
Drawn up in rancks, and files, the bearded spikes
Guard it from birds as with a stand of pikes.
When of the Vine I speak, I seem inspir'd,
And with delight, as with her juice am fir'd;   120
At Nature's God-like power I stand amaz'd,
Which such vast bodies hath from Attoms rais'd.
The kernel of a grape, the fig's small grain
Can cloath a Mountain, and o'reshade a Plaine:[25]
But thou (dear Vine) forbid'st me to be long,
Although thy trunck be neither large, nor strong,
Nor can thy head (not helpt) it self sublime,
Yet like a Serpent, a tall tree can climb,
Whate're thy many fingers can intwine
Proves thy support, and all its strength is thine,   130
Though Nature gave not legs, it gave thee hands,
By which thy prop the proudest Cedar stands;
As thou hast hands, so hath thy off-spring wings,
And to the highest part of Mortals springs,[26]
But lest thou should'st consume thy wealth in vain,
And starve thy self, to feed a numerous train,

[25] A rhetorical heightening of *Omitto enim vim ipsam omnium, quae generantur e terra; quae ex fici tantulo grano aut ex acini vinaceo aut ex ceterarum frugum aut stirpium minutissimis seminibus tantos truncos ramosque procreet.*

[26] This couplet is not suggested in the original.

Or like the Bee (sweet as thy blood) design'd
To be destroy'd to propagate his kind,
Lest thy redundant, and superfluous juyce,
Should fading leaves instead of fruits produce,   140
The Pruner's hand with letting blood must quench
Thy heat, and thy exub'rant parts retrench:
Then from the joynts of thy prolifick stemme
A swelling knot is raised (call'd a gemme)
Whence, in short space it self the cluster shews,
And from earths moisture mixt with Sun-beams grows,
I' th' Spring, like youth, it yields an acid taste,
But Summer doth, like age, the sourness waste,
Then cloath'd with leaves from heat, and cold secure,
Like Virgins,[27] sweet, and beauteous, when mature.[28]   150
On fruits, flowrs, herbs, and plants, I long could dwell
At once to please my eye, my taste, my smell,
My Walks of trees, all planted by my hand[29]
Like Children of my own begetting stand,
To tell the several nature of each earth,
What fruits from each most properly take birth:
And with what arts to inrich every mold,
The dry to moysten and to warm the cold.
But when we graft, or Buds inoculate,
Nature by Art we nobly meliorate,   160
As *Orpheus* Musick wildest beasts did tame,
From the sowr Crab the sweetest Apple came:
The Mother to the Daughter goes to School,
The species changed, doth her laws o're-rule;
Nature her self doth from her self depart,
(Strange transmigration) by the power of Art.
How little things, give law to great? we see

[27] The similes "like youth," "like age," "like virgins" are not in the original.
[28] Short passage omitted.
[29] 153-172 greatly expanded from *Nec vero segetibus solum et pratis et vineis et arbustis res rusticae laetae sunt, sed hortis etiam et pomariis, tum pecudum pastu, apium examinibus, florum omnium varietate. Nec consitiones modo delectant, sed etiam insitiones, quibus nihil invenit agri cultura sollertius.*

The small Bud captivates the greatest Tree.
Here even the Power Divine we imitate,
And seem not to beget, but to create.   170
Much was I pleas'd with fowls and beasts, the tame
For food and profit, and the wild for game.
Excuse me when this pleasant string I touch,
(For age, of what delights it, speaks too much)
Who, twice victorious *Pyrrhus* conquered,
The *Sabines* and the *Samnites* captive led,
Great *Curius,* his remaining dayes did spend,
And in this happy life his triumphs end.[30]
My Farm stands neer, and when I there retire,
His, and that Age's temper I admire,   180
The *Samnites* chiefs, as by his fire he sate,
With a vast sum of Gold on him did wait,
Return, said he, Your Gold I nothing weigh,
When those, who can command it, me obey:
This my assertion proves, he may be old
And yet not sordid, who refuses Gold.
In Summer to sit still, or walk, I love,[31]
Neer a cool Fountain, or a shadie Grove,
What can in Winter render more delight?
Then the high Sun at noon, and fire at night,   190
While our old friends, and neighbours feast, and play,
And with their harmless mirth turn night to day,
Unpurchas'd plenty our full tables loads,
And part of what they lent, returns to our Gods.
That honour, and authority which dwells
With age, all pleasures of our youth excells,
Observe, that I that Age have only prais'd
Whose pillars were on youth's foundations rais'd,
And that (for which I great applause receiv'd)
As a true maxime hath been since believ'd.   200
That most unhappy age great pity needs,

[30] Curius conquered the Sabines and the Samnites as well as Pyrrhus.
[31] 187-196. A summary of a long passage, omitting anecdotes of many eminent men who enjoyed the pleasures of agriculture.

Which to defend it self, new matter pleads,
Not from gray hairs authority doth flow,
Nor from bald heads, nor from a wrinckled brow,
But our past life, when virtuously spent,
Must to our age those happy fruits present,
Those things to age most Honorable are,
Which easie, common, and but light appear,
Salutes, consulting, complement, resort,
Crouding attendance to, and from the Court,   210
And not on *Rome* alone this honour waits,
But on all Civill, and well-govern'd States.
Lysander pleading in his City's praise,
From thence his strongest argument did raise,
That *Sparta* did with honour Age support,
Paying them just respect, at Stage, and Court,
But at proud *Athens* Youth did Age out-face,
Nor at the Playes, would rise, or give them place,
When an *Athenian* Stranger of great age,
Arriv'd at *Sparta*, climbing up the Stage,   220
To him the whole Assembly rose, and ran
To place and ease this old and reverend man,[32]
Who thus his thanks returns, the *Athenians* know
What's to be done, but what they know, not do.
Here our great Senat's Orders I may quote,
The first in age is still the first in vote,
Nor honour, nor high-birth, nor great command
In competition with great years may stand.
Why should our Youths short, transient pleasures, dare
With Age's lasting honours to compare?   230
On the World's Stage, when our applause grows high,
For acting here, life's Tragick Comedy,
The lookers on will say we act not well,
Unless the last the former Scenes excell:

[32] *Cum Athenis ludis quidam in theatrum grandis natu venisset, magno consessu locum nusquam ei datum a suis civibus; cum autem ad Lacedaemonios accessisset, qui legati cum essent, certo in loco consederant, consurrexisse omnes illi dicunter et senem sessum recepisse.*

But Age is froward, uneasie, scrutinous,
Hard to be pleas'd, and parcimonious;
But all those errors from our Manners rise,
Not from our years, yet some Morosities
We must expect, since jealousie belongs
To age, of scorn, and tender sense of wrongs,   240
Yet those are mollify'd, or not discern'd,
Where civil arts and manners have been learn'd,
So the Twins humours in our *Terence,* are[33]
Unlike, this harsh, and rude, that smooth and faire,
Our nature here, is not unlike our wine,
Some sorts, when old, continue brisk, and fine,
So Age's gravity may seem severe,
But nothing harsh, or bitter ought to'appear,
Of Age's avarice I cannot see
What colour, ground, or reason there should bee,   250
Is it not folly? when the way we ride
Is short, for a long voyage to provide.
To Avarice some title Youth may own,[34]
To reap in Autumn, what the Spring had sown;
And with the providence of Bees, or Ants,
Prevent[35] with Summers plenty, Winters wants,
But Age scarce sows, till Death stands by to reap,
And to a strangers hand transfers the heap;
Affraid to be so once, she's always poor,
And to avoid a mischief, makes it sure   260
Such madness, as for fear of death to dy,
Is, to be poor for fear of Poverty.

THE FOURTH PART

Now against (that which terrifies our age)
The last, and greatest grievance we engage,

[33] *1669, Marginal note,* In his Comedy called Adelphi.
[34] 253-262 added by Denham.
[35] *1669,* prevents.

To her, grim death appears in all her shapes,
The hungry grave for her due tribute gapes,
Fond, foolish man! with fear of death surpriz'd
Which either should be wisht for, or despis'd,
This, if our Souls with Bodies, death destroy,
That, if our Souls a second life enjoy,
What else is to be fear'd? when we shall gain
Eternal life, or have no sence of pain,   10
The youngest in the morning are not sure,
That till the night their life they can secure
Their age stands more expos'd to accidents
Then our's, nor common cure[36] their fate prevents:
Death's force (with terror) against Nature strives,
Nor one of many to ripe age arrives,
From this ill fate the world's disorders rise,
For if all men were old they would be wise,
Years, and experience, our fore-fathers taught,
Them under Laws, and into Cities brought: 20
Why only should the fear of death belong
To age? which is as common to the young:
Your hopefull Brothers, and my Son, to you
(*Scipio*) and me, this maxime makes too true,
But vigorous Youth may his gay thoughts erect
To many years, which Age must not expect,
But when he sees his airy hopes deceiv'd,
With grief he saies, who this would have believ'd?
We happier are then they, who but desir'd
To possess that, which we long since acquir'd.   30
What if our age to *Nestor's* could extend?[37]
'Tis vain to think that lasting, which must end;
And when 'tis past, not any part remains
Thereof, but the reward which virtue gains.
Dayes, Months, and years, like running waters flow,
Nor what is past, nor what's to come we know,

[36] Care?
[37] Illustration of Nestor substituted for Arganthonius, King of Tartessus.

Our date how short soe're must us content,
When a good Actor doth his part present,
In ev'ry Act he our attention draws,
That at the last he may find just applause,   40
So (though but short) yet we must learn the art
Of virtue, on this Stage to act our part;
True wisdome must our actions so direct,
Not only the last Plaudite to expect;
Yet grieve no more though long that part should last,
Then Husbandmen, because the Spring is past,
The Spring, like Youth, fresh blossoms doth produce,
But Autumne makes them ripe, and fit for use:
So Age a Mature Mellowness doth set
On the green promises of youthfull heat.   50
All things which Nature did ordain, are good,
And so must be receiv'd, and understood,
Age, like ripe Apples, on earth's bosom drops,
Whil'st force our youth, like fruits untimely crops;
The sparkling flame of our warm blood expires,
As when huge streams are pour'd on raging fires,
But age unforc'd falls by her own consent,
As Coals to ashes, when the Spirit's spent;
Therefore to death I with such joy resort,
As Seamen from a Tempest to their Port,   60
Yet to that Port our selves we must not force,
Before our Pilot Nature steers our course,
Let us the Causes of our fear condemn,
Then death at his approach we shall contemn,
Though to our heat of youth our age seems cold,
Yet when resolv'd, it is more brave and bold.
Thus *Solon* to *Pisistratus* reply'd,
Demanded, on what succour he rely'd,
When with so few he boldly did ingage,
He said, he took his courage from his Age.   70
Then death seems welcome, and our Nature kind,
When leaving us a perfect sense and mind;

She (like a Workman in his Science skill'd)
Pulls down with ease, what her own hand did build.
That Art which knew to joyn all parts in one,
Makes the least violent separation.
Yet though our Ligaments betimes grow weak,
We must not force them till themselves they break.
Pythag'ras bids us in our Station stand,
Till God our General shall us disband.   80
Wise *Solon* dying, wisht his friends might grieve,
That in their memories he still might live.
Yet wiser *Ennius* gave command to all
His friends, not to bewail his funeral;
Your tears for such a death in vain you spend,
Which strait in immortality shall end.
In death if there be any sense of pain,
But a short space, to age it will remain.
On which without my fears, my wishes wait,
But timorous youth on this should meditate: 90
Who for light pleasure this advice rejects,
Finds little, when his thoughts he recollects.
Our death (though not its certain date) we know,
Nor whether it may be this night, or no:
How then can they contented live? who fear
A danger certain, and none knows how near.
They erre, who for the fear of death dispute,
Our gallant actions this mistake confute.
Thee (*Brutus*) *Rome's* first Martyr I must name,
The *Curtii* bravely div'd the Gulph of Flame: 100
Attilius sacrific'd himself, to save
That faith, which to his barb'rous foes he gave;
With the two *Scipio's* did thy Uncle fall,
Rather to fly from Conquering *Hannibal*.
The great *Marcellus* (who restored *Rome*)[38]
His greatest foes with Honour did intomb.
Their Lives how many of our Legions threw,

[38] Illustration of Lucius Paullus omitted.

Into the breach? whence no return they knew;
Must then the wise, the old, the learned fear,
What not the rude, the young, th' unlearn'd forbear?   110
Satiety from all things else doth come,
Then life must to it self grow wearisome.
Those Trifles wherein Children take delight,
Grow nauceous to the young man's appetite,
And from those gaieties our youth requires,
To exercise their minds, our age retires.
And when the last delights of Age shall die,
Life in it self will find satietie.
Now you (my friends) my sense of death shall hear,
Which I can well describe, for he stands near.   120
Your Father *Lælius*, and yours *Scipio*,
My friends, and men of honour I did know;
As certainly as we must die, they live
That life which justly may that name receive.
Till from these prisons of our flesh releas'd,
Our souls with heavy burdens lie oppress'd;
Which part of man from Heaven falling down,
Earth in her low Abysse, doth hide, and drown.
A place so dark to the Celestial light,
And pure, eternal fires quite opposite.   130
The Gods through humane bodies did disperse
An heavenly soul, to guide this Universe;
That man, when he of heavenly bodies saw
The Order, might from thence a pattern draw:
Nor this to me did my own dictates show
But to the old Philosophers I owe.
I heard *Pythagoras*, and those who came
With him, and from our Countrey took their Name.
Who never doubted but the beams divine
Deriv'd from Gods, in mortal breasts did shine.   140
Nor from my knowledge did the Antients hide
What *Socrates* declar'd, the hour he dy'd,
He th' Immortality of Souls proclaim'd,

(Whom th' Oracle of men the wisest nam'd)
Why should we doubt of that? whereof our sence
Finds demonstration from experience;
Our minds are here and there, below, above;
Nothing that's mortal can so swiftly move.
Our thoughts to future things their flight direct,
And in an instant all that's past collect,   150
Reason, remembrance, wit, inventive art,
No nature, but immortal, can impart.
Man's Soul in a perpetual motion flowes,
And to no outward cause that Motion owes;
And therefore, that, no end can overtake,
Because our minds cannot themselves forsake.
And since the matter of our Soul is pure,
And simple, which no mixture can endure
Of parts, which not among themselves agree;
Therefore it never can divided be.   160
And Nature shews (without Philosophy)
What cannot be divided, cannot die.
We even in early infancy discern,
Knowledge is born with babes before they learn;
Ere they can speak, they find so many wayes
To serve their turn, and see more Arts than dayes,
Before their thoughts they plainly can expresse,
The words and things they know are numberlesse;
Which Nature only, and no Art could find,
But what she taught before, she call'd to mind.   170
This to his Sons (as *Xenophon* records)
Of the great *Cyrus* were the dying words;
Fear not when I depart (nor therefore mourn)
I shall be no where, or to nothing turn:
That Soul, which gave me life, was seen by none,
Yet by the actions it design'd, was known;
And though its flight no mortal eye shall see,
Yet know, for ever it the same shall be.
That Soul, which can immortal glory give,

To her own Vertues must for ever live.   180
Can you believe, that man's all-knowing mind
Can to a mortal body be confin'd?
Though a foul, foolish prison her immure
On earth, she (when escap'd) is wise, and pure.
Man's body when dissolv'd is but the same
With beasts, and must return from whence it came;
But whence into our bodys reason flowes,
None sees it, when it comes, or where it goes.
Nothing resembles death so much as sleep,
Yet then our minds themselves from slumber keep.   190
When from their fleshly bondage they are free,
Then what divine, and future things they see?
Which makes it most apparent whence they are,
And what they shall hereafter be declare.[39]
This Noble Speech the dying *Cyrus* made.
Me (*Scipio*) shall no argument perswade,
Thy Grandsire, and his Brother, to whom Fame
Gave from two conquer'd parts o' th' World, their Name,
Nor thy great Grandsire, nor thy Father *Paul*,
Who fell at *Cannæ* against *Hannibal*;   200
Nor I (for 'tis permitted to the ag'd
To boast their actions) had so oft ingag'd
In Battels, and in Pleadings, had we thought,
That only Fame our vertuous actions bought,
'Twere better in soft pleasure and repose
Ingloriously our peaceful eyes to close:
Some high assurance hath possest my mind,
After my death, an happier life to find.
Unless our Souls from the Immortals came,
What end have we to seek Immortal Fame?   210
All vertuous spirits some such hope attends,
Therefore the wise his dayes with pleasure ends.
The foolish and short-sighted die with fear,
That they go no where, or they know not where.

[39] Last few lines of Cyrus's speech omitted.

The wise and vertuous Soul with cleerer eyes
Before she parts, some happy Port discries.
My friends, your Fathers I shall surely see,
Nor only those I lov'd, or who lov'd me;
But such as before ours did end their daies:
Of whom we hear, and read, and write their praise.   220
This I believe, for were I on my way,
None should perswade me to return, or stay:
Should some God tell me, that I should be born,
And cry again, his offer I should scorn;
Asham'd when I have ended well my race,
To be led back, to my first starting place.
And since with life we are more griev'd than joy'd,
We should be either satisfi'd, or cloy'd;
Yet will not I my length of dayes deplore,
As many wise and learn'd have done before: 230
Nor can I think such life in vain is lent,
Which for our Countrey and our friends is spent.
Hence from an Inne, not from my home, I pass,
Since Nature meant us here no dwelling place.
Happy when I from this turmoil set free,
That peaceful and divine assembly see:
Not only those I nam'd I there shall greet,
But my own gallant vertuous *Cato* meet.
Nor did I weep, when I to ashes turn'd
His belov'd body, who should mine have burn'd: 240
I in my thoughts beheld his Soul ascend,
Where his fixt hopes our Interview attend:
Then cease to wonder that I feel no grief[40]
From Age, which is of my delights the chief.
My hope's, if this assurance hath deceiv'd,
(That I Man's Soul Immortal have believ'd)
And if I erre, no Pow'r shall dispossess
My thoughts of that expected happiness.
Though some minute Philosophers pretend,

[40] A few lines omitted.

That with our dayes our pains and pleasures end.   250
If it be so, I hold the safer side,
For none of them my Error shall deride.
And if hereafter no rewards appear,[41]
Yet Vertue hath it self rewarded here.
If those who this Opinion have despis'd,
And their whole life to pleasure sacrific'd;
Should feel their error, they when undeceiv'd,
Too late will wish, that me they had believ'd.
If Souls no Immortality obtain,
'Tis fit our bodies should be out of pain.   260
The same uneasiness, which every thing
Gives to our Nature, life must also bring.
Good Acts (if long) seem tedious, so is Age
Acting too long upon this Earth her Stage.
Thus much for Age, to which when you arrive,
That Joy to you, which it gives me, 'twill give.

THE SOPHY[1]

THE PROLOGUE

Hither ye come, dislike, and so undo
The Players, and disgrace the Poet too;
But he protests against your votes, and swears

[41] 253-258 added by Denham.

[1] For an account of the source, etc., see p. 45. I have not strictly followed
the line arrangement of the 1668 edition, but have tried in a few places to
correct what seem arbitrary divisions of lines.

In the 1642 edition, between the *dramatis personae* and the text of the
play, are printed two prologues:

THE PROLOGUE AT COURT

Had not obedience ov'rrul'd the author's feare
And judgement too, this humble peece had nere
Approacht so high a majestie, not writ
By the exact and subtile rules of wit,
Ambitious for the splendor of this night,

He'll not be try'd by any, but his Peers;
He claims his priviledge, and sayes 'tis fit
Nothing should be the Judge of wit, but Wit.
Now you will all be Wits, and be I pray;
And you that discommend it, mend the Play:
'Tis the best satisfaction, he knows then

    But fashion'd up in hast for his owne delight.
    This, by my Lord, with as much zeale as ere
    Warm'd the most loyall heart, is offered here
    To make this night your pleasure, although we
    Who are the actors feare 'twill rather be
    Your patience; and if any mirth, we may
    Sadly suspect 'twill rise quite the wrong way.
    But you have mercy, Sir, and from your eye,
    Bright Madam, never yet did lightning flye,
    But vitall beames of favour such as give
    A growth to all who can deserve to live.
    Why should the author tremble then, or we
    Distresse our hopes, and such tormentors be
    Of our owne thoughts, since in those happie times
    We live when mercies greater than the crimes.

THE PROLOGUE AT THE FRYERS [BLACK FRIARS]

    Ere we begin, that no man may repent
    Two shillings and his time, the author sent
    The prologue with the errors of his play
    That who will may take his money and away.
    First for the plot: 'tis no way intricate
    By crosse deceits in love, nor so high in state
    That we might have given out in our play-bill
    This day's the Prince writ by Nick Machivill.
    The language too is easie, such as fell
    Unstudyed from his pen, not like a spell,
    Bygge with misterious words, such as inchant
    The halfe-witted, and confound the ignorant.
    Then what must needes afflict the amorist,
    No virgin here in breeches casts a mist
    Before her lover's eyes, no ladies tell
    How their blood boyles, how high their veines doe swell.
    But what is worse, no bawdy mirth is here
    (The wit of bottle ale and double beere)
    To make the wife of citizen protest,
    And country justice sweare 'twas a good jest.
    Now, sirs, you have the errors of his wit;
    Like or dislike, at your own perills be 't.

His turn will come, to laugh at you agen.
But Gentlemen, if ye dislike the Play,
Pray make no words on't till the second day,
Or third be past: For we would have you know it,
The loss will fall on us, not on the Poet:
For he writes not for money, nor for praise,
Nor to be call'd a Wit, nor to wear Bayes:
Cares not for frowns or smiles: so now you'll say,
Then (why the Devil) did he write a Play?
He says, 'twas then with him, as now with you,
He did it when he had nothing else to do.

ACTORS

Scena *Persia*.

Abbas, King of *Persia*.
Mirza, the Prince, his Son.
Erythœa, the Princess, his Wife.
Haly, the King's Favourite. ⎫
Mirvan, Haly's Confident. ⎭ Enemies to the Prince.
Abdall, ⎫
Morat, ⎭ Two Lords, Friends to the Prince.
Caliph.
Solyman, a foolish Courtier.
Soffy, the Prince his Son, now King of *Persia*.
Fatyma, his Daughter.
2 *Turkish Bashawes.*
3 *Captains.*
2 *Women.*
Physician.
Tormentors.

THE SOPHY

Actus Primus.

Enter Abdall *and* Morat.

Mor. My Lord, you have good intelligence,
    What news from the Army,
    Any certainty of their design or strength?
Abd. We know not their design: But for their strength,
    The disproportion is so great, we cannot but
    Expect a fatal consequence.
Mor. How great my Lord?
Abd. The Turks are fourscore thousand Foot,
    And fifty thousand Horse. And we in the whole
    Exceed not forty thousand.   10
Mor. Me-thinks the Prince should know
    That Judgment's more essential to a General,
    Than Courage, if he prove victorious
    'Tis but a happy rashness.
Abd. But if he lose the battel, 'tis an error
    Beyond excuse, or remedy, considering
    That half the Lesser *Asia* will follow
    The Victors fortune.
Mor. 'Tis his single vertue
    And terror of his name, that walls us in   20
    From danger, were he lost, the naked Empire
    Would be a prey expos'd to all Invaders.
Abd. But is't not necessary
    The King should know his danger?
Mor. To tell him of so great a danger,
    Were but to draw a greater on our selves:
    For though his eye is open as the mornings,
    Towards lusts & pleasures, yet so fast a lethargy
    Has seiz'd his powers towards publick cares and dangers,
    He sleeps like death.   30
Abd. He's a man of that strange composition,

Made up of all the worst extremities
Of youth, and age.

Mor. And though
He feels the heats of youth, and colds of age,
Yet neither tempers, nor corrects the other;
As if there were an Ague in his nature
That still inclines to one extream.

Abd. But the *Caliph,* or *Haly,* or some that know
His softer hours, might best acquaint him with it. 40

Mor. Alas, they shew him nothing
But in the glass of flattery, if any thing
May bear a shew of glory, fame, or greatness,
'Tis multiplied to an immense quantity,
And stretcht even to Divinity:
But if it tend to danger, or dishonour,
They turn about the Perspective, and shew it
So little, at such distance, so like nothing,
That he can scarce discern it.

Abd. 'Tis the fate of Princes, that no knowledge 50
Comes pure to them, but passing through the eies
And ears of other men, it takes a tincture
From every channel; and still bears a relish
Of Flattery, or private ends.

Mor. But danger and necessity
Dare speak the truth.

Abd. But commonly
They speak not till it is too late:
And for *Haly,*
He that shall tell him of the Princes danger, 60
But tells him that himself is safe.

Scena Secunda.

Enter King, Princess, and Solyman.

King. Clear up, clear up, sweet *Erythœa,*
That cloud that hangs upon thy brow presages

A greater storm than all the Turkish power
Can throw upon us, me-thinks I see my fortune
Setling her looks by thine, and in thy smile
Sits victory, and in thy frown our ruine:
Why should not hope as much erect our thoughts,
As fear deject them; why should we
Anticipate our sorrows? 'Tis like those
That die for fear of death: 10
What is 't you doubt, his courage or his fortune?
Prin. Envy it self could never doubt his courage.
King. Then let not love do worse, by doubting that
Which is but valours slave; a wise, well-temper'd valour,
For such is his, those Giants death and danger,
Are but his Ministers, and serve a Master
More to be fear'd than they; & the blind Goddess
Is led amongst the Captives in his triumph.
Prin. I had rather she had eyes, for if she saw him
Sure she would love him better; but admit   20
She were at once a Goddess, and his slave,
Yet fortune, valour, all is overborn
By numbers: as the long resisting Bank
By the impetuous Torrent.
King. That's but rumour:
Ne're did the Turk invade our Territory,
But Fame and Terrour doubled still their files:
But when our Troops encountred, then we found
Scarce a sufficient matter for our fury.

One brings word of a Messenger.[2]

Solyman conduct him in, 'tis surely from the Prince.   30

Enter Post, and delivers a Letter.

King. Give it our Secretaries, I hope the Prince is well.

[2] *1642,* But heark, a post!
              A Horn within.

Post. The Letter will inform you.

> *Enter a Mess. Ex. Princess. Enter Lords.*

Mess. Sir, the Lords attend you.

King. What news from the Army?

Lord. Please you to hear the Letter.

King. Read it.

Lord. The Turk enraged with his last years overthrow, hath
    re-enforc't his Army with the choice of all his Janizars, and
    the flow'r of his whole Empire, we understand by some
    fugitives, that he hath commanded the Generals to return 40
    with victory, or expect a shameful death: what I shall
    further do, (their numbers five times exceeding ours) I
    desire to receive directions from your Majesties com-
    mand.

King. Send away all our Guards
    Let fresh supplies of victuals, and of money—

Lord. Your Treasures
    Are quite exhausted, the Exchequer's empty.

King. Send to the Bankers.

Abd. Sir, upon your late demands[3]   50
    They answered they were poor.

King. Sure the Villains hold a correspondence
    With the enemy, and thus they would betray us:
    First give us up to want, then to contempt,
    And then to ruine; but tell those sons of earth

---

[3] *1642:*

King. Let twenty thousand men be raised,
    Let fresh supplyes of victuals, and of money
    Be sent with speed.

Lord. Sir, your Treasures
    Are quite exhausted, the Exchequer's empty.

King. Talke not to me of Treasures, or Exchequers:
    Send for five hundred of the wealthiest Burgers,
    Their shops and ships are my Exchequer.

Abd. 'Twere better you could say their hearts. [*Abd. aside.*]
    Sir upon your late demands, etc.

I'le have their money, or their heads.[4]
'Tis my command, when such occasions are
No Plea must serve; 'tis cruelty to spare.

Another Messenger. Exeunt Lords.

King. The Prince transported with his youthful heat,
    I fear hath gon too far: 'Tis some disaster,   60
    Or else he would not send so thick: well, bring him in;
    I am prepar'd to hear the worst of evils.

Enter Solyman and two Captains. Cap. kisses his hand.

King. What is the Prince besieged in his Trenches,
    And must have speedy aid, or die by famine?
    Or hath he rashly tri'd the chance of War,
    And lost his Army, or his[5] Liberty?
    Tell me what Province they demand for ransom:
    Or if the worst of all mishaps hath fallen,
    Speak, for he could not die unlike himself:
    Speak freely; and yet me-thinks I read   70
    Something of better fortune in thy looks,
    But dare not hope it.
Cap. Sir, the Prince lives.
King. And hath not lost his honour?
Cap. As safe in honour as in life.
King. Nor liberty?
Cap. Free as the air he breaths.
King. Return with speed:
    Tell him he shall have money, victuals, men,
    With all the haste they can be levied. *Farewel.*   80

Offers to go.

---

  [4] *1668* has the stage direction, *Wind a horn.* This was struck out in the errata.
    1671, as above.
    1684, as above.
  [5] *1668,* and his. This was corrected in the errata.
    1671, as above.
    1684, as above.

Cap. But Sir, I have one word more.

King. Then be brief.

Cap. So now you are prepar'd; and I may venture.

King. What is't?

Cap. Sir, a Fathers love mixt with a Father's[6] care,
　This shewing dangers greater, and that nearer,
　Have rais'd your fears too high; and those remov'd,
　Too suddenly would let in such a deluge
　Of joy, as might oppress your aged spirits,
　Which made me gently first remove your fears,　　　　90
　That so you might have room to entertain
　Your fill of joy: Your Son's a Conquerour.

King. Delude me not with fained hopes, false joys,
　It cannot be. And if he can but make
　A fair Retreat, I shall account it more
　Than all his former conquests, (those huge numbers
　Arm'd with despair) the flow'r of all the Empire.

Cap. Sir, I have not us'd to tell you tales or fables,
　And why should you suspect your happiness,
　Being so constant. On my life 'tis true Sir.　　　　100

King. Well, I'le no more suspect
　My fortune, nor thy faith:
　Thou and thy news most welcom: *Solyman*
　Go call the *Princess* and the *Lords,* they shall
　Participate our joyes, as well as cares.

Enter Princess and Lords.

King. Fair daughter, blow away those mists & clouds,
　And let thy eyes shine forth in their full lustre;
　Invest them with thy loveliest smiles, put on
　Thy choycest looks: his coming will deserve them.

Princess. What, is the Prince return'd with safety?　　　　110
　'Tis beyond[7] belief or hope.

King. I, sweet *Erythœa;*
　Laden with spoyls and honour: all thy fears,

[6] *1642*, princes.
[7] *1642*, above.

Thy wakeful terrors, and affrighting dreams,
Thy morning sighs, and evening tears have now
Their full rewards. And you my Lords,
Prepare for Masques & Triumphs: Let no circumstance
Be wanting, that becomes
The greatness of our State, or Joy.
Behold he comes.   120

Enter Prince with Captains, and two Captive Bashawes.

King. Welcom brave son, as welcom to thy father
    As *Phœbus* was to *Jove,* when he had slain
    Th' ambitious Giants that assail'd the sky;
    And as my power resembles that of *Joves,*
    So shall thy glory like high *Phœbus* shine
    As bright and as immortal.
Prince. Great Sir, all acquisition
    Of Glory as of Empire, here I lay before
    Your Royal feet, happy to be the Instrument
    To advance either: Sir I challenge nothing,   130
    But am an humble suitor for these prisoners,
    The late Commanders of the Turkish powers,
    Whose valours have deserv'd a better fortune.
King. Then what hath thine deserv'd? th'are thine brave *Mirzah,*
    Worthy of all thy Royal Ancestors,
    And all those many Kingdoms, which their vertue,
    Or got, or kept, though thou hadst not been born to't.
    But daughter still your looks are sad,
    No longer I'le defer your joys, go take him
    Into thy chast embrace, and whisper to him   140
    That welcom which those blushes promise.

Exit King.

Prince. My *Erythœa,* why entertain'st thou with so sad a brow
    My long-desir'd return? thou wast wont
    With kisses and sweet smiles, to welcom home
    My victories, though bought with sweat and bloud;
    And long expected.

Princess. Pardon Sir;
    'Tis with our souls
    As with our eyes, that after a long darkness
    Are dazled at the approach of sudden light: 150
    When i' th' midst of fears we are surpriz'd
    With unexpected happiness: the first
    Degrees of joy are meer astonishment.
    And 'twas so lately in a dreadful dream
    I saw my Lord so near destruction,
    Deprived of his eyes, a wretched Captive;
    Then shriekt my self awake, then slept again
    And dream't the same; my ill presaging fancy
    Suggesting still 'twas true.

Prince. Then I forgive thy sadness, since love caus'd it,   160
    For love is full of fears; and fear the shadow
    Of danger, like the shadow of our bodies,
    Is greater then, when that which is the cause
    Is farthest off.

Princess. But still there's something
    That checks my joys, nor can I yet distinguish
    Which is an apparition, this, or that.

Prince. An apparition?
    At night I shall resolve that doubt, and make
    Thy dreams more pleasing.   170

        Exeunt. Enter Haly and Mirvan.

Mir. The time has been, my Lord,
    When I was no such stranger to your thoughts,
    You were not wont to wear upon your brow
    A frown, or smile, but still have thought me worthy,
    At least to know the cause.

Ha. 'Tis true,
    Thy breast hath ever been the Cabinet
    Where I have lockt my secrets.

Mir. And did you ever find
    That any art could pick the lock, or power   180
    Could force it open.

Ha. No, I have ever found thee
    Trusty and secret. But is't observ'd i'th' Court
    That I am sad?
Mir. Observ'd? 'tis all mens wonder and discourse,
    That in a Joy so great, so universal,
    You should not bear a part.
Ha. Discour'st of too?
Mir. Nothing but treason
    More commonly, more boldly spoken.   190
    So singular a sadness
    Must have a cause as strange as the effect:
    And grief conceal'd, like hidden fire consumes;
    Which flaming out, would call in help to quench it.
Ha. But since thou canst not mend it,
    To let thee know it, will but make thee worse;
    Silence and time shall cure it.
Mir. But in diseases when the cause is known,
    'Tis more than half the cure: you have my Lord
    My heart to counsel, and my hands to act,   200
    And my advice and actions both have met
    Success in things unlikely.
Ha. But this
    Is such a secret, I dare hardly trust it
    To my own soul. And though it be a crime
    In friendship to betray a trusted Counsel,
    Yet to conceal this were a greater crime,
    And of a higher nature.
Mir. Now I know it,
    And your endeavour to conceal it,   210
    Speaks it more plainly. 'Tis some plot upon the Prince.
Ha. Oh thou hast touch't my Sore, and having searcht it,
    Now heal it if thou canst: The Prince hates[8] me,
    Or loves me not, or loves another better;
    Which is all one. This being known in Court,
    Has rendred me despis'd, and scorn'd of all:

[8] *1642,* doth hate.

For I that in his absence
Blaz'd like a star of the first magnitude,
Now in his brighter sun-shine am not seen:
No applications now, no troops of suitors;   220
No power, no not so much as to do mischief.

Mir. My Lord, I am asham'd of you,
So ill a master in an art, so long
Profest, and practiz'd by you, to be angry,
And angry with a Prince. And yet to shew it
In a sad look, or womanish complaint:
How can you hope to compass your designs,
And not dissemble 'em. Go flatter & adore him,
Stand first among the crowd of his admirers.

Ha. Oh I have often spread those nets, but he   230
Hath ever been too wise to think them real.

Mir. However,
Dissemble still, thank him for all his injuries;
Take 'em for favours; if at last
You cannot gain him; some pretty nimble poyson
May do the feat. Or if he will abroad,
Find him some brave and honourable danger.

Ha. Have I not found him out as many dangers
As *Juno* did for *Hercules:* yet he returns
Like *Hercules,* doubled in strength and honour.   240

Mir. If danger cannot do it, then try pleasure,
Which when no other enemy survives,
Still conquers all the Conquerers. Endeavour
To soften his ambition into lust,
Contrive fit opportunities, and lay
Baits for temptation.

Ha. Ile leave nothing unattempted:
But sure this will not take; for all his Passions,
Affections, and Faculties are slaves
Only to his ambition.   250

Mir. Then let him fall by his own greatness,
And puffe him up with glory, till it swell

And break him. First, betray him to himself,
Then to his ruine: From his virtues suck a poyson,
As Spiders do from flowers; praise him to his Father,
You know his nature: Let the Princes glory
Seem to eclipse, and cast a cloud on his;
And let fall something that may raise his jealousie:
But lest he should suspect it, draw it from him
As Fishers do the bait, to make him follow it.   260
Ha. But the old King is so suspitious.
Mir. But withall
    Most fearful: He that views a Fort to take it,
    Plants his Artillery 'gainst the weakest part:
    Work on his fears, till fear hath made him cruel;
    And cruelty shall make him fear again.
    Methinks (my Lord) you that so oft have sounded
    And fathom'd all his thoughts, that know the deeps
    And shallows of his heart, should need no instruments
    To advance your ends; his passions, and his fears   270
    Lie Liegers for you in his brest, and there
    Negotiate your affairs.

      Enter King, Solyman, and Lords to them.

King. Solyman, Be it your care to entertain the Captains
    And the Prisoners, & use them kindly.
Sol. Sir, I am not for entertainments now I am melancholy.
King. What, griev'd for your good fortune?
Sol. No Sir, but now the wars are done, we have no pretences
    To put off Creditors: I am haunted Sir.
King. Not with Ghosts.
Sol. No Sir,   280
    Material and Substantial Devils.
King. I know the cause, what is't thou ow'st them?
Sol. Not much Sir, but so much as spoils me for a good fellow;
    'Tis but 2000 Dollars. A small sum—to you Sir.
King. Well, it shall be paid.
Sol. Then if the Devil come, for drinking let me alone with him.
    Well, Drink, I love thee but too well already,

But I shall love thee better hereafter: I have often
Drunk my self into debt, but never out of debt till now.

Exeunt. Finis Actus primi.

Actus Secundus.

Scena Prima.

Enter Prince, Haly, Captains and Prisoners, Bashawes.

Prince. Pray let these strangers find such entertainment[9]
    As you would have desir'd,
    Had but the chance of war determin'd it
    For them, as now for us. And you brave enemies
    Forget your Nation, and ungrateful Master;
    And know that I can set so high a price
    On valour, though in foes, as to reward it
    With trust and honour.
1 Bashaw. Sir, your twice conquered Vassals,
    First by your courage, then your clemency,   10
    Here humbly vow to sacrifice their lives,
    (The gift of this your unexampled mercy)
    To your commands and service.
Prince to Haly. I pray (my Lord) second my suit,
    I have already mov'd the King in private,

---

[9] *1642:*
Prince. Captaines, me-thinkes you looke like fishes out of water,
    I see the Court is not your element:
    You must to the warres againe.
1 Cap. Faith Sir, These young Gallants are so taken up with their Mistresses;
    I doubt their edge is taken off from the warres.
2 Cap. I, and their backes too.
1 Cap. But for us old ones we're weary of being laught at by these Court
    hobby-horses, for making legges, and kissing hands unhandsomely.
2 Cap. And to be censured by the criticks, because our legges are bigger then
    the Court standard, and therefore out of fashion.
1 Cap. And such a gigling, because ones band's unpin'd; anothers beard not
    well turn'd up: And such a fiddle faddle, 'tis not to be endur'd.
Prince. Well, howsoevèr you are dealt with,
    Pray let these strangers finde such entertainment, etc.

That in our next years expedition they may have
Some command.

Ha. I shall, my Lord,
And glad of the occasion.   *aside.*
I wonder Sir, you'll leave the Court, the sphere   20
Where all your graces in full lustre shine.

Prince. I *Haly,* but the reputation
Of virtuous actions past, if not kept up
With an access, and fresh supply of new ones,
Is lost and soon forgotten: and like Palaces,
For want of habitation and repair,
Dissolve to heaps of ruine.

Ha. But can you leave, Sir,
Your old indulgent Father, and forsake
The embraces of so fair, so chast a Wife?   30
And all the beauties of the Court besides,
Are mad in love, and dote upon your person:
And is 't not better sleeping in their arms,
Than in a cold Pavilion in the Camp?
Where your short sleeps are broke and interrupted
With noises and alarms.

Prince. Haly, Thou know'st not me, how I despise
These short and empty pleasures; and how low
They stand in my esteem, which every Peasant,
The meanest Subject in my Fathers Empire   40
Enjoys as fully, in as high perfection
As he or I; and which are had in common
By beasts as well as men: wherein they equal,
If not exceed us; pleasures to which we're led
Only by sence, those creatures which have least
Of reason, most enjoy.

Ha. Is not
The Empire you are born. to, a Scene large enough
To exercise your virtues? There are virtues
Civil as well as military; for the one   50
You have given the world an ample proof already:

Now exercise the other, 'tis no less
To govern justly, make your Empire flourish
With wholesom laws, in riches, peace & plenty,
Than by the expence of wealth and bloud to make
New acquisitions.
Prince. That I was born so great, I owe to Fortune,
    And cannot pay that debt, till vertue set me
    High in example, as I stand[10] in title;
    Till what the world calls fortune's gifts, my actions   60
    May stile their own rewards, and those too little.
    Princes are then themselves, when they arise
    More glorious in mens thoughts than in their eyes.
Ha. Sir, your fame
    Already fills the world, and what is infinite
    Cannot receive degrees, but will swallow
    All that is added; as our Caspian Sea
    Receives our Rivers, and yet seems not fuller:
    And if you tempt her more, the wind of fortune
    May come about, and take another point   70
    And blast your glories.
Prince. No,
    My glories are past danger, they're full blown:
    Things that are blasted, are but in their bud;
    And as for fortune, I nor love, nor fear her:
    I am resolv'd, go *Haly,* flatter still your aged Master,
    Still sooth him in his pleasures, and still grow
    Great by those arts.
    Well, farewell Court,
    Where vice not only hath usurp't the place,   80
    But the reward, and even the name of vertue.[11]

[10] *1668,* am. This was corrected in the errata.
1671, as above.
1684, as above.
[11] *1642,*
    But the reward, and even the name of vertue;
    Wee'le goe and hunt, it is a Princely sport
    And much resembles warre.

Ha. Still, still,
    Slighted and scorn'd; yet this affront
    Hath stampt a noble title on my malice,
    And married it to Justice. The King is old,
    And when the Prince succeeds,
    I'me lost past all recovery: then I
    Must meet my danger, and destroy him first;
    But cunningly, and closely, or his son
    And wife, like a fierce Tygress will devour me.   90
    There's danger every way; and since 'tis so,
    'Tis brave, and noble, when the falling weight
    Of my own ruine crushes those I hate:
    But how to do it, that's the work; he stands
    So high in reputation with the people,
    There's but one way, and that's to make his father
    The instrument, to give the name, and envy
    To him; but to my self the prize and glory.
    He's old and jealous, apt for suspitions,
    'Gainst which Tyrants ears   100
    Are never clos'd. The Prince is young,
    Fierce, and ambitious, I must bring together

Cap. Such warres as ours,
    Where we have us'd to follow chases.
Prince. It shews us pretty dangers, and acquaints us
    With scituations, while I view the hills,
    The thickets, and the rivers; here me-thinkes,
    With best advantage I could pitch my campe;
    Here range my Army, there the battaile joyne;
    Here make a safe retreat, and there enclose
    The enemie, as beasts within a toyle:
    And yet I can observe the chased Stagge,
    How he can cast about to seeke his safety;
    And when he sees his death is unavoydable,
    How he will weepe. I can observe the Dogs too,
    How some in swiftnesse, some in scent excell;
    Others in cry: But let us lose no time,
    Me-thinkes the Courts a prison.
                    Exeunt. Manet Haley.
Haly. Still, still, etc.

All these extreams, and then remove all Mediums,
That each may be the others object.

Enter Mirvan.

Mir. My Lord,
Now if your plots be ripe, you are befriended
With opportunity; the King is melancholy,
Apted for any ill impressions.
Make an advantage of the Princes absence,
Urge some suspected cause of his departure,   110
Use all your art: he's coming.

Exit Mir. Enter King.

Ha. Sir, have you known an action of such glory
Less swell'd with ostentation, or a mind
Less tainted with felicity? 'Tis a rare temper in the Prince.
King. Is it so rare to see a son so like
His Father? Have not I performed actions
As great, and with as great a moderation?
Ha. I Sir, but that's forgotten.
Actions o'th' last Age are like Almanacks o'th' last Year.
King. 'Tis well; but with all his conquests, what I get in Empire   120
I lose in fame: I think my self no gainer.
But am I quite forgotten?
Ha. Sir, you know
Age breeds neglect in all, and actions
Remote in time, like objects
Remote in place, are not beheld at half their greatness;
And what is new, finds better acceptation,
Than what is good or great: yet some old men
Tell Stories of you in their chimney corners.
King. No otherwise.   130
Ha. They're all so full of him: some magnifie
His courage, some his wit, but all admire
A greatness so familiar.
King. Sure *Haly*
Thou hast forgot thy self: art thou a Courtier,

Or I a King? my ears are unacquainted
With such bold truths; especially from thee.
Ha. Sir, when I am call'd to 't, I must speak
    Boldly and plainly.
King. But with what eagerness, what circumstance,   140
    Unaskt, thou tak'st such pains to tell me only
    My son's the better man.
Ha. Sir, where Subjects want the priviledge
    To speak; there Kings may have the priviledge,
    To live in ignorance.
King. If 'twere a secret that concern'd my life
    Or Empire, then this boldness might become thee;
    But such unnecessary rudeness savours
    Of some design.
    And this is such a false and squint-eyed praise,   150
    Which seeming to look upwards on his glories,
    Looks down upon my fears; I know thou hat'st him;
    And like infected persons fain wouldst rub
    The ulcer of thy malice upon me.
Ha. Sir, I almost believe you speak your thoughts,
    But that I want the guilt to make me fear it.
King. What mean these guilty blushes then?
Ha. Sir, if I blush, it is because you do not,
    To upbraid so try'd a servant, that so often
    Have wak'd that you might sleep; and been expos'd   160
    To dangers for your safety.
King. And therefore think'st
    Thou art so wrapt, so woven into all
    My trusts and counsels, that I now must suffer
    All thy Ambition aims at.
Ha. Sir, if your love grows weary,
    And thinks you have worn me long enough, I'me willing
    To be left off; but he's a foolish Sea-man,
    That when his Ship is sinking, will not
    Unlade his hopes into another bottom.   170
King. I understand no Allegories.

Ha. And he's as ill a Courtier, that when
    His Master's old, desires not to comply
    With him that must succeed.
King. But if he will not be comply'd with?
Ha. Oh Sir,
    There's one sure way, and I have known it practiz'd
    In other States.
King. What's that?
Ha. To make   180
    The Fathers life the price of the sons favour,
    To walk upon the graves of our dead Masters
    To our own security.

King starts and scratches his head.

Ha. aside. 'Tis this must take: Does this plainness please you Sir?
King. Haly: thou know'st my nature, too too apt
    To these suspitions; but I hope the question
    Was never mov'd to thee.
Ha. In other Kingdoms, Sir.
King. But has my Son no such design?
Ha.   Alas,   190
    You know I hate him; and should I tell you
    He had, you'd say it was but malice.
King. No more of that good *Haly,* I know thou lov'st me:
    But lest the care of future safety tempt thee
    To forfeit present loyalty; or present loyalty
    Forfeit thy future safety,
    Ile be your reconciler: call him hither.
Ha. Oh Sir, I wish he were within my call, or yours.
King. Why where is he?
Ha. He has left the Court, Sir.   200
King. I like not these Excursions, why so suddenly?
Ha. 'Tis but a sally of youth, yet some say he's discontented.
King. That grates my heart-strings. What should discontent him?
    Except he think I live too long.
Ha. Heaven forbid:
    And yet I know no cause of his departure;

I'me sure he's honoured, and lov'd by all;
The Souldiers god, the Peoples Idol.

King. I, *Haly,*
The Persians still worship the rising sun.   210
But who went with him?

Ha. None but the Captains.

King. The Captains? I like not that.

Ha. Never fear it, Sir:
'Tis true, they love him but as their General, not their Prince.
And though he be most forward and ambitious,
'Tis temper'd with so much humility.

King. And so much the more dangerous;
There are some that use
Humility to serve their pride, and seem   220
Humble upon their way, to be the prouder
At their wisht journeys end.

Ha. Sir, I know not
What ways or ends you mean; 'tis true
In popular States, or where the Princes Title
Is weak, & must be propt by the peoples power;
There by familiar ways 'tis necessary
To win on mens affections. But none of these
Can be his end.

King. But there's another end.   230
For if his glories rise upon the ruines
Of mine, why not his greatness too?

Ha. True Sir,
Ambition is like love, impatient
Both of delays and rivals. But Nature.—

King. But Empire.—

Ha. I had almost forgot Sir, he has
A suit to your Majesty.

King. What is't?

Ha. To give the Turkish prisoners some command   240
In the next action.

King. Nay, then 'tis too apparent,

He fears my Subjects loyalty,
And now must call in strangers; come deal plainly,
I know thou canst discover more.
Ha. I can discover (Sir)
The depth of your great judgment in such dangers.
King. What shall I do *Haly?*
Ha. Your wisdom is so great, it were presumption
For me to advise.   250
King. Well, we'll consider more of that, but for the present
Let him with speed be sent for. *Mahomet,* I thank thee
I have one faithful servant, honest *Haly.*

Exit King. Enter Mirvan.

Mir. How did he take it?
Ha. Swallow'd it as greedily
As parched earth drinks rain.
Now the first part of our design is over,
His ruine; but the second, our security,
Must now be thought on.
Mir. My Lord, you are too sudden; though his fury   260
Determine rashly, yet his colder fear
Before it executes, consults with reason,
And that not satisfied with shews, or shadows,
Will ask to be convinc'd by something real;
Now must we frame some plot, and then discover it.
Ha. Or intercept some Letter, which our selves
Had forg'd before.
Mir. And still admire the miracle,
And thank the providence.
Ha. Then we must draw in some body   270
To be the publick Agent, that may stand
'Twixt us and danger, and the peoples envy.
Mir. Who fitter than the grand *Caliph?*
And he will set a grave religious face
Upon the business.
Ha. But if we cannot work him,

For he's so full of foolish scruples;
Or if he should prove false, and then betray us.
Mir. Betray us? sure (my Lord) your fear has blinded
    Your understanding; for what serves the King?   280
    Will not his threats work more than our perswasions,
    While we look on, and laugh, and seem as ignorant
    As unconcern'd; and thus appearing friends
    To either side, on both may work our ends.

Enter Mess.

Mess. My Lord, the Turkish *Bashaws*
    Desire access.
Ha. Admit 'em, I know their business.
Mir. They long to hear with what success you mov'd
    The King in their behalf.
Ha. But now they're come, I'le make 'em do my business   290
    Better than I did theirs. *Mirvan*, leave us a while.[12]

Ex. Mir. Enter two Bashaws.

Ha. My Lords, my duty and affection to the Prince,
    And the respects I owe to men of honour,
     Extort a secret from me, which yet I grieve to utter:
    The Prince departing, left to me the care
    Of your affairs, which I, as he commanded,
    Have recommended to the King, but with so unlookt for
    A success—
1 Bas. My Lord, fear not to speak our doom, while we
    Fear not to hear it: we were lost before,   300
    And can be ready now to meet that fate
    We then expected.
Ha. Though he that brings unwelcom news
    Has but a losing Office, yet he that shews
    Your danger first, and then your way to safety,
    May heal that wound he made. You know the King
    With jealous eyes hath ever lookt awry

---

[12] *1668, Mir.* Leave us a while. It is obvious, however, that this is part of
Haly's speech.

On his Sons actions, but the fame and glory
Of the last war hath rais'd another spirit;
Envy and Jealousie are twin'd together,   310
Yet both lay hid in his dissembled smiles,
Like two concealed serpents, till I, unhappy I,
Moving this question, trod upon them both,
And rouz'd their sleeping angers; then casting from him
His doubts, and straight confirm'd in all his fears,
Decrees to you a speedy death, to his own son
A close restraint: but what will follow
I dare not think; you by a sudden flight
May find your safety.

2 Bas. Sir, Death and we are not such strangers,   320
That we should make dishonour, or ingratitude
The price of life; it was the Princes gift,
And we but wear it for his sake and service.

Ha. Then for his sake and service
Pray follow my advice: though you have lost the favour
Of your unworthy Master; yet in the Provinces
You lately governed, you have those dependances
And interests, that you may raise a power
To serve the Prince: Ile give him timely notice
To stand upon his guard.   330

1 Bas. My Lord, we thank you,
But we must give the Prince intelligence,
Both when, and how to imploy us.

Ha. If you will write,
Commit it to my care and secrecy,
To see it safe convey'd.

2 Bas. We shall my Lord.

Ex.

Ha. These men were once the Princes foes, and then
Unwillingly they made him great: but now
Being his friends, shall willingly undo him;   340
And which is more, be still his friends.
What little Arts govern the world! we need not

.An armed enemy, or corrupted friend;
When service but misplac'd, or love mistaken
Performs the work: nor is this all the use
I'le make of them; when once they are in Arms,
Their Master shall be wrought to think these forces
Rais'd against him; and this shall so endear me
To him, that though dull vertue and the gods
O'recome my subtle mischief, I may find   350
A safe retreat, and may at least be sure,
If not more mighty, to be more secure.

Exeunt.

Finis Actus Secundi.

Actus Tertius.

Scena Prima.

Enter King *and* Haly.

King. But *Haly,* what confederates has the Prince
        In his conspiracy?
Ha. Sir, I can yet suspect
        None but the Turkish prisoners, and that only
        From their late sudden flight.
King. Are they fled? For what?
Ha. That, their own fears best know; their entertainment
        I'me sure was such as could not minister
        Suspition, or dislike: but sure they're conscious
        Of some intended mischief, and are fled   10
        To put it into act.
King. This still confirms me more;
        But let 'em be pursu'd: let all the passages
        Be well secur'd, that no intelligence
        May pass between the Prince and them.
Ha. It shall be done, Sir.
King. Is the *Caliph* prepar'd?

Ha. He's without, Sir,
    And waits your pleasure.
King. Call him.   20

           Enter Haly *and* Caliph.

King. I have a great design to act, in which
    The greatest part is thine. In brief 'tis this,
    I fear my Sons high spirit; and suspect
    Designs upon my Life and Crown.
Ca. Sure, Sir, your fears are causeless;
    Such thoughts are strangers to his noble soul.
King. No, 'tis too true; I must prevent my danger,
    And make the first attempt: there's no such way
    To avoid a blow, as to strike first, and sure.
Ca. But, Sir, I hope my function shall exempt me   30
    From bearing any part in such designs.
King. Your function! (*Laughs*) Do you think that Princes
    Will raise such men so near themselves for nothing?
    We but advance you to advance our purposes:
    Nay, even in all Religions,
    Their Learned'st, and their seeming holiest men, but serve
    To work their Masters ends; and varnish o're
    Their actions, with some specious pious colour:
    No scruples; do 't, or by our holy Prophet,
    The death my rage intends to him, is thine.   40
Ca. Sir, 'tis your part to will, mine to obey.
King. Then be wise and sudden.

      Enter Lords as to Council, Ab., Mor.

Ca. My Lords, it grieves me to relate the cause
    Of this Assembly; and 'twill grieve you all:
    The prince you know stands high in all those graces
    Which Nature, seconded by fortune, gives:
    Wisdom he has, and to his Wisdom Courage;
    Temper to that, and unto all, Success.
    But Ambition, the disease of Virtue, bred
    Like surfets from an undigested fulness,   50

Meets death in that which is the means of life.
Great *Mahomet,* to whom our Soveraigns life,
And Empire is most dear, appearing, thus
Advis'd me in a Vision; Tell the King,
The Prince his Son attempts his Life & Crown;
And though no creature lives that more admires
His vertues, nor affects his person more
Than I; yet zeal and duty to my Soveraign
Have cancell'd all respects; nor must we slight
The Prophets Revelations.   60

Abd. Remember, Sir, he is your Son,
Indeared to you by a double bond,
As to his King, and Father.[13]

King. And the remembrance of that double bond
Doubles my sorrows. 'Tis true,
Nature and duty bind him to Obedience;
But those being placed in a lower sphere,
His fierce ambition, like the highest mover,
Has hurried with a strong impulsive motion
Against their proper course. But since he has forgot   70
The duty of a son, I can forget
The affections of a Father.

Abd. But, Sir, in the beginning of diseases
None try the extreamest remedies.

King. But when they're sudden,
The cure must be as quick; when I'me dead, you'll say,
My fears have been too slow: Treasons are acted,
As soon as thought, though they are ne're believed
Until they come to act.

Mor. But consider, Sir,   80
The greatness of the attempt, the people love him;
The lookers on, and the enquiring vulgar

13   "He's here in double trust;
       First as I am his kinsman and his subject,
       Strong both against the deed; then as his host . . ."
                          Macbeth, Act I, Sc. vii, ll. 12-14.

Will talk themselves to action: thus by avoyding
A danger but suppos'd, you tempt a real one.
King. Those Kings whom envy, or the peoples murmur
 Deters from their own purposes, deserve not
 Nor know not their own greatness;
 The peoples murmur, 'tis a sulphurous vapour
 Breath'd from the bowels of the basest earth;
 And it may soyl, and blast things near it self: 90
 But ere it reach the region we are plac'd in,
 It vanishes to ayr; we are above
 The sence or danger of such storms.
Ca.[14] True Sir, they are but storms while Royalty
 Stands like a Rock, and the tumultuous vulgar,
 Like billows rais'd with wind, (that's with opinion)
 May roar, and make a noise, and threaten;
 But if they rowl too near, they're dash't in pieces
 While they stand firm.
Abd. Yet Sir, Crowns are not plac'd so high,   100
 But vulgar hands may reach 'em.
King. Then 'tis when they are plac'd on vulgar heads.
Abd. But Sir,
 Look back upon your self; why should your son
 Anticipate a hope so near, so certain?
 We may wish and pray
 For your long life: but neither prayers nor power
 Can alter Fates decree, or Natures Law.
 Why should he ravish then that Diadem
 From your gray temples, which the hand of time 110
 Must shortly plant on his?
King. My Lords,
 I see you look upon me as a Sun
 Now in his West, half buryed in a cloud,
 Whose rays the vapours of approaching night
 Have rendred weak and faint: But you shall find
 That I can yet shoot beams, whose heat can melt

[14] All the texts read "Cap."

.The waxen wings of this ambitious Boy.
Nor runs my bloud so cold, nor is my arm
So feeble yet, but he that dares defend him,   120
Shall feel my vengeance, and shall usher me
Into my grave.
Ab.   Sir, we defend him not,
Only desire to know his crime: 'Tis possible
It may be some mistake, or mis-report,
Some false suggestion, or malicious scandal:
Or if ambition be his fault, 'twas yours;
He had it from you when he had his being:
Nor was't his fault, nor yours, for 'tis in Princes
A crime to want it; from a noble spirit
Ambition can no more be separated,   130
Than heat from fire: Or if you fear the Vision,
Will you suspect the noble Prince, because
This holy man is troubled in his sleep?
Because his crazy stomach wants concoction,
And breeds ill fumes; or his melancholy spleen
Sends up phantastick vapours to his brain:
Dreams are but dreams, these causeless fears become not
Your noble soul.
King.   Who speaks another word
Hath spoke his last: Great *Mahomet* we thank thee,
Protector of this Empire, and this life,   140
Thy cares have met my fears; this on presumptions
Strong and apparent, I have long presag'd:
And though a Prince may punish what he fears,
Without account to any but the Gods;
Wise States as often cut off ills that may be,
As those that are; and prevent purposes
Before they come to practise; and foul practises
Before they grow to act. You cannot but observe
How he dislikes the Court, his rude departure,
His honour from the people and the souldiers,   150
His seeking to oblige the Turks, his prisoners,

Their sudden and suspected flight:
And above all, his restless towring thoughts.[15]

King. If the business be important,
Admit him.

Enter Messenger[16] with a letter.

Mess.[17]   Sir, upon your late command
To guard the passages, and search all packets,
This to the Prince was intercepted.

King opens it, and reads it to himself.

King.   Here *Abdal*, read it.

Abdal reads. The Letter.

Ab. reads. Sir, we are assured how unnaturally your fathers in-
tentions are towards you, and how cruel towards us; we
have made an escape, not so much to seek our own, as to be   160
instruments of your safety: We will be in arms upon the
borders, upon your command, either to seek danger with you,
or to receive you if you please, to seek safety with us.

King. Now my Lords,
Alas my fears are causless, and ungrounded,
Fantastick dreams, and melancholick fumes
Of crazy stomacks, and distempered brains:
Has this convinc'd you?

Mor. Sir, we see
Some reason you should fear, but whom, we know not;   170
'Tis possible these Turks may play the Villains,
Knowing the Prince, the life of all our hopes,
Staff of our Age, and pillar of our Empire;
And having fail'd by force, may use this Art

---

[15] *1668* has the stage direction, *A horn winded without*. This was struck out
in the errata.
1671, as above.
1684, as above.
[16] *1668, post*. This was corrected in the errata.
1671, as above.
1684, as above.
[17] *1668, Post*. Here corrected to conform to change under note 16 above.

To ruine him, and by their treason here
To make their peace at home.
Now should this prove a truth, when he has suffered
Death, or disgrace, which are to him the same;
'Twill be too late to say you were mistaken;
And then to cry him mercy: Sir, we beseech you   180
A while suspend your doom, till time produce
Her wonted off-spring, Truth.
King.   And so expecting
The event of what you think, shall prove the experiment
Of what I fear; but since he is my son,
I cannot have such violent thoughts toward him,
As his towards me: he only shall remain
A prisoner till his death or mine enlarge him.

Ex. Lords. Man. Haly. Solyman peeps in.

King. Away, away, we're serious.
Sol. But not so serious to neglect your safety.
King. Art thou in earnest?   190
Sol. Nay Sir, I can be serious as well as my betters.
King. What's the matter?
Sol. No, I am an inconsiderable fellow, and know nothing.
King. Let's hear that nothing then.
Sol. The Turks, Sir.
King. What of them?
Sol. When they could not overcome you by force, they'll do it by
    treachery.
King. As how?
Sol. Nay I can see as far into a milstone, as another man.   200
    They have corrupted some ill-affected persons.
King. What to do?
Sol. To nourish Jealousies 'twixt you and your Son.
King. My son! Where is he?
Sol. They say he's posting hither.
King. Haly, we are betrayed, prevented, look
    To the Ports, and let

The Guards be doubled: how far's his Army hence?
Is the City in arms to joyn with him?

Sol. Arms? and joyn with him? I understand you not.   210

King. Didst thou not say the Prince was coming?

Sol. I heard some foolish people say you had sent for him,
as a Traytor, which to my apprehension was on purpose
spoken to make you odious, and him desperate; and so
divide the people into faction. A Plot of dangerous con-
sequence, as I take it, Sir.

King. And is this all, thou sawcy trifling fool?[18]

Haly. Sir, this seeming fool is a concealed dangerous
knave; Under that safe disguise he thinks he may say
or do any thing: you'll little think him the chief con-   220
spirator, the only spy t'inform the Prince of all is
done in Court.

King. Let him be rack't,[19] till he confess
The whole conspiracy.

Sol. Rackt![20] I have told you all I know, and more;
There's nothing more in me, Sir, but may be squeezed
out without racking, only a stoop or two of Wine;
and if there had not been too much of that, you had
not had so much of the other.

King. That's your cunning, sirrah.   230

Sol. Cunning, Sir! I am no Politician; and was ever
thought to have too little wit, and too much plain deal-
ing for a States-man.

Exit.

King. Away with him.

Ha.   But something must be done, Sir,
To satisfie the people:
'Tis not enough to say he did design,
Or plot, or think, but did attempt some violence;
And then some strange miraculous escape:

[18] *1642*, adds, away with him!
[19] *1642*, adds, and tortured.
[20] *1642*, adds, and Tortured.

For which our Prophet must have publick thanks: 240
And this false colour shall delude the eyes
Of the amused[21] vulgar.
King.   'Tis well advis'd.

Enter Mess.

Mess. Sir, his Highness is return'd.
King. And unconstrain'd? But with what change of countenance
    Did he receive the message?
Mess. With some amazement;
    But such as sprung from wonder, not from fear;
    It was so unexpected.
King. Leave us.
    Haly, I ever found thee honest; truer to me   250
    Than mine own bloud, and now's the time to shew it:
    For thou art he my love and trust hath chosen
    To put in action my design: surprize him
    As he shall pass the Galleries. I'le place
    A guard behind the Arras; when thou hast him,
    Since blinded with ambition, he did soar
    Like a seel'd Dove; his crime shall be his punishment
    To be depriv'd of sight, which see perform'd
    With a hot steel: Now as thou lov'st my safety
    Be resolute, and sudden.
Ha.   'Tis severe;   260
    But yet I dare not intercede, it shall be done:
    But is that word irrevocable?
King. I, as years, or ages past; relent not, if thou do'st—

Exit King. Enter Mirvan.

Mir. Why so melancholy? is the design discovered?
Ha. No, but I am made the instrument,
    That still endeavoured to disguise my plots
    With borrowed looks, and make 'em walk in darkness,

[21] *1668,* amazed. This was corrected in the errata.
1671, as above.
1684, as above.

To act 'em now my self; be made the mark
For all the peoples hate, the Princes[22] curses,
And his sons rage, or the old Kings inconstancy.   270
For this to Tyranny belongs,
To forget service, but remember wrongs.

Mir. But could you not contrive
Some fine pretence to cast it on some other?

Ha. No, he dare trust no other: had I given
But the least touch of any private quarrel,
My malice to his son, not care of him,
Had then begot this service.

Mir. 'Tis but t'other plot, my Lord; you know
The King by other wives had many sons: 280
Soffy is but a Child, and you already
Command the Emperours Guard; procure for me
The Government o'th' City; when he dies,
Urge how unfortunate those States have been
Whose Princes are but children: then set the Crown
Upon some others head, that may acknowledge
And owe the Empire to your gift.

Ha. It shall be done; *Abdal,* who commands
The City, is the Princes friend, and therefore
Must be displac'd, and thou shalt straight succeed him.   290
Thou art my better Genius, honest *Mirvan;*
Greatness we owe to Fortune, or to Fate;
But wisdom only can secure that state.

    Ex. Enter Prince at one door, and Princess at another.

Princess. You're double welcom now (my Lord) your coming
Was so unlookt for.

Prince. To me I'me sure it was;
Know'st thou the cause? for sure it was important,
That calls me back so suddenly.

Princess. I am so ignorant,
I knew not you were sent for.   300
Waking I know no cause, but in my sleep

22 *1668,* Princess.

My fancy still presents such dreams, and terrors,
As did *Andromache's* the night before
Her *Hector* fell; but sure 'tis more than fancy.
Either our Guardian Angels, or the Gods
Inspire us, or some natural instinct
Fore-tells approaching dangers.
Prince. How does my Father?
Princess. Still talks and plays with *Fatyma,* but his mirth
   Is forc'd, and strain'd: In his look appears   310
   A wild distracted fierceness; I can read
   Some dreadful purpose in his face; but where
   This dismal cloud will break, and spend his fury,
   I dare not think: pray heaven make false his fears.
   Sometimes his anger breaks through all disguises,
   And spares not gods, nor men; and then he seems
   Jealous of all the world: suspects, and starts,
   And looks behind him.

Enter Morat, as in haste.

Mor. Sir, with hazard of my life I've ventur'd
   To tell you, you are lost, betray'd, undone;   320
   Rouze up your courage, call up all your counsels,
   And think on all those stratagems which nature
   Keeps ready to encounter sudden dangers.
Prince. But pray (my Lord) by whom? for what offence?
Mor. Is it a time for story, when each minute
   Begets a thousand dangers? the gods protect you.

Ex.

Prince. This man was ever honest, and my friend,
   And I can see in his amazed look,
   Something of danger; but in act or thought,
   I never did that thing should make me fear it.   330
Princess. Nay, good Sir, let not so secure a confidence
   Betray you to your ruine.
Prince.   Prethee woman
   Keep to thy self thy fears, I cannot know

There is such a thing in nature.[23] I stand so strong,
Inclosed with a double guard of Vertue,
And Innocence, that I can look on dangers,
As he that stands upon a Rock
Can look on storms and tempests. Fear & guilt
Are the same thing; & when our actions are not,
Our fears are crimes.   340
And he deserves it less that guilty bears
A punishment, than he that guiltless fears.

Ex. Enter Haly and Torturers.

Ha. This is the place appointed, assist me courage!
This hour ends all my fears; but pause a while:
Suppose I should discover to the Prince
The whole conspiracy, and so retort it
Upon the King; it were an handsom plot,
But full of difficulties, and uncertain;
And he's so fool'd with down-right honesty,
He'l ne're believe it; and now 'tis too late;   350
The guards are set, and now I hear him coming.

Enter Prince, stumbles at the entrance.

Prince. 'Tis ominous, but I will on; destruction
O'retakes as often those that fly, as those
That boldly meet it.
Ha. By your leave Prince, your father greets you.
Prince. Unhand me traytors.

Haly casts a scarf over his face.

Ha. That title is your own, and we are sent
To let you know it.
Prince. Is not that the voice of *Haly?*[24]

---

[23] *1668,* That there is such a thing. This was corrected in the errata.
1671, as above.
1684, as above.
[24] *1668,* adds, that thunders in my ears? This was struck out in the errata.
1671, as above.
1684, as above.

Ha. I, vertuous Prince, I come to make you exercise   360
　　One vertue more, your patience. (Heat the Irons quickly.)
Prince. Insolent villain, for what cause?
Ha. Only to gaze upon a while, until your eyes are out.
Prince. O villain, shall I not see my Father,
　　To ask him what's my crime? who my accusers?
　　Let me but try if I can wake his pity
　　From his Lethargick sleep.
Ha. It must not be, Sir.
Prince. Shall I not see my wife, nor bid farewell
　　To my dear Children?   370
Ha. Your pray'rs are all in vain.
Prince. Thou shalt have half my Empire *Haly*, let me
　　But see the Tyrant, that before my eyes are lost,
　　They may dart poys'nous flashes like the Basilisk,
　　And look him dead: These eyes that still were open,
　　Or to fore-see, or to prevent his dangers,
　　Must they be closed in eternal night?
　　Cannot his thirst of bloud be satisfied
　　With any but his own? And can his tyranny
　　Find out no other object but his Son?   380
　　I seek not mercy; tell him, I desire
　　To die at once, not to consume an age
　　In lingring deaths.
Ha. Our ears are charm'd: Away with him.
Prince. Can ye behold (ye Gods) a wronged Innocent?
　　Or sleeps your Justice, like my Fathers Mercy?
　　Or are you blind? as I must be.

Finis Actus Tertii.

Actus Quartus.

Enter Abdal and Morat.

Ab. I ever fear'd the Princes too much greatness
　　Would make him less: the greatest heights are near
　　The greatest precipice.

Mor. 'Tis in worldly accidents
 As in the world it self, where things most distant
 Meet one another: Thus the East and West,
 Upon the Globe, a Mathematick point
 Only divides: Thus happiness and misery,
 And all extreams are still contiguous.
Ab. Or, if 'twixt happiness and misery there be   10
 A distance, 'tis an Aery *Vacuum;*
 Nothing to moderate, or break the fall.
Mor. But oh this Saint-like Devil!
 This damned *Caliph,* to make the King believe
 To kill his son, 's religion.
Ab. Poor Princes, how they are mis-led!
 While they, whose sacred Office 'tis to bring
 Kings to obey their God, and men their King;
 By these mysterious links to fix and tie
 Them to the foot-stool of the Deity;   20
 Even by these men, Religion, that should be
 The curb, is made the spur to tyranny:
 They with their double key of conscience bind
 The Subjects souls, and leave Kings unconfin'd;
 While their poor Vassals sacrifice their blouds
 T' Ambition; and to Avarice, their goods:
 Blind with Devotion. They themselves esteem
 Made for themselves, and all the world for them;
 While heavens great Law, given for their guide, appears
 Just, or unjust, but as it waits on theirs: 30
 Us'd, but to give the eccho to their words,
 Power to their wills, and edges to their swords.
 To varnish all their errors, and secure
 The ills they act, and all the world endure.
 Thus by their arts Kings aw the world, while they,
 Religion, as their Mistress, seem t' obey;
 Yet as their slave command her: while they seem
 To rise to heaven, they make heaven stoop to them.
Mor. Nor is this all, where feign'd devotion bends

The highest things, to serve the lowest ends: 40
For if the many-headed beast hath broke,
Or shaken from his neck the royal yoke,
With popular rage, Religion doth conspire,
Flows into that, and swells the torrent higher;
Then powers first pedigree from force derives,
And calls to mind the old prerogatives
Of free-born man; and with a saucy eye
Searches the heart and soul of Majesty:
Then to a strict account, and censure brings
The actions, errors, and the end of Kings;   50
Treads on authority, and sacred Laws;
Yet all for God, and his pretended cause,
Acting such things for him, which he in them,
And which themselves in others will condemn;
And thus engag'd, nor safely can retire,
Nor safely stand, but blindly bold aspire,
Forcing their hopes, even through despair, to climb
To new attempts; disdain the present time,
Grow from disdain to threats, from threats to arms;
While they (though sons of peace) still sound th'alarms: 60
Thus whether Kings or people seek extreams,
Still conscience and religion are their Theams:
And whatsoever change the State invades,
The pulpit either forces, or perswades.
Others may give the fewel, or the fire;
But they the breath, that makes the flame, inspire.[25]
Ab. This, and much more is true, but let not us
Add to our ills, and aggravate misfortunes
By passionate complaints, nor lose our selves,
Because we have lost him; for if the Tyrant   70
Were to a son so noble, so unnatural;
What will he be to us, who have appear'd
Friends to that son?

[25] 17-66 reprinted as separate poem with the title "Verses" in *The Fifth Part of Miscellany Poems . . . Publish'd by Mr. Dryden . . . the Fourth Edition,* 1716. *The Fifth Edition,* 1727.

Mor.   Well thought on, and in time;
 Farewel, unhappy Prince, while we thy friends,
 As strangers to our Countrey, and our selves,
 Seek out our safety, and expect with patience
 Heavens Justice.

Ab. Let's rather act it, than expect it:
 The Princes injuries at our hands require
 More than our tears, and patience: 80
 His Army is not yet disbanded,
 And only wants a head; thither we'll fly,
 And all who love the Prince, or hate the Tyrant,
 Will follow us.

Mor. Nobly resolv'd; and either we'll restore
 The Prince, or perish in the brave attempt.
 Ye Gods, since what we mean to execute,
 Is your high office (to avenge the innocent)
 Assist us with a fortune, equal to
 The justice of our action; lest the world   90
 Should think it self deluded, and mistrust
 That you want will, or power to be just.

Ex. Enter Haly.

Ha. 'Tis done, and 'twas my master-piece, to work
 My safety 'twixt two dangerous extreams;
 Now like a skilful sayler have I past
 Scylla and *Charybdis,* I have scap't the rock
 Of steep Ambition, and the gulf of Jealousie,
 A danger less avoyded, 'cause less fear'd.

Enter Mirvan.

Mir. What's done, my Lord?
Ha.   Enough, I warrant you;
 Imprison'd, and depriv'd of sight.   100

Mir. No more? This but provokes him: Can you think
 Your self secure, and he alive?

Ha. The rest o'th' business will do it self;
 He can as well endure a prison, as a wild Bull the net:

There let him struggle, and toyl himself to death,
And save us so much envy.
Mir. But if his Father should relent, such injuries
Can receive no excuse or colour, but to be
Transfer'd upon his Counsellours; and then
The forfeiture of them redeems his errour. 110
Ha. We must set a mark upon his passion,
And as we find it running low,
What ebbs from his, into our rage shall flow.
Why, should we be more wicked
Than we must needs?
Mir. Nay, if you stick at Conscience,
More gallant actions have been lost, for want of being
Compleatly wicked, than have been perform'd
By being exactly vertuous. 'Tis hard to be
Exact in good, or excellent in ill;
Our will wants power, or else our power wants skill. 120

Ex. Enter Solyman, and Tormentors.

Sol. But Gentlemen, was the King in earnest?
I can scarce believe it.
Tor. You will when you feel it.
Sol. I pray, have any of you felt it, to tell me what it is?
Tor. No, Sir, but
Some of your fellow Courtiers can tell you,
That use something like it, to mend their shapes.
'Twill make you so straight and slender!
Sol. Slender! because I was slender in my wits, must I be
drawn slender in my waste? I'de rather grow wise, and 130
corpulent, like him they call *Abdomen*.[26]
Tor. Come, Sir, 'tis but a little stretching.
Sol. No, no more's hanging; and sure this will be the death of
me: I remember my Grandmother died of Convulsion fits.
Tor. Come, Sir, prepare, prepare.
Sol. I, for another world: I must repent first.
Tor. Quickly then.

[26] *1642*, omits, like him they call abdomen.

Sol. Then first I repent that sin of being a Courtier. And
    secondly, the greatest sin one can commit in that place,
    the speaking of truth.   140

Tor. Have you no more sins?

Sol. Some few trifles more, not worth the remembring; drink-
    ing, and whoring, and swearing, and such like: but for
    those let 'em pass.

Tor. Have you done now?

Sol. Only some good counsel to the standers by.

Tor. We thank you for that, Sir.

Sol. Nay, Gentlemen, mistake me not; 'tis not that I love
    you, but because 'tis a thing of course for dying men.

Tor. Let's have it then.   150

Sol. First then, if any of you are fools (as I think that
    but a needless question) be fools still, and labour
    still in that vocation, then the worst will be but whip-
    ping; where, but for seeming wise, the best is racking.
    But if you have the luck to be Court-fools, those that
    have either wit or honesty, you may fool withal, and spare
    not: but for those that want either, you'll find it rather
    dangerous than otherwise; I could give you a modern in-
    sance[27] or two, but let that pass: but if you happen to
    be State-fools, then 'tis but fooling on the right side,   160
    and all's well; then you shall at least be wise mens fel-
    lows, if not wise mens masters. But of all things take
    heed of giving any man good counsel, you see what I have
    got by it; and yet like a fool, must I be doing on 't again.

Tor. Is this all?

Sol. All, but a little in my own behalf. Remember, Gentle-
    men, I am at full growth, and my joynts are knit; and
    yet my sinews are not Cables.

Tor. Well, we'll remember 't.

Sol. But stay, Gentlemen, what think you of a bottle now?   170

Tor. I hope you are more serious.

---

27   "Full of wise saws and modern instances."
                           As You Like It, Act II, Sc. vii, l. 156.

Sol. If you knew but how dry a thing this sorrow is, espe-
cially meeting with my constitution; which is as
thirsty as any Serving-mans.

Tor. Let him have it, it may be 'twill make him confess.

Sol. Yes, I shall, I shall lay before you all that's within
me, and with most fluent utterance. Here's to you
all Gentlemen, and let him that's good natur'd in
his drink, pledge me.

(*Drinks*)

So, me-thinks I feel it in my joynts   180
already, it makes 'em supple.

(*Drinks again*)

Now I feel it in my brains,
it makes 'em swim.[28]

Tor. Hold, Sir, you have no measure of your self.

Sol. What do you talk of measure, you'll take measure
of me with a vengeance?

Tor. You are witty, Sir.

Sol. Nothing but a poor clinch; I have a thousand of them
(a trick I learn't amongst the States-men.)

(*Drinks again*)

Well rack, I defie thee, do thy worst; I would thou wer't
Man, Gyant, or Monster. Gentlemen, now if I happen to   190
fall asleep upon this Engine, pray wake me not to sud-
denly; you see here's good store of wine, and if it be
over-rackt, 'twill come up with lees and all; there I
was with you again, and now I am for you.

Exeunt. Enter Prince, being blind, solus.

Prince. Nature,
How didst thou mock mankind to make him free
And yet to make him fear; or when he lost
That freedom, why did he not lose his fear?

---

[28] *1642*, adds as if the racke would be a shipwracke, and transposes the two
following pairs of speeches.

That fear of fears, the fear of what we know not,
While yet we know it is in vain to fear it: 200
Death, and what follows death, 'twas that that stamp't
A terrour on the brow of Kings; that gave
Fortune her Deity, and *Jove* his thunder.
Banish but fear of death, those Giant names
Of Majesty, Power, Empire, finding nothing
To be their object, will be nothing too:
Then he dares yet be free that dares to die,
May laugh at the grim face of Law and scorn
The cruel wrinkle of a Tyrants brow:
But yet to die so tamely,   210
O'recome by passion and misfortune,
And still unconquer'd by my foes, sounds ill;
Below the temper of my spirit:
Yet to embrace a life so poor, so wretched,
So full of deaths, argues a greater dulness;
But I am dead already, nor can suffer
More in the other world. For what is Hell,
But a long sleepless night? and what's their torment,
But to compare past joyes with present sorrows?
And what can death deprive me of? the sight   220
Of day, of children, friends, and hope of Empire;
And whatsoever others lose in death,
In life I am depriv'd of; then I will live
Only to die reveng'd: nor will I go
Down to the shades alone.
Prompt me some witty, some revengeful Devil,
His Devil that could make a bloudy feast
Of his own son, and call the gods his guests;
Hers that could kill her aged Sire, and cast
Her Brothers scatter'd limbs to Wolves and Vultures;   230
Or his that slew his Father, to enjoy
His mothers bed; and greater than all those,
My fathers Devil.
Come mischief, I embrace thee; fill my soul:

And thou Revenge ascend, and bear the Scepter
O're all my passions; banish thence
All that are cool, and tame.
Know old Tyrant,
My heart's too big to break, I know thy fears
Exceed my sufferings; and my revenge,   240
Though but in hope, is much a greater pleasure
Than thou canst take in punishing. Then my anger
Sink to the Center of my heart, and there
Lie close in ambush, till my seeming patience
Hath made the cruel Tyrant as secure,
Though with as little cause, as now he's jealous.
Who's[29] there?

                    Enter two or three.

            I find my nature would return
To her old course, I feel an inclination
To some repose; welcome thou pleasing slumber:
A while embrace me in thy leaden arms,   250
And charm my careful thoughts:
Conduct me to my bed.

            Exit. Enter King, Haly and Caliph.

King. How do's the Prince? how bears he his restraint?
Ha. Why, Sir, as all great spirits
            Bear great and sudden changes, with such impatience
            As a *Numidian* Lion, when first caught,
            Endures the toyl that holds him.
            He would think of nothing
            But present death, and sought all violent means
            To compass it. But time hath mitigated   260
            Those furious heats, he now returns to food
            And sleep, admits the conversation
            Of those that are about him.

[29]*1668,* whose.
1671, who's.
1684, whose.

King. I would I had not
    So easily believ'd my fears, I was too sudden;
    I would it were undone.
Cal.   If you lament it,
    That which now looks like Justice, will be thought
    An inconsiderate rashness.
King. But there are in nature
    Such strong returns! That I punisht him,   270
    I do not grieve; but that he was my Son.
Ha. But it concerns you to bear up your passion,
    And make it good; for if the people know,
    That you have cause to grieve for what is done,
    They'll think you had no cause at first to do it.
King to the Ca. Go visit him from me, and teach him patience;
    Since neither all his fury, nor my sorrow
    Can help what's past, tell him my severity
    To him shall in some measure be requited,
    By my indulgence to his children. And if he   280
    Desire it, let them have access to him:
    Endeavour to take off his thoughts from revenge,
    By telling him of Paradise, and I know not
    What pleasures in the other world.
Cal.   I shall, Sir.

Ex. King and C. Ma. Haly. Enter Mirvan.

Ha. Mirvan, The King relents, and now there's left
    No refuge but the last; he must be poysoned:
    And suddenly, lest he survive his Father.
Mir. But handsomly, lest it appear.
Ha.   Appear!
    To whom? you know there's none about him
    But such as I have plac't; and they shall say   290
    'Twas discontent, or abstinence.
Mir. But at the best
    'Twill be suspected.
Ha.   Why though't be known,
    We'll say he poysoned himself.

Mir. But the curious will pry further
  Than bare report, and the old King's suspitions
  Have piercing eyes.
Ha. But those nature
  Will shortly close: you see his old disease
  Grows strong upon him.   300
Mir. But if he should recover?
Ha. But I have cast his Nativity; he cannot, he must not.
  I'th' mean time I have so besieg'd him,
  So blockt up all the passages, and plac'd
  So many Centinels and Guards upon him,
  That no intelligence can be convey'd
  But by my instruments. But this business will require
  More heads and hands than ours: Go you to the prison,
  And bring the Keeper privately to me,
  To give him his instructions.   310

    Ex. several ways. Enter Prince and Caliph.

Cal. Sir, I am
  Commanded by the King to visit you.
Prince. What, to give a period to my life,
  And to his fears? You're welcome; here's a throat,
  A heart, or any other part, ready to let
  In death, and receive his commands.
Ca.   My Lord,
  I am no messenger, nor minister
  Of death, 'tis not my function.
Prince. I should know that voice.
Ca. I am the *Caliph*, and am come to tell you, your Father 320
  Is now return'd to himself: Nature has got
  The victory o're passion, all his rigour
  Is turn'd to grief and pity.
Prince.   Alas good man!
  I pity him, and his infirmities;
  His doubts, and fears, and accidents of age,
  Which first provok'd his cruelty.
Ca. He bid me tell you,

His love to yours should amply recompence
His cruelty to you: And I dare say 'tis real;
For all his thoughts, his pleasures, and delights,   330
Are fixt on *Fatyma*: when he is sad,
She comforts him; when sick, she's his Physitian,
And were it not for the delight he takes
In her, I think hee'd die with sorrow.
Prince. But how, are his affections fixt so strangely
On her alone? sure 'tis not in his nature;
For then he had lov'd me, or hated her,
Because she came from me.
Ca.   'Tis her desert,
She's fair beyond comparison, and witty
Above her age; and bears a manly spirit   340
Above her sex.
Prince.   But may not I admire her?
Is that too great a happiness? pray let
Her make it her next suit to be permitted
To visit me her self.
Ca. She shall, Sir: I joy to see your mind
So well compos'd; I fear'd I should have found
A tempest in your soul, and came to lay it.
I'le to the King; I know to him that news
Will be most acceptable.
Prince. Pray do, and tell him   350
I have cast off all my passions, and am now
A man again; fit for society
And conversation.
Ca. I will Sir.

Exit.

Prince. I never knew my self till now; how on the sudden
I'me grown an excellent dissembler, to out-do
One at the first, that has practiz'd it all his life:
So now I am my self again, what is 't
I feel within? Me thinks some vast design
Now takes possession of my heart, and swells   360

My labouring thoughts above the common bounds
Of humane actions, something full of horror
My soul hath now decreed, my heart does beat,
As if 'twere forging thunder-bolts for *Jove*,
To strike the Tyrant dead: So now, I have it,
I have it, 'tis a gallant mischief,
Worthy my Father, or my Fathers Son.
All his delight's in *Fatyma*, poor innocent!
But not more innocent than I, and yet
My Father loves thee, and that's crime enough.   370
By this act, old Tyrant,
I shall be quit with thee: while I was virtuous,
I was a stranger to thy bloud, but now
Sure thou wilt love me for this horrid crime,
It is so like thy own. In this I'm sure,
Although in nothing else, I am thy Son:
But when 'tis done, I leave him yet that remedy
I take my self, Revenge; but I as well
Will rob him of his anger, as his joy,
And having sent her to the shades, I'le follow her.   380
But to return again, and dwell
In his dire thoughts, for there's the blacker hell.

Enter Messenger.

Mess. Sir, your wife the Princess is come to visit you.
Prince. Conduct her in; now to my disguise again.

Enter Princess.

Princess. Is this my Lord the Prince?
Prince. That's *Erythæa*, or some Angel voyc't
    Like her. 'Tis she, my strugling soul would fain
    Go out to meet and welcome her. *Erythæa!*
    No answer but in sighs (dear *Erythæa?*)
    Thou cam'st to comfort, to support my sufferings,   390
    Not to oppress me with a greater weight,
    To see that my Unhappiness
    Involves thee too.

Princess. My Lord, in all your triumphs and your glories,
      You call'd me into all your joys, and gave me
      An equal share, and in this depth of misery
      Can I be unconcern'd? you needs must know,
      You needs must hope I cannot; or which is worse,
      You must suspect my love: for what is love
      But sympathy? And this I make my happiness,   400
      Since both cannot be happy,
      That we can both be miserable.

Prince. I prithee do not say thou lovest me;
      For love, or finds out equals, or makes 'em so:
      But I am so cast down, and fal'n so low,
      I cannot rise to thee, and dare not wish
      Thou should'st descend to me; but call it pity,
      And I will own it then, that Kings may give
      To beggars, and not lessen their own greatness.

Princess. Till now I thought virtue had stood above   410
      The reach of fortune; but if virtue be not,
      Yet love's a greater Deity: whatever fortune
      Can give or take, love wants not, or despises;
      Or by his own omnipotence supplies:
      Then like a God with joy beholds
      The beauty of his own Creations.
      Thus what we form and image to our fancies,
      We really possess.

Prince. But can thy imagination
      Delude it self, to fix upon an object   420
      So lost in miseries, so old in sorrows;
      Paleness and death hang on my cheek, and darkness
      Dwells in my eyes;[30] more chang'd from what I was
      In person than in fortune.

[30]   "Art thou so bare, and full of wretchedness,
         And fear'st to die? famine is in thy cheeks,
         Need and oppression starveth in thine eyes,
         Contempt and beggary hang upon thy back."
                          Romeo and Juliet, Act V, Sc. i, ll. 68-71.

Princess. Yet still the same to me: alas my Lord,
    These outward beauties are but the props and scaffolds
    On which we built our love, which now made perfect,
    Stands without those supports: nor is my flame
    So earthy as to need the dull material fuel
    Of eyes, or lips, or cheeks, still to be kindled,   430
    And blown by appetite, or else t' expire:
    My fires are purer, and like those of Heaven,
    Fed only, and contented with themselves,
    Need nothing from without.
Prince. But the disgrace that waites upon misfortune,
    The meer reproach, the shame of being miserable,
    Exposes men to scorn and base contempt,
    Even from their nearest friends.
Princess. Love is so far from scorning misery,
    That he delights in 't, and is so kindly cruel,   440
    Sometimes to wish it, that he may be alone;
    Instead of all, of fortunes, honours, friends, which are
    But meer diversions from loves proper object,
    Which only is it self.
Prince.   Thou hast almost
    Taught me to love my miseries, and forgive
    All my misfortunes. I'le at least forget 'em;
    We will revive those times, and in our memories
    Preserve, and still keep fresh (like flowers in water)
    Those happier days: when at our eyes our souls
    Kindled their mutual fires, their equal beams   450
    Shot and returned, till linkt, and twin'd in one,
    They chain'd our hearts together.
Princess. And was it just, that fortune should begin
    Her tyranny, where we began our loves?
    No, if it had, why was not I blind too?
    I'm sure if weeping could have don't, I had been.
Prince. Think not that I am blind, but think it night,
    A season for our loves, and which to lovers
    Ne're seems too long; and think of all our miseries,

But as some melancholy dream which has   460
Awak't us, to the renewing of our joys.
Princess. My Lord, this is a temper
    Worthy the old Philosophers.
Prince. I but repeat that lesson
    Which I have learnt from thee. All this morality
    Thy love hath taught me.
Princess.   My Lord, you wrong your virtue,
   T' ascribe the effect of that to any cause
    Less noble than it self.
Prince.   And you your love,
    To think it is less noble, or less powerful,
    Than any the best virtue: and I fear thy love   470
    Will wrong it self; so long a stay will make
    The jealous King suspect we have been plotting:
    How do the pledges of our former love;
    Our Children?
Princess. Both happy in their Grandsires love, especially
    The pretty *Fatyma;* yet she
    According to her apprehension feels
    A sence of your misfortunes.
Prince. But let her not too much express it,
    Lest she provoke his fury.   480
Princess. She only can allay it
    When 'tis provok't; she
    Plays with his rage, and gets above his anger;
    As you have seen a little boat
    To mount and dance upon the wave, that threatens
    To overwhelm it.
Prince. To threaten is to save, but his anger
    Strikes us like thunder, where the blow out-flies
    The loud report, and even prevents mens fears.
Princess. But then like thunder   490
    It rends a Cedar, or an Oak, or finds
    Some strong resisting matter; women and children
    Are not Subjects worthy a Princes anger.

Prince. Whatsoever
    Is worthy of their love is worth their anger.
Princess. Love's a more natural motion; they are angry
    As Princes, but love as men.
Prince.   Once more I beg,
    Make not thy love thy danger.
Princess. My Lord, I see with what unwillingness
    You lay upon me this command, and through your fears   500
    Discern your love, and therefore must obey you.

Exit.

Prince. Farewell my dearest *Erythœa.*
    There's a strange musick in her voice, the story
    Of *Orpheus,* which appears so bold a fiction,
    Was prophecy'd of thee; thy voyce has tam'd
    The Tygers and the Lions of my soul.

Enter Messenger.

Mess. Sir, your daughter *Fatyma.*
Prince. Conduct her in; how strangely am I tempted
    With opportunity, which like a sudden gust
    Hath swell'd my calmer thoughts into a tempest?   510
    Accursed opportunity!
    The Midwife and the Bawd to all our vices,
    That work'st our thoughts into desires, desires
    To resolutions; those being ripe, and quickned,
    Thou giv'st 'em birth, and bring'st 'em forth to action.

Enter Fat. and Messenger.

Prince. Leave us, O opportunity!
    That when my dire and bloudy resolutions,
    Like sick and froward children
    Were rockt asleep by reason or religion,
    Thou like a violent noise cam'st rushing in,   520
    And mak'st 'em wake and start to new unquietness.
    Come hither, pretty *Fatyma,*
    Thy Grandsires darling, sit upon my knee:
    He loves thee dearly.

Fat. I, Father, for your sake.

Prince.   And for his sake
    I shall requite it. O virtue, virtue,
    Where art thou fled? thou wert my Reasons friend;
    But that like a deposed Prince has yielded
    His Scepter to his base usurping vassals;
    And like a traytor to himself, takes pleasure   530
    In serving them.

Fat.   But Father, I desir'd
    Him that you might have liberty, and that
    He would give you your eyes again.

Prince. Pretty Innocence!
    'Tis not i' th' art, nor power of man to do it.

Fat. Must you never see again then, Father?

Prince. No, not without a miracle.

Fat.   Why Father, I
    Can see with one eye, pray take one of mine.

Prince. I would her innocent prate could overcome me:
    O what a conflict do I feel! how am I   540
    Tost like a ship 'twixt two encountring tides!
    Love that was banisht hence, would fain return
    And force an entrance, but revenge
    (That's now the Porter of my soül) is deaf,
    Deaf as the Adder, and as full of poyson.
    Mighty revenge! that single canst o'rethrow
    All those joynt powers, which nature, vertue, honour,
    Can raise against thee.

Fat. What do you seek for, your handkerchief? pray use mine;
    To drink the bloudy moisture from your eyes;   550
    I'le shew 't my Grandfather, I know
    'Twill make him weep. Why do you shake Father?
    Just so my Grandsire trembled at the instant
    Your sight was ta'ne away.

Prince. And upon the like occasion.

Fat. O Father, what means the naked knife?

Prince. 'Tis to requite thy Grandsires love. Prepare
    To meet thy death.
Fat. O, 'tis I, 'tis I,
    Your daughter *Fatyma!*
Prince.   I therefore do it.   560
Fat. Alas, was this the blessing my mother sent me to receive?
Prince. Thy Mother! *Erythœa!* There's something
    In that that shakes my resolution.
    Poor *Erythœa,* how wretched shall I make thee,
    To rob thee of a Husband and a Child?
    But which is worse, that first I fool'd and won thee
    To a belief that all was well; and yet
    Shall I forbear a crime for love of thee,
    And not for love of virtue? But what's virtue?
    A meer imaginary sound, a thing   570
    Of speculation; which to my dark soul,
    Depriv'd of reason, is as indiscernable
    As colours to my body, wanting sight.
    Then being left to sense, I must be guided
    By something that my sense grasps and takes hold of;
    On then my love, and fear not to encounter
    That Gyant, my revenge (alas poor *Fatyma*)
    My Father loves thee, so do's *Erythœa:*
    Whether shall I by justly plaguing
    Him whom I hate, be more unjustly cruel   580
    To her I love? Or being kind to her,
    Be cruel to my self, and leave unsatisfied
    My anger and revenge? but Love, thou art
    The nobler passion, and to thee I sacrifice
    All my ungentle thoughts. *Fatyma* forgive me,
    And seal it with a kiss: What is 't I feel?
    The spirit of revenge re-inforcing
    New Arguments. Fly *Fatyma,*
    Fly while thou may'st, nor tempt me to new mischief,
    By giving means to act it; to this ill   590
    My will leads not my power, but power my will.

Ex. Fat.

O what a tempest have I scap't, thanks to Heaven,
And *Erythæa's* love!
No: 'twas a poor, a low revenge, unworthy
My virtues, or my injuries, and
As now my fame, so then my infamy,
Would blot out his; And I in stead of his Empire,
Shall only be the heir of all his curses.
No: I'le be still my self, and carry with me
My innocence to th' other world, and leave   600
My fame to this: 'twill be a brave revenge
To raise my mind to a constancy, so high,
That may look down upon his threats, my patience
Shall mock his fury; nor shall he be so happy
To make me miserable: and my sufferings shall
Erect a prouder Trophy to my name,
Than all my prosperous actions: Every Pilot
Can steer the ship in calms, but he performs
The skilful part, can manage it in storms.

Finis Actus Quarti.

Actus Quintus.

Enter Prince.

Prince. If happiness be a substantial good,
          Not fram'd of accidents, nor subject to 'em,
          I err'd to seek it in a blind revenge,
          Or think it lost in loss of sight, or Empire;
          'Tis something sure within us, not subjected
          To sense or sight, only to be discern'd
          By reason, my soul's eye, and that still sees
          Clearly, and clearer for the want of these;
          For gazing through these windows of the body,
          It met such several, such distracting objects;   10
          But now confin'd within it self, it sees

A strange, and unknown world, and there discovers
Torrents of Anger, Mountains of Ambition;
Gulfes of Desire, and Towers of Hope, huge Giants,
Monsters, and savage Beasts; to vanquish these,
Will be a braver conquest than the old
Or the new world.
O happiness of blindness! now no beauty
Inflames my lust, no others good, my envy,
Or misery, my pity: no mans wealth   20
Draws my respect, nor poverty my scorn;
Yet still I see enough. Man to himself
Is a large prospect, rays'd above the level
Of his low creeping thoughts; if then I have
A world within my self, that world shall be
My Empire; there I'le raign, commanding freely,
And willingly obey'd, secure from fear
Of forraign forces, or domestick treasons,[31]
And a hold a Monarchy more free, more absolute
Than in my Fathers seat; and looking down   30
With scorn or pity, on the slippery state
Of Kings, will tread upon the neck of fate.

       Ex. Enter Bashaws disguis'd, with Haly.

1 Bash. Sir, 'tis of near concernment, and imports
    No less than the Kings life and honour.
Ha. May not I know it?
1 Bash. You may, Sir. But in his presence we are sworn
    T' impart it first to him.
Ha. Our Persian State descends not
    To Interviews with strangers: But from whence
    Comes this discovery, or you that bring it?   40
2 Bash. We are, Sir, of *Natolia.*

[31]   "Treason has done his worst; nor steel **nor** prison,
       Malice domestic, foreign levy, nothing
       Can touch him further."
                 Macbeth, Act III, Sc. ii, ll. 24-26.

Ha. Natolia? Heard you nothing
    Of two Villains that lately fled from hence?
1 Bash. The *Bashaws,* Sir?
Ha. The same.
2 Bash. They are nearer than you think for.
Ha. Where?
1 Bash. In *Persia.*
Ha. In arms again to 'tempt another slavery?
2 Bash. No, Sir,   50
    They made some weak attempts, presuming on
    The reputation of their former greatness:
    But having lost their fame and fortunes, 'tis
    No wonder they lost their friends; now hopeless and forlorn
    They are return'd, and somewhere live obscurely,
    To expect a change in *Persia;* nor wil't be hard
    To find 'em.
Ha.   Do 't, and name your own rewards.
2 Bash. We dare do nothing till we have seen the King,
    And then you shall command us.
Ha. Well, though 'tis not usual,   60
    Ye shall have free access.

Exit Haly. Enter King and Haly.

1 Bash. Sir, there were two Turkish prisoners lately fled
    From hence for a suppos'd conspiracy
    Between the Prince and them.
King.   Where are the Villaines?
1 Bash. This is the Villain, Sir;

They pull off their disguises.

    And we the wrongfully accus'd: You gave
    Life Sir, and we took it
    As a free noble gift; but when we heard
    'Twas valued at the price of your Sons honour,
    We came to give it back, as a poor trifle,   70
    Priz'd at a rate too high.

King. Haly,
 I cannot think my favours plac'd so ill,
 To be so ill requited; yet their confidence
 Has something in't that looks like innocence.
Ha. aside. Is't come to that? then to my last and surest refuge.
King. Sure if the guilt were theirs, they could not charge thee
 With such a gallant boldness: If 'twere thine,
 Thou could'st not hear 't with such a silent scorn;
 I am amaz'd.   80
Ha. Sir,
 Perplex your thoughts no further, they have truth
 To make 'em bold; and I have power to scorn it:
 'Twas I, Sir, that betray'd him, and you, and them.
King. Is this impudence, or madness?
Ha. Neither: a very sober, and sad truth—
 To you, Sir.
King. A Guard there.

     Enter Mirvan, and others.

King. Seize him.
Ha. Seize them; now   90
 Though 'tis too late to learn, yet know 'gainst you
 Are King again, what 'tis to let your Subjects
 Dispose all offices of trust and power:
 The beast obeys his keeper, and looks up,
 Not to his masters, but his feeders hand;
 And when you gave me power to dispense
 And make your favours mine, in the same hour
 You made your self my shadow: and 'twas my courtesie
 To let you live, and raign so long.
King.   Without there!

   Enter two or three, and joyn with the others.

What none but Traytors? Has this Villain   100
Breath'd treason into all, and with that breath,
Like a contagious vapour, blasted Loyalty?

       Sure Hell it self hath sent forth all her Furies,
       T' inhabit and possess this place.
Ha. Sir, passions without power,
       Like seas against a rock, but lose their fury.
       Mirvan, Take these Villains, and see 'em strangled.
1 Bash. Farewell, Sir, commend us to your son, let him know,
       That since we cannot die his servants,
       We'll die his Martyrs.   110
King. Farewell, unhappy friends,
       A long farewell, [32] and may you find rewards
       Great as your Innocence; or which is more,
       Great as your wrongs.
2 Bash. Come, thou art troubled,
       Thou dost not fear to dye?
1 Bash. No, but to lose my death,
       To sell my life so cheap, while this proud villain
       That takes it must survive.
2 Bash. We shall not lose our deaths,   120
       If Heaven can hear the cries of guiltless blood,
       Which sure it must; for I have heard th' are loud ones:
       Vengeance shall overtake thee.
Ha. Away with 'em.
King. Stay, *Haly,* they are innocent; yet life,
       When 'tis thy gift,
       Is worse than death, I disdain to ask it.
1 Bash. And we to take it.
Ha.   Do not ask it, Sir,
       For them to whom you owe your ruine, they have undone you,
       Had not they told you this, you had liv'd secure,   130
       And happy in your ignorance; but this injury,
       Since 'tis not in your nature to forgive it,
       I must not leave it in your power to punish it.
King. Heaven, though from thee I have deserv'd this plague,
       Be thou my Judge and Witness, from this villain

[32]   "So farewell to the little good you bear me,
       Farewell, a long farewell to all my greatness!"
                   King Henry VIII, Act III, Sc. ii, l. 351.

'Tis undeserv'd.
Had I but felt your vengeance from some hand
That first had suffer'd mine, it had been justice:
But have you sent this sad return of all
My love, my trust, my favours?   140
Ha. Sir, there's a great resemblance
Between your favours, and my injuries;
Those are too great to be requited, these
Too great to be forgiven: and therefore
'Tis but in vain to mention either.
King. Mirza, Mirza,
How art thou lost by my deceiv'd credulity?
I'le beg thy pardon.
Ha. Stay, Sir, not without my leave:
Go some of you, and let the people know   150
The King keeps state, and will not come in publick:
If any great affairs, or State addresses,
Bring 'em to me.
King.   How have I taught the villain
To act my part? But oh, my son, my son,
Shall I not see thee?
Ha. For once you shall, Sir,
But you must grant me one thing.
King. Traytor, dost thou mock my miseries?
What can I give but this unhappy life?
Ha. Alas! Sir,   160
It is but that I ask, and 'tis my modesty
To ask it, it being in my power to take it:
When you shall see him, Sir, to dye for pity,
'Twere such a thing, 'twould so deceive the world,
And make the people think you were good natur'd;
'Twill look so well in story, and become
The stage so handsomly.
King. I ne're deny'd thee any thing, and shall not now
Deny thee this, though I could stand upright
Under the tyranny of age and fortune;   170

Yet the sad weight of such ingratitude
Will crush me into earth.

Ha. Lose not your tears, but keep
　　Your lamentations for your son, or sins:
　　For both deserve 'em: but you must make haste, Sir,
　　Or he'l not stay your coming.

　　　　　　He looks upon a watch.

'Tis now about the hour the poyson
Must take affect.

King. 　　　　　　Poyson'd? oh Heaven!

Ha. Nay, Sir, lose no time in wonder, both of us
　　Have much to do; if you will see your Son,　　　　180
　　Here's one shall bring you to him.

　　　　　　Exit King.

Some unskilful Pylot had shipwrackt here;
But I not only against sure
And likely ills have made my self secure:
But so confirm'd, and fortify'd my state,
To set it safe above the reach of Fate.

　　　Exit Haly. Enter Prince led, Servant at the other door,
　　　　　　Princess and Soffy.

Serv. Sir, the Princess and your Son.

Prince. Soffy, thou com'st to wonder at
　　Thy wretched father: why dost thou interrupt
　　Thy happiness, by looking on an object　　　　190
　　So miserable?

Princess. My Lord, methinks there is not in your voice
　　The vigour that was wont, nor in your look
　　The wonted chearfulness. Are you well, my Lord?

Prince. No: but I shall be, I feel my health a coming.

Princess. What's your disease, my Lord?

Prince. Nothing, but I have tane a Cordial,
　　Sent by the King or *Haly,* in requital
　　Of all my miseries, to make me happy:

The pillars of this frame grow weak,   200
    As if the weight of many years oppress 'em;
    My sinews slacken, and an Icy stiffness
    Benums my blood.
Princess.   Alas, I fear he's poysoned:
    Call all the help that Art, or Herbs, or Minerals
    Can minister.
Prince. No, 'tis too late:
    And they that gave me this, are too well practis'd
    In such an Art, to attempt and not perform.
Princess. Yet try my Lord, revive your thoughts, the Empire
    Expects you, your Father's dying.   210
Prince. So when the ship is sinking,
    The winds that wrackt it cease.
Princess. Will you be the scorn of fortune,
    To come near a Crown, and only near it?
Prince. I am not fortunes scorn, but she is mine,
    More blind than I.
Princess. O tyranny of Fate! to bring
    Death in one hand, and Empire in the other;
    Only to shew us happiness, and then
    To snatch us from it.   220
Prince. They snatch me to it;
    My soul is on her journey, do not now
    Divert, or lead her back, to lose her self
    I' th' amaze, and winding labyrinths o' th' world:
    I preethee do not weep, thy love is that
    I part with most unwillingly, or otherwise
    I had not staid till rude necessity
    Had forc'd me hence.
    Soffy, be not a man too soon,
    And when thou art, take heed of too much vertue;   230
    It was thy Fathers, and his only crime,
    'Twill make the King suspitious; yet ere time,
    By natures course has ripened thee to man,
    'Twill mellow him to dust; till then forget

I was thy Father, yet forget it not,
My great example shall excite thy thoughts
To noble actions. And you, dear *Erythœa*,
Give not your passions vent, nor let blind fury
Precipitate your thoughts, nor set 'em working,
Till time shall lend 'em better means and instruments   240
Than lost complaints. Where's pretty *Fatyma?*
She must forgive my rash ungentle passion.

Princess. What do you mean, Sir?

Prince. I am asham'd to tell you.
I prethee call her.

Princess. I will, Sir, I pray try if sleep will ease
Your torments, and repair your wasted spirits.

Prince. Sleep to those empty lids
Is grown a stranger, and the day and night,
As undistinguisht by my sleep, as sight.   250
O happiness of poverty! that rests
Securely on a bed of living turfe,
While we with waking cares and restless thoughts,
Lye tumbling on our downe, courting the blessing
Of a short minutes slumber, which the Ploughman
Shakes from him, as a ransom'd slave his fetters:[33]
Call in some Musick, I have heard soft airs
Can charm our senses, and expel our cares.
Is *Erythœa* gone?

Serv.   Yes, Sir.

Prince.   'Tis well:
I would not have her present at my death.   260

Enter Musick.

Morpheus,[34] *the humble God, that dwells*
In cottages and smoakie cells,

---

[33] *Cf. Henry IV, Part II*, Act III, Sc. i, ll. 9-14; and *Henry V*, Act IV, Sc. i.
[34] *1668*, Somnus. This was corrected in the errata.
1671, as above.
1684, as above.
This song was separately printed. See p. 90.

Hates gilded roofs and beds of down;
And though he fears no Princes frown,
Flies from the circle of a Crown.

Come, I say, thou powerful God,
And thy Leaden charming Rod,
Dipt in the Lethæan Lake,
O're his wakeful temples shake,
Lest he should sleep and never wake.   270

Nature (alas) why art thou so
Obliged to thy greatest Foe?
Sleep that is thy best repast,
Yet of death it bears a taste,
And both are the same thing at last.

Serv. So now he sleeps, let's leave him
To his repose.

Enter King.

King. The horrour of this place presents
The horrour of my crimes, I fain would ask
What I am loth to hear; but I am well prepar'd: 280
They that are past all hope of good, are past
All fear of ill: and yet if he be dead,
Speak softly, or uncertainly.
Phy. Sir, he sleeps.
King. O that's too plain, I know thou mean'st his last,
His long, his endless sleep.
Phy. No, Sir, he lives; but yet
I fear the sleep you speak of will be his next:
For nature, like a weak and weary traveller,
Tir'd with a tedious and rugged way,   290
Not by desire provokt, but even betray'd
By weariness and want of spirits,
Gives up her self to this unwilling slumber.
King. Thou hast it, *Haly*, 'tis indeed a sad
And sober truth, though the first

And only truth thou ever told'st me:
And 'tis a fatal sign, when Kings hear truth,
Especially when flatterers dare speak it.
Prince. I thought I heard my Father, does he think the poyson
Too slow, and comes to see the operation?   300

Prince Awakes.

Or does he think his engine dull, or honest?
Less apt to execute, than he to bid him:
He needs not, 'tis enough, it will succeed
To his expectation.[35]
King. 'Tis indeed thy Father,
Thy wretched Father; but so far from acting
New cruelties, that if those already past,
Acknowledg'd and repented of, can yet
Receive a pardon, by those mutual bonds
Nature has seal'd between us, which though I   310
Have cancell'd, thou hast still preserv'd inviolate;
I beg thy pardon.
Prince. Death in it self appears
Lovely and sweet, not only to be pardoned,
But wisht for, had it come from any other hand,
But from a Father; a Father,
A name so full of life, of love, of pity:
Death from a Fathers hand, from whom I first
Receiv'd a being, 'tis a preposterous gift,
An act at which inverted Nature starts   320
And blushes to behold her self so cruel.
King. Take thou that comfort with thee, and be not deaf to truth:
By all that's holy, by the dying accents
Of thine, and my last breath, I never meant,
I never wisht it: sorrow has so over-fraught
This sinking bark, I shall not live to shew
How I abhor, or how I would repent

---

[35]   "No, 'tis not so deep as a well, nor so wide
as a church-door; but 'tis enough, 'twill serve."
Romeo and Juliet, Act III, Sc. i, l. 99.

My first rash crime; but he that now
Has poyson'd thee, first poyson'd me with jealousie,
A foolish causless jealousie.   330
Prince. Since you believe my innocence,
I cannot but believe your sorrow:
But does the villain live? A just revenge
Would more become the sorrows of a King,
Than womanish complaints.
King.   *O Mirza, Mirza!*
I have no more the power to do it,
Than thou to see it done: My Empire *Mirza,*
My Empire's lost: thy vertue was the rock
On which it firmly stood, that being undermin'd,
It sunk with its own weight; the villain whom   340
My breath created, now braves it in my Throne.
Prince. O for an hour of life; but 'twill not be:
Revenge and justice we must leave to Heaven.
I would say more, but death has taken in the outworks,
And now assails the fort; I feel, I feel him
Gnawing my heart-strings: Farewel, and yet I would. . . .
                                        Dies.

King. O stay, stay but a while, and take me with thee;
Come Death, let me embrace thee, thou that wert
The worst of all my fears, art now the best
Of all my hopes. But Fate, why hast thou added   350
This curse to all the rest? the love of life;
We love it, and yet hate it; death we loath,
And still desire; flye to it, and yet fear it.

                    Enter Princess and Soffy.

Princess. He's gone, he's gone for ever:
O that the poyson had mistaken his,
And met this hated life; but cruel Fate
Envyed so great a happiness: Fate that still
Flies from the wretched, and pursues the blest.
Ye Heavens! But why should I complain to them

That hear me not, or bow to those that hate me?   360
Why should your curses so out-weigh your blessings?
They come but single, and long expectation
Takes from their value: but these fall upon us
Double and sudden.

Sees the King.

Yet more of horrour, then farewel my tears,
And my just anger be no more confin'd
To vain complaints, or self-devouring silence;
But break, break forth upon him like a deluge,
And the great spirit of my injur'd Lord
Possess me, and inspire me with a rage   370
Great as thy wrongs, and let me call together
All my Souls powers, to throw a curse upon him
Black as his crimes.
King.   O spare your anger, 'tis lost;
For he whom thou accusest has already
Condemn'd himself, and is as miserable
As thou canst think, or wish him; spit upon me,
Cast all reproaches on me, womans wit
Or malice can invent, I'le thank thee for them;
Whate're can give me a more lively sence
Of my own crimes, that so I may repent 'em.   380
Princess. O cruel Tyrant! could'st thou be so barbarous
To a Son as noble as thy self art vile?
That knew no other crime, but too much vertue;
Nor could deserve so great a punishment
For any fault, but that he was thy Son?
Now not content to exceed all other Tyrants,
Exceed'st thy self: first robbing him of sight,
Then seeming by a fain'd and forc'd repentance,
To expiate that crime, didst win him to
A false security, and now by poyson   390
Hast rob'd him of his life.
King. Were but my soul as pure
From other guilts as that, Heaven did not hold

One more immaculate. Yet what I have done,
He dying did forgive me, and hadst thou been present,
Thou wouldst have done the same: for thou art happy,
Compar'd to me; I am not only miserable,
But wicked too; thy miseries may find
Pity, and help from others; but mine make me
The scorn, and the reproach of all the world;   400
Thou, like unhappy Merchants, whose adventures
Are dasht on rocks, or swallowed up in storms,
Ow'st all thy losses to the Fates: but I
Like wastful Prodigals, have cast away
My happiness, and with it all mens pity:
Thou seest how weak and wretched guilt can make,
Even Kings themselves, when a weak womans anger
Can master mine.
Princess. And your sorrow
As much o'recomes my anger, and turns into melting pity.   410
King. Pity not me, nor yet deplore your husband;
But seek the safety of your son, his innocence
Will be too weak a guard, when nor my greatness,
Nor yet his fathers vertues could protect us.
Go on my Boy, the just revenge of all

To Soffy.

Our wrongs I recommend to thee and Heaven;
I feel my weakness growing strong upon me:

Exeunt.

Death, thou art he that wilt not flatter Princes,
That stoops not to authority, nor gives
A specious name to tyranny; but shews   420
Our actions in their own deformed likeness.
Now all those cruelties which I have acted,
To make me great, or glorious, or secure,
Look like the hated crimes of other men.

Enter Physician.

King. O save, save me! who are those that stand,
    And seem to threaten me?
Phy. There's no body, 'tis nothing
    But some fearful dream.
King. Yes, that's my brothers ghost, whose birth-right stood
    'Twixt me and Empire, like a spreading Cedar   430
    That grows to hinder some delightful prospect,
    Him I cut down.
    Next my old Fathers Ghost, whom I impatient
    To have my hopes delay'd, hastned by violence
    Before his fatal day;
    Then my enraged Son, who seems to becken,
    And hale me to him. I come, I come, ye Ghosts,
    The greatest of you all; but sure one hell's
    Too little to contain me, and too narrow
    For all my crimes.   440

Dies.

Enter Mirvan and Haly at several doors.

Haly. Go muster all the City-Bands; pretend it
    To prevent sudden tumults, but indeed
    To settle the succession.
Mir. My Lord,
    You are too sudden, you'l take 'em unprepar'd;
    Alas, you know their consciences are tender.
    Scandal and scruple must be first remov'd,
    They must be pray'd and preach'd into a tumult:
    But for succession,
    Let us agree on that; there's *Calamah*   450
    The eldest Son by the Arabian Lady,
    A gallant youth.
Ha. I, too gallant, his proud spirit will disdain
    To owe his greatness to anothers gift:
    Such gifts as Crowns, transcending all requital,
    Turn injuries. No, *Mirvan;*
    He must be dull and stupid, lest he know
    Wherefore we made him King.

Mir. But he must be good natur'd, tractable,
          And one that will be govern'd.   460
Ha.   And have so
          Much wit to know whom he's beholding to.
Mir. But why, my Lord, should you look further than your self?
Ha. I have had some such thoughts; but I consider
          The Persian State will not endure a King
          So meanly born; no, I'le rather be the same I am,
          In place the second, but the first in power:
          Solyman the Son of the *Georgian* Lady
          Shall be the man: what noyse is that?

                         Enter Messenger.

Mess. My Lord, the Princes late victorious Army
          Is marching towards the Palace, breathing nothing   470
          But fury and revenge; to them are joyn'd
          All whom desire of change, or discontent,
          Excites to new attempts, their Leaders
          Abdal and *Morat*.
Ha. Abdal and *Morat!* *Mirvan*, we are lost,
          Fallen from the top
          Of all our hopes, and cast away like Saylers,
          Who scaping Seas, and Rocks, and Tempests, perish
          I' th' very Port; so are we lost i' th' sight
          And reach of all our wishes.   480
Mir. How has our intelligence fail'd us so strangely?
Ha. No, no, I knew they were in mutiny;
          But they could ne're have hurt us,
          Had they not come at this instant period,
          This point of time: had he liv'd two days longer,
          A pardon to the Captains, and a largess
          Among the Souldiers, had appeas'd their fury:
          Had he dy'd two days sooner, the succession
          Had as we pleas'd, been settled, and secur'd
          By *Soffy's* death. Gods, that the world should turn   490
          On minutes, and on moments!
Mir. My Lord, lose not yourself

In passion, but take counsel from necessity;
I'le to 'em, and will let them know
The Prince is dead, and that they come too late
To give him liberty; for love to him
Has bred their discontents: I'le tell them boldly,
That they have lost their hopes.

Ha.   And tell them too,
As they have lost their hopes o' th' one, they have lost
Their fears o' th' other: tell their Leaders we desire   500
Their counsel in the next succession;
Which if it meet disturbance,
Then we shall crave assistance from their power,
Which Fate could not have sent in a more happy hour.

Exit Mirvan. Enter Lords, Caliph.

Cal. My Lord, ye hear
The news, the Princes Army is at the gate.
Ha. I, I hear it, and feel it here; (*Aside.*)
But the succession, that's the point that first
Requires your counsel.
Cal. Who should succeed, but *Soffy?*   510
Ha. What! in such times as these, when such an Army
Lies at our gates, to chuse a Child our King?
You, my Lord *Caliph,* are better read in story,
And can discourse the fatal consequences
When Children reign.
Cal.   My Lords, if you'l be guided
By reason and example—

Enter Abdal and Morat.

Ha. My Lords,
You come most opportunely, we were entring
Into dispute about the next succession.
Ab. Who dares dispute it? we have a powerful argument   520
Of forty thousand strong, that shall confute him.
Cal. A powerful argument indeed.
Ab. I, such a one as will puzzle all your Logick

And distinctions to answer it;
And since we came too late for the performance
Of our intended service to the Prince,
The wronged Prince, we cannot more express
Our loyalty to him, than in the right
Of his most hopeful Son.
Ha. But is he not too young?   530
Mor. Sure you think us so too; but he, and we
　Are old enough to look through your disguise,
　And under that to see his Fathers Enemies.
　A Guard there.

Enter Guard.

Mor. Seize him, and you that could shew reason or example.
Ha. Seize me! for what?
Ab. Canst thou remember such a name as *Mirza,*
　And ask for what?
Ha. That name I must remember, and with horrour;
　But few have dyed for doing,   540
　What they had dy'd for if they had not done:
　It was the Kings command, and I was only
　Th' unhappy minister.
Ab. I, such a minister as wind to fire,
　That adds an accidental fierceness to
　Its natural fury.
Mor. If 'twere the Kings command, 'twas first thy malice
　Commanded that command, and then[36] obey'd it.
Ha. Nay, if you have resolv'd it, truth and reason
　Are weak and idle arguments; but let   550
　Me pity the unhappy instruments
　Of Princes wills, whose anger is our fate,
　And yet their love's more fatal than their hate.
Ab. And how well that love hath been requited,
　Mirvan your Confident, by torture has confest.
Mor. The story of the King, and of the Bashaws.

[36] All the texts follow this reading. In the 1668 table of errata "then" is
corrected to "they," but the change destroys the meaning of the passage.

Ha. Mirvan, poor-spirited wretch, thou hast deceiv'd me;
    Nay then farewel my hopes, and next my fears.

Enter Soffy.

Soffy. What horrid noyse was that of drums and trumpets,
    That struck my Ear? What mean these bonds? Could not   560
    My Grandsires jealousie be satisfied
    Upon his Son, but now must seize
    His dearest Favourite? Sure my turn comes next.
Ab. 'Tis come already, Sir; but to succeed
    Him, not them: Long live King *Soffy!*

Without Drums and Trumpets.

Soffy. But why are these men prisoners?
Ab. Let this inform you.
Soffy. But is my Grandsire dead?
Ab. As sure as we are alive.
Soffy. Then let 'em still be prisoners, away with 'em;   570
    Invite our Mother from her sad retirement,
    And all that suffer for my Fathers love,
    Restraint or punishment.

Enter Princess.

So.   Dear Mother, make
    Our happiness compleat, by breaking through
    That cloud of sorrow,
    And let us not be wanting to our selves,
    Now th' heavens have done their part,
    Lest so severe and obstinate a sadness
    Tempt a new vengeance.
Princess. Sir, to comply with you I'le use a violence   580
    Upon my nature; Joy is such a forrainer,
    So meer a stranger to my thoughts, I know
    Not how to entertain him; but sorrow
    Is[37] made by custom so habitual,
    'Tis now part of my nature.

[37] *1668,* Ill.

Sṗ. But can no pleasure, no delight divert it?
   Greatness, or power, which women most affect,
   If that can do it, rule me, and rule my Empire.
Princess. Sir,
   Seek not to rob me of my tears, Fortune   590
   Her self is not so cruel; for my counsels
   Then may be unsuccessful, but my prayers
   Shall wait on all your actions.

            Enter Solyman, as from the Rack. Guard.

So.[38] Alas poor *Solyman*, how is he altered?
Sol. Why, because I would not accuse your Father, when your
   Grandfather saw he could not stretch my conscience, thus
   he has stretcht my carkass.
Mor. I think they have stretcht his wit too.
Sol. This is your Fathers love that lyes thus in my bones;[39]
   I might have lov'd all the Pocky Whores in Persia, and   600
   have felt it less in my bones.
So. Thy faith and honesty shall be rewarded
   According to thine own desire.
Sol. Friend, I pray thee tell me where-about my knees are,
   I would fain kneel to thank his Majesty: Why Sir, for
   the present my desire is only to have a good Bone setter,
   and when your Majesty has done that office to the Body
   Politick, and some skilful man to this body of mine (which
   if it had been a Body Politick, had never come to this) I
   shall by that time think on something for my suffering: 610
   But must none of these great ones be Hang'd for their vil-
   lanies?

---

[38] *1642:*
So. Alas, poore *Solyman*, how is he altered?
Sol. I know not, Sir, it is an art your Grandfather had to make me grow, I
   think he took me for some crooked Lady, I'm sure the engine is better for
   the purpose, than steele bodies, or bolsters.
So. But for what cause was all this crueltie?
Sol. Why, because I would not accuse your father, when he saw he could not
   stretch my conscience, etc.
   [39] *1642*, joynts.

Aside.

Mor. Yes certainly.

Sol. Then I need look no further, some of their estates will
　　serve my turn.

So. Bring back those villains.

Enter Haly and Caliph.

Now to your tears, dear Madam, and the Ghost
Of my dead Father, will I consecrate
The first fruits of my justice: Let such honours
And funeral rites, as to his birth and vertues　　　　　620
Are due, be first performed, then all that were
Actors, or Authors of so black a deed,
Be sacrific'd as Victims to his Ghost:
First thou, my holy Devil, that couldst varnish
So foul an act with the fair name of Piety:
Next thou, th' abuser of thy Princes ear.

Cal. Sir, I beg your mercy.

Ha. And I a speedy death, nor shall my resolution
Disarm it self, nor condescend to parley
With foolish hope.　　　　　630

So. 'Twere cruelty to spare 'em, I am sorry
I must commence my reign in blood, but duty
And justice to my fathers soul exact
This cruel piety; let's study for
A punishment, a feeling one,
And borrow from our sorrow so much time,
T'invent a torment equal to their crime.

Exeunt.

FINIS

THE EPILOGUE

'Tis done, and we alive again, and now
There is no Tragedy, but in your brow.
And yet our Author hopes you are pleas'd, if not;
This having fail'd, he has a second Plot:
'Tis this; the next day send us in your friends,
Then laugh at them, and make your selves amends.
Thus, whether it be good or bad, yet you
May please your selves, and you may please us too:
But look you please the Poet, lest he vow
A full revenge upon you all, but how?
'Tis not to kill you all twenty a day,
He'll do't at once, a more compendious way;
He means to write again; but so much worse,
That seeing that, you'l think it a just curse
For censuring this: 'Faith give him your applause,
As you give Beggars money; for no cause,
But that he's troublesome, and he has swore,
As Beggars do, he'l trouble you no more.

APPENDICES

Appendix A.

NEW POEMS

THESE consist of eleven poems, in Denham's hand, written on the end papers of a copy of the 1668 edition of his poems. Eight of them, published anonymously in 1653, can for the first time be ascribed to him.[1] The other three are entirely new. Now part of the Osborn collection in the Yale University Library, this volume was recently acquired by Mr. James M. Osborn. In an article in the T.L.S.[2] Mr. Osborn described its acquisition and the authentication of the handwriting and printed excerpts from six of the eight anonymous poems,[3] excerpts from two of the three unknown poems, and the full text of the third, the *Elegy on Sir William Davenant*. The text here printed is that of the ms. with the contractions expanded and the punctuation supplied. The readings of the 1653 edition are recorded as variants, differences of spelling, capitalization, and punctuation being ignored. Some of the changes correct obvious printer's errors, and others seem to reflect the mood of the moment. A few improve the rhythm or the sense, although in poems of such poor literary quality this is faint praise.

The most interesting thing about them is the fact of their existence. Why did Denham copy them into his book? The reason for the *Elegy* is clear. Davenant died on April 7, 1668, and Denham wished to preserve this newly composed tribute to his friend, which is, as Mr. Osborn justly observes, "written with a gentler touch"[4] than the earlier poems. These are also concerned with Davenant and were probably copied for that reason, to accompany the *Elegy*. In 1651 Davenant published *Gondibert: an Heroick Poem*, the solemn pretentiousness of which aroused the mirth of

---

[1] In the first edition of this book I tentatively ascribed four to him, two rightly and two wrongly.

[2] James M. Osborn, "New Poems by Sir John Denham," T.L.S., Sept. 1, 1966, p. 788.

[3] Because of the confusion of the ms. Mr. Osborn noticed only six previously printed poems.

[4] Osborn, *op. cit.*

his contemporaries. Of it Aubrey says (*Brief Lives,* ed. A. Clark, I, 207), "The courtiers with the Prince of Wales could never be at quiet about this piece, which was the occasion of a very witty but satericall little booke of verses in 8vo. about 4 sheetes writt by George, Duke of Buckes, Sir John Denham etc." The pamphlet to which Aubrey refers is CERTAIN/VERSES/WRITTEN/By severall of the/*Authors Friends;*/TO BE/RE-PRINTED/WITH THE/Second Edition/OF/*GONDIBERT.*/*LONDON,* Printed in the Year, 1653. Of this Aubrey says further (*Brief Lives,* ed. A. Clark, I, 221), "In the verses against Gondibert, most of them are Sir John's. He was satyricall when he had a mind to it."

Four authors seem to have been involved in this production. Aubrey mentions Denham and the Duke of Buckingham. A third was probably Lord Crofts,[5] who is the supposed speaker of one of the ms. poems, and with whom Denham was intimate. It is useless to speculate on the identity of the fourth. These men refer to themselves on the title page as the author's friends and in the text as his four best friends. (One wonders what the unfortunate Davenant's enemies would have considered witty). In his 1668 edition Denham does include a mild burlesque of *Gondibert,*[6] but he omits these far more stinging attacks. His motive was probably kindness, since, considering other poems in the volume, it could hardly have been a sense of insufficient poetical merit. To satirize Davenant anonymously at the time *Gondibert* was being written was admissible; to continue the satire under his own name fifteen years later was not. After Davenant's death, however, kindness need no longer restrain him and he could acknowledge his productions, which he evidently felt were worth reproducing.[7] The textual variants may have been introduced when he copied the poems into the 1668 edition, but it seems more likely that they had been made in a copy of the 1653 publication, or in his original ms. The two satires not included in 1653 doubtless date from the same year or shortly after.[8]

[5] See p. 107.   [6] See p. 133.
[7] One, "As Martial's" etc. is canceled with a pen stroke. Why?
[8] We must assume that Denham copied only his own work. Otherwise we would not have assigned to him the poem "Denham come helpe to laugh," in the ms. titled "Lord Crofts." It must, however, be classed with "I am old Davenant," supposedly spoken by him.

POEMS PRINTED IN 1653

ON GONDIBERT
THE PREFACE, BEING PUBLISHED
BEFORE THE BOOKE WAS WRITTEN[1]
UPON THE PREFACE

Room Room[2] for the best of Poets heroick,
If you will[3] believe two wits and a Stoick.
Farwell[4] the Iliads and farwell[5] Aeneidos;
Ye both[6] must give place to Gondiberteidos,
For to Homer and Virgill he has a just pyque
Because one's writ in Latin the other in Greek:
Besides an old grudg (our Criticks say[7] so)
To[8] Ovid because his sirname is[9] naso.
If fiction the fame of a Poet raises,[10]
What Poets are you that have writ his praises?
But we Justly quarell at this our defeat;
You give us a stomack, he gives us no meat.
A preface to no booke, a porch to no house:
Now see[11] the mountaine, but where is the mouse?
But Virginia[12] now must breed up the Brat
From whence 'twill return an Indian[13] rat,
For Daphne, alas,[14] is gone from among us,
With thirty-two slaves, to plant mundungus.

I
After so many sad mishaps,
Of drinking, riming, and of claps,
I Pity most thy Last relaps:
2
That having past the Soldiers pains,
The Statesmens arts, the seamens gains,
With gondibert to break thy brains.

---

[1] Omitted. [2] Second Room omitted. [3] you'l. [4] Down go. [5] down go
the. [6] All. [7] they say. [8] With. [9] was. [10] thus raises. [11] Here is.
[12] Oh, America. [13] West-Indy. [14] Will to Virginia.

3

And so incessantly to ply it,
To sacrifice thy sleep, thy diet,
Thy business; and what's more, our quiet.

4

And all this stir to make a story,
Not much superior to John Dory,
Which thus in short[1] I lay before ye.

5

All in the Land of Lombardie,
A Wight there was of Knights degree,
Sir gondibert ycleap't was hee;

6

This Gondibert as sayth[2] our Author
Got the good will of a Kings daughter,
A shame it seems the Devill ought her.

7

Though hee in fight was most audacious,
Of person hee was most ungracious,[3]
And in his ale most pernicatious.

8

And by a most unhappy Fate[4]
Hee[5] in a drunken street debate
One night had[6] gott a broken pate.

9[7]

And so succeeded his disaster:
Being sure of the daughter of his Master,
Hee sold his Princess for a Plaister,

[1] brief.
[2] says.
[3] Of person he was not ungratious, Grave in Debate, in Fight audacious.
[4] And this was cause of his sad Fate.
[5] For.
[6] he.
[7] Stanzas 7 and 9 are transposed.

10

For being cured, hee would not tarry,
But needs the simpling Girle would marry,
Of Astragon th Apothecary.

11

To make the story[8] more Romancy,
Both wise and rich you must him fancy,
But hee in both fell[9] short of Plancy.

12

But for the Lady hee did woo so,
To say the truth shee was but so so,
Not much unlike her of Toboso.

13

Her beuty though twas not exceeding,
Yet what in Face or Shape was needing,
Shee made it up with parts and breeding.

14

Though all the knowledge[10] shee was rich in,
Both of the Dayry and the kitchin,
Yet shee had knowledge more bewitching,

15

For shee had learned her Fathers skill,
Both of th'Alimbeck and the still,
The purge, the poltice, and the Pill.

16

But her cheife talent was a Glyster,
And such a hand to administer,
That[11] on the breech it raisd no blister.

17

So well shee handle[d] Gondebart,
That though shee did not hurt that part,
Shee raisd[12] a blister on his heart.

[8] thing yet.
[9] came.
[10] science.

18

Into the Garden of her Father,
Garden (saith[13] I) the[14] backside rather,
One night shee went a rose to gather.

19

Her Gallant[15] was not farr behind.
Full soon hee had her in the wind,
For love can smell though hee bee blind.

20

Her business shee had finisht scarcely,
When on a gentle bed of Parsely
Full soft and fayre[16] hee made her arse ly.

Raised by a Prince of Lambard blood
An antique Fabrick long hath stood,
Of Podian flint and Parian freestone,
Mingled as well[1] as you shall see stone,
A part whereof hyght Cripples Region
Contains of halfe men a whole Legion.
Thes men had[2] been from ancient Lore
For three swift Centuries and more
Friends to the debtors and the drinkers,
And foes both to[3] the Smiths and Clinkers.
When in the Churchyard or the Alley
Occasion serves, then forth they salley
Both horse and foot; but now I wrong 'um,
There's nether horse nor foot among 'um;
But those which[4] are for horse accounted
Are on tall wooden Engins mounted,
On which (in Lombard Author's Notion)
They abuse the property of Motion.
But for the foot tis more unproper,
For they moved not on foot, but Crupper;

11 As.   12 made.   13 said.   14 or.   15 The Knight he.   16 fair and soft.
1 Omitted.   2 Who still have.   3 unto.   4 that.

And having nether Legg nor Stumpe,
Advance themselves on hip[5] and rump.
A stand they make; a stand d'you call't?
The word of Art is make a halt.
Then steps forth a grave Eastern Cripple,
One that could fight and talke, and tipple.
Brave Freinds, quoth hee, powr is a Liquor
Makes force[6] more strong, and witt the[7] quicker;
Powr is a tree, whose boughs and branches
Serve us instead of Legges and Hanches;
Powr is a Hill, to whose command
Men walke by sea, and saile by land.
But what is[8] power unlesse wee know it?
And knowledge what, unlesse we show it?
Behold the Knight who late did marry
The daughter of our Pothecary
Hurried to durance like a stinkard
By Goltho[?][9] Smith and Borgia Clinkard,
Where[10] him like to a Civill sheep
In jayle (nice Statesmens pound) they'l keep.
This said, you might have seen (for such is
The force of Eloquence) their crutches
Indu'd with speed[11] in th'eyes and Noses
(Of such as had them) flames and roses.
Their nervs of wire new heat makes limber,
And rage even animates their timber.
Then like a Pack of Rhegian hounds,
Pursuing ore th'Illyrian Grounds,
A Thuscan[12] Stagg, if in the wind
A flock of Rhegian Sheep they find,
Calebrian Swine or Paduan[13] Goats,
In blood they bath their Canon throats.
And on their[14] trembling entrails hasten
Their well experienc't teeth to fasten,

---

[5] hand.   [6] hands.   [7] more.   [8] what's our.   [9] Oswald.   [10] And.
[11] diligence.   [12] Tuscan.   [13] pagan.   [14] the.

With such Croatian rage the stout
Bold[15] Cripples did the Baillifes rout.
The Bailiffs being fled, or dead all,
The Knight pluck[t][16] out an Antique medall
On the reverse whereof was graved
Th' alliance betwixt Christ and David.[17]
Quoth hee of rescued knighthood carry
This just reward, broach of Canary,
Or Belgian Brandywine, the Vessell
Wherewith the Argonauts of Tessell
When Mars or[18] Neptune them ingages
Inflame their flegmatick Courages.
Thus reskuing Gondibert, they save him,
Then to Cowlane[19] Coachman gave him.
Hee safe returning[20] joy and mirth a-
bounded twixt Arstragon and Birtha.
Thus leave wee them in Humour jolly
Free from old Roman Melancholly.

Thou hadst[1] not been so[2] long neglected
But now thy four best Freinds expected
Thou wouldst in time have stood corrected.

But since that Planet governs still
Which guids[3] thy toedious fustian quill,
Gainst Nature's and the Muses will,[4]

---

[15] grave.   [16] pulls.   [17] Marginal note: Cross and Harp.   [18] and.
[19] a Berkshire.   [20] return'd   here.
[1] hast.
[2] thus.
[3] rules.
[4] A stanza is omitted in the ms.
> When by thy friends advice and care
> Twas hopd in time thou woldst despaire
> To give ten pounds to write it faire.

Least thou to all the world should show it
Wee thought twas time[5] to lett thee know it:
Thou art a damnd insipid Poet.

This[6] for the present shall suffice;
Tis[?] with thy Museful[?] freinds advise.
A word's enough unto the wise.

SONG[1]

I am old Davenant
    With my fustian Quill.
Though skill I have not,
    I must be riming still
        On Gondibart
Which is not worth a Fart.

    Waller and Cowley
Tis true did praise[2] my book,
    But how untruly
All those may know who look;
    Nor can old Hobbs
Defend me from dry bobbs.

Then no more Ill dabble
    Nor pump Fancy dry
To compose a Fable
    Shall make Will Crofts to cry,
        O gentle knight
Thou writst for those[3] who shite.

[5] it fit.
[6] This stanza is unprinted.
[1] The Author upon himself.
[2] have prais'd.
[3] to them.

UPON THE PREFACE OF GONDIBERT
MARS. EPIG.
LASCIVA EST NOBIS PAGINA VITA PROBA EST
As Martials Life was grave and sad,
Wanting the myrth his verses had:
Even so this our Long Preface shows
What ere we want our Book has nose.[4]

To the Tune of Fortunes might[?][1]
Of all ill Poets by their Lumber known
Who ne're Fames favors wore, yet sought them long,
Sir Daphne gives precedency to none
And makes[2] most business for abstersive song.[3]

Rhime was his studied Art, rhime which was bad,
Rhime meant for spells the Devill himselfe to charm,[4]
Rime wrought with Fustian, lind with bombast plad,
Might without Indian Gowne keep th'author warm[5]

[4] This whole poem is canceled with a pen stroke.
[1] An Essay in Explanation of Mr. *Hobbs,* where he tells the Author,
*The Vertues you distribute there among so many Noble persons, represent
the Image but of one Mans Vertue to my Fancy, which is your own.*
[2] breeds.
[3] a stanza is omitted:
       From untaught Childhood, to mistaking Man,
       An ill-performing Agent to the Stage;
       With *Albovin* in *Lumber* he began,
       With *Gondibert* in *Lumber* ends his rage.
[4] charms to keep th' devil in aw.
[5] Rime which with Fustian lin'd & Nonesense clad,
  More needful is, than Finger, Shirt or Straw.
Two further stanzas are omitted:
       To conquer Reason, Nature's common gift,
       Fein'd Art, sophisticated Rime devis'd,
       While those who cannot their weak judgements lift
       To discern sense, and[6] with hard words surpris'd.

       Yet Laws of Verse rescue but doubtfully
       From one ill Poet all good Poets fame;
       Till against Rime, the wise Rimes help apply,
       Which soberly tells *Will* he is to blame.
[6] are?

LORD CROFTS[1]

Denham come helpe[2] to laugh
    At old Daph,
Whose Fancies are lighter than Chaffe.
    He abuses
    All our Muses
And would it [not][3] make a man laugh till he burst
That he would be though[t] of Poets the first,
    Who[4] is of all rimers the worst?
Daphne wast[5] thou not content
    For to vent
    Thy Fancies without our consent?
    But hadst the face
    In thy preface
To raile[6] at all those who had written before
When we thy best friends to the number of four
Had advisd[7] thee to scrible no more.

POEMS PREVIOUSLY UNPRINTED

SONG
To the Tune of Walsingham

As I came from Lombardy
    With my fustian Style,
Hoping to make merry England
    An Important Isle,

First I sojournd in fayre France
    All in Paris towne,
Where I stanzaes did compose
    In my Indian Gowne.

---

[1] Upon the Author.   [2] helpe me.   [3] it not.   [4] That.   [5] wert.   [6] laugh.
[7] Advisd.

But they so their patience tryed
  Who the Stanzaes did see
Gentle reader none was found
  But the Lord Harley.

Then with my dear Gondibert
  And my face so flatt
Was I taken on the salt seas
  By a false Pyrate.

Gentle Pyrate, then said I,
  Saw you my true love
As my Shipp you rifled have
  Both below and above.

Thirty slaves and two, said hee,
  There were great and small,
But of womankind saw I not
  One, amongst them all.

Nor woman nor womans child
  Makes me thus complaine,
But my owne dear Gondibert,
  The babe of my braine.

TO THE TUNE OF ARTHUR OF BRADLY

Sir William's no more a Poet;
Hee cares not who doth know it,
Tho hangman hath burnt his book,
And now hes turned a cooke.

For the Honour of Will of Avenant
  Ho brave Will of Avenant
  Heigh brave Will of Avenant Ho.

In Rhine no more hee rages,
But serves up good Pottages
And cares for the Muses no more
Than they did for him before.

For the Honour etc.

With old Bards no more hee Justles,
But serves up his dish of Museles,
And as for his sauce to a Pike
Toby[?] never made the like.

For the Honour etc.

His vocation[?] all has fled.
Hee will seasone his heifers head
And with redlegd Partridge fills
Our bellies from Genoa Hills.

For the Honour etc.

His Guests are cheerfull and merry
With Burgundy Rhenish and sherry;
And their merriment not to defeat
He vows no more verse to repeat.

For the Honour etc.[1]

ELEGY ON SIR WILLIAM D'AVENANT

Though hee is dead th' Imortall name
Of William who from Avenant came,
Who mixt with English Lombard Flame,
Shall live in the records of Fame.

[1] Four illegible lines, apparently of a different poem, are written across this stanza.

Hee lyes who sayth hee wanted witt
Both for the table and the Pitt,
Which like his Face had never splitt
Had Nasute Judgment steered it.

Industrious to a Prodigie,
Of that nor th' Important bee
Nor the Grave Ant had more than hee,
As by his labourd lines you see.

Had hee to Law become a Drudge
And touched on the temple Rudge
And learned to Westminster to trudge,
Hee had long since gone forth a Judge.

Had hee with some good trade began
When into riming rage he ran,
Hee had been Maire or Alderman,
But still his Muse did him trepan.

Twelve lustres his Icarian quill,
Striving to toppe the Muses Hill,
Weary about the middel stood still.
Will lov'd them but they lov'd not Will.

Hee out of breath himselfe did run
When with high vappour hee begun
By aemulating Doctor Donne
(I meane the Father not the Sonne).

Now roosting in the Poets nest,
Amongst his kindred hee doth rest
Wit Haut gousts. They their wellcome guest
In limbo Poetarum feast.

First in the broad Elysian streets
Hee his old Father Johnson meets;
Then him his Cousin Shakespeare greets,
But his Freind Suckling Lent him sheets.

Cowley a Fayre appartment keepes;
Receiving him with joy he weepes.
Into his bed Sir William creepes
And now in Abrahams bosome sleeps.

His Freind hee to the Ancients shows;
Their former Feuds hee doth compose.
To shew they are no longer Foes
Noso has lent him halfe his Nose.

In Poetry hee raised a Scisme
Gainst the old Bards of Paganisme,
Styld by the Modernes D'avenantisme,
Condemn'd for want of Syllogisme.

And yet I feare thy want of breath
Will prove the English Stages death.
Could I to thee new life bequeath
No other head should were the wreath.

Appendix B.

WORKS ATTRIBUTED TO DENHAM

THE/True PRESBYTERIAN/WITHOUT DISGUISE:/OR A /CHARACTER/OF A/*Presbyterians Ways and Actions,*/By Sir *JOHN DENHAM,* Knight/(Motto)/Text. Folio sheet./*LONDON;* Printed for *J.B.* 1680.

Reprinted in *The Secret History of the Calves-Head club* . . . *with a Character of a Presbyterian written by Sir John Denham* Knight, 1706, sixth edition, and in subsequent editions of 1707, 1709, 1713, and 1714.

I reject this as genuine work of Denham for the following reasons:

- (1) It was first published as a folio sheet eleven years after his death.
- (2) There was contemporary doubt of its authenticity. "The name of Sir John Denham is set to this poem, but then question'd by many whether ever he was the author of it," Wood, *Athenae Oxoniensis,* 1721, II, 424.
- (3) It is not characteristic of Denham's style:
  - (a) It is loose, and lacking in strength, terseness or antithesis.
  - (b) It has eleven feminine couplets as against only one in all Denham's authentic work (*Progress of Learning,* ll. 207-208).

HIS M-Y'S MOST GRACIOUS SPEECH TO BOTH HOUSES OF P-T

A witty prose satire on Charles II attributed to Denham by Edmund Goldsmid in *Bibliotheca Curiosa. Some Political Satires of the Seventeenth Century,* 1885. Goldsmid gives no evidence to support his attribution, nor does the piece contain any internal evidence of authorship. I have been unable to discover the original.

THE/LAWREL/AND the/AX:/A/FABLE. Folio sheet, undated.

MADAM/Semphronia's Farewel,/OR AN/ELEGY/*Written by* D. P. Folio sheet, undated.

An Exact/COPY OF A/LETTER,/Sent to *William Laud* late Archbishop of *Canterbury*, now Prisoner in the Tower/*November* the 5. 1641. At which his Lordship taking exceptions, the Author/ visited him in his owne person: and having admittance to him, had some/private discourse with him; concerning the cruelty, in which he for-/merly raigned in his power. The substance whereof is truly compo-/sed by the Author himselfe. Wherein doth appeare a sign of com-/plying with the time, and some hopes of his Repentance./ (Cut)/*London Printed for H.W. and T.B.* 1641.

These three items were attributed to Denham in the catalogue of the Wrenn Library, now at the University of Texas. Neither of the poems is in Denham's style; neither contains any indication of his authorship; indeed, the title of *Madam Semphronia* bears direct evidence to the contrary. The prose pamphlet also contains no definite evidence of Denham's authorship. We know from *The Sophy,* written about this time, that Denham was interested in religious questions, and it is possible that he is the author, but there is no evidence one way or the other.

Through the kindness of Mr. Thomas J. Wise, from whom Wrenn bought many books and pamphlets, I can understand in part how these came to be attributed to Denham. In a letter of Feb. 26, 1923, Wise writes, "As you are aware, it is frequently the case that when one buys an old folio volume of pamphlets in order to obtain a Prior or a Pope, there are many pieces of old literature bound with it of which the origin is unknown. One point upon which Wrenn and I never agreed was the method of dealing with these waifs and strays. I advocate leaving them alone to await some chance revelation of their authorship. It was his (very proper) ambition to gather in this class of literature in order that it might be made available in America. But instead of leaving the question of authorship entirely open, whenever there was the smallest suggestion of the identity of the author of any particular poem or tract, he insisted upon its being placed temporarily under the name of that author. As a temporary measure this was all right; and had Wrenn lived to print his own catalogue he would have explained how each came to be so attributed. But he died, and left his work half-finished, and his son had just to catalogue

the books as they stood. . . . Many times at my house we have
gone over a bundle of these anonymous things that had accumu-
lated, and if (for instance) Aiken said, 'That may be by Gay,'
or 'Prior may have had a hand in this,' down they went under
the names of Gay and Prior—but only as a temporary make-shift."

This letter indicates that the same method was followed in the
case of these items.

UPON HER MAJESTY'S NEW BUILDINGS AT SOMERSET HOUSE

This was attributed to Denham by Sir Sidney Lee in the *Diction-
ary of National Biography*. It first appeared anonymously as a
broadside in 1665, but was included in the third, 1668, edition of
Waller's poems, during the life of both Denham and Waller, and in
all subsequent editions of Waller.

VERSES

A poem with this title appears as Denham's in *The Fifth Part of
Miscellany Poems . . . Publish'd by Mr Dryden . . . The Fourth
Edition*, 1716. This is merely a section of *The Sophy*, Act IV, ll. 17-
66.

DIRECTIONS TO A PAINTER

These poems appeared under Denham's name but I consider his
authorship impossible.

Waller began the series of "Directions" by his poem, *Instructions
to a Painter for the drawing of the posture and progress of His Ma*ties
*forces at sea under command of his Highness Royal. Together with the
battel and victory obtained over the Dutch, June 3, 1665.* This poem
is a fulsome eulogy of the Duke of York.

Next came THE/Second Advice/*TO A*/PAINTER,/For Drawing
the/HISTORY/Of our/*NAVALL* Business;/*In Imitation of Mr.*
WALLER./Being the last Work of Sir JOHN DENHAM./Printed in
the Year, 1667. This is a poem of 340 lines, beginning "Nay Painter,
if thou dar'st, design that fight." It satirizes the conduct of the Duke
of York in the battle of Lowestoft, June, 1665, which Waller had
lauded, and the Earl of Sandwich's conduct before Bergen in August

of the same year. It is possible that this is the poem referred to by
Pepys, December 14, 1666, when he says, "And here I met with, sealed
up, from Sir H. Cholmly, the lampoone, or the Mocke-Advice to a
Paynter, abusing the Duke of York and my Lord Sandwich, Pen, and
the King himself, in all the matters of the navy and warr."

Next came THE/Second, and Third Advice/*TO A/PAINTER,*/
For Drawing the/HISTORY/Of our/*NAVALL* Actions,/The two
last Years, 1665 And 1666./ *In Answer to Mr.* WALLER./(Motto)/
A. Breda, 1667.

It consists of (1) a reprint of the *Second Advice,* "Nay painter"
etc., under the heading THE/Second Advice/*TO A*/PAINTER,/
FOR/Drawing the History of our/*NAVALL* Bussiness;/*In Answer
to Mr.* Waller.; and (2) the poem beginning "Sandwich in Spain
now and the Duke in love," under the heading THE/Third Advice/
TO A PAINTER,/On our last Summers Success,/with *French* and
Dutch./1666./Written by the same Hand as the former was. The
subject of the *Third Advice* is the four days' battle of the Downs,
June, 1666.

Finally came DIRECTIONS/TO A/PAINTER/FOR/Describing
our Naval Business:/In Imitation of Mr. *WALLER.*/BEING/The
Last Works/OF/Sir JOHN DENHAM./Whereunto is annexed,/
CLARINDONS House-Warming./By an Unknown AUTHOR./
Printed in the Year 1667. This contains, (1) the *Second Advice,*
"Nay painter," (2) the *Third Advice,* "Sandwich in Spain now," and
(3) two new sections: "Draw England ruined by what was giv'n be-
fore," which describes the ascent of the Thames by the Dutch, June,
1667; and "Painter where wast thy former work did cease?" which
treats of the events following the Treaty of Breda, July 31, 1667.

Considering the poems as a whole, we can find four arguments
against Denham's authorship: (1) There had always been doubt of
their authenticity. Wood says, ". . . to which directions, tho' Sir
John Denham's name is set, yet they were thought by many to have
been written by Andr. Marvell Esq.";[1] and in the reprint of the
Directions in *Poems on Affairs of State,* 1703, vol. I, we find this
note in the table of contents: "Said to be written by Sir John Denham,

[1] *Athenae Oxoniensis,* 1721, II, 424.

but believed to be writ by Mr. Milton";[2] (2) the events described in some of the poems fall within the period of Denham's insanity. This will be treated in greater detail below; (3) evidence of style points to the conclusion that the poems are not the work of one man; (4) it is incredible that Denham, holding the office of Surveyor-General and being a favorite at court, should have openly published under his own name poems attacking state policies and high officials, and even the King himself. It would, however, be very natural for some-one else to shelter himself under Denham's well-known name. Nor could Denham have written the poems without intending to have them published; such a proceeding would have been not only dangerous, but pointless, as the very *raison d'être* of such political satires is publicity.

Considering the poems separately in their chronological order, we come first to the *Second Advice*. Stylistically, this might perhaps be Denham's; there are but three feminine rhymes; there are no full stops within the line; the proportion of open to closed couplets is only about one to ten; and the lines have a tendency toward an-tithesis which is more pronounced than in the other poems. It is, how-ever, like the others, full of elisions (see the second quotation below) which are entirely uncharacteristic of Denham. The first part, dealing with the battle of Lowestoft, is evidently written with Waller's poem in mind, which gives point to the couplet occurring near the end:

> Now may historians argue con and pro;
> Denham says thus, though always Waller so.

The appearance of Denham's name in the text might under other circumstances be considered a bit of evidence supporting his author-ship, but here it seems merely put in as a blind.

Apart from style, there are two serious difficulties: (1) We do not know when Denham recovered from his fit of insanity. He was striken in April, 1666, and we hear no more of him until June, 1667. How long during this interval his attack lasted, and how severe it was, is unknown. It is true that the events described took place in the summer of 1665, but I imagine that the poem was not written

---

[2] This may be a reproduction of Wood's statement with the blunder of Milton for Marvell.

much before its publication, for the reason given above, that work of this character finds its way early into print. In any event, if this is the first of three editions dated 1667, it must have been published fairly early in the year and we may well hesitate to assign a poem to Denham when the last we have heard of him is that he thinks himself the Holy Ghost.[3] (2) The poem continues, after the couplet quoted above, as follows:

> And he good man, in his long sheet and staff,
> This pennance did for Cromwel's epitaph;
> And his next theam must be o' th' Duke's mistress,
> Advice to draw Madam l'Edificatress.

The Duke of York's mistress was Lady Denham. The "Lady Builder" could refer to no one else, and Pepys in 1665 and 1666 has frequent references to the affair. Although Denham was perhaps a complaisant husband, it seems impossible that he should thus refer to his wife's infidelity.

We come next to the *Second and Third Advice*. This is probably the poem referred to by Pepys, January 20, 1666/7: "He did lend me 'The Third Advice to a Paynter,' a bitter satyre upon the service of the Duke of Albermarle last year." It consists of a reprint of the *Second Advice,* and in addition the *Third Advice,* beginning, "Sandwich in Spain now and the Duke in love." I do not consider this poem Denham's for the following reasons: (1) The proportion of open couplets is almost double that of the *Second Advice,* being about two to ten. (2) The naval battle that the poem describes took place in June, 1666, only two months after the violent outbreak of his insanity, so that the above objections apply with still more force here. (3) The phrase "the Duke in love" refers to the intrigue of the Duke with Lady Denham. (See above.)

Lastly, we come to the *Directions to a Painter*. This contains the *Second* and the *Third Advice* and two other poems in addition, dealing with the events of the summer of 1667: "Draw England ruin'd by what was giv'n before," and "Painter, where wast thy former work did cease?" My reasons for rejecting these poems are two: (1)

---

[3] Mr. T. W. Baldwin in *Modern Language Notes,* December, 1927, p. 508, shows this argument to be of no value, by proving that Denham had recovered his sanity by September, 1666.

their attacks on the King; (2) their style. In the first, the proportion
of feminine rhymes is higher than in the *Second Advice,* and the ratio
of open and closed couplets is almost four to ten. In the second, the
difference is even more marked. There are thirteen feminine rhymes,
at least twenty full stops within the line, and the ratio of open and
closed couplets is about three to four.

To sum up: the *Second Advice,* judged merely by its style, might
possibly be by Denham, though it has uncharacteristic points, but his
authorship is made very doubtful by (1) the fact that he may have
been insane at the time the poem was written or published, and (2)
the reference to his wife's intrigue; the *Third Advice* has not so strong
a stylistic argument in its favor, and is open to the same two ob-
jections that the *Second Advice* is; the *Directions* have none of the
characteristics of Denham's mature style, are prosodically markedly
different from the two earlier poems of the series, and openly attack
the King. The tone of the whole series is that of an irresponsible free-
lance critic, rather than a courtier and a dependent of the King.

For further information on later "Advices" and "Directions" see
Pepys' *Diary,* Wheatley edition of 1920, VI, 101, note.

Appendix C.

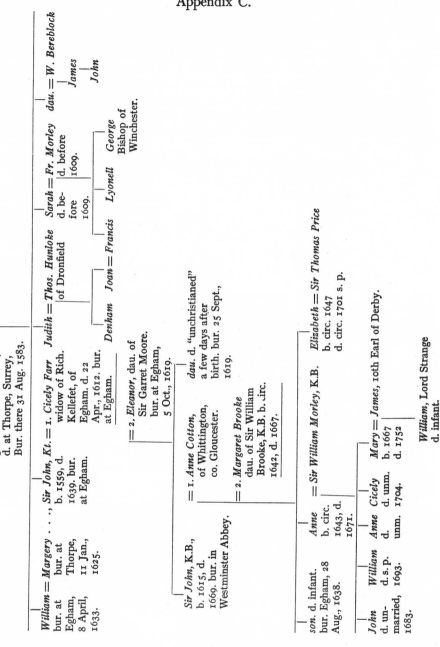

William Denham = Joane . . . .
goldsmith of London,
d. at Thorpe, Surrey,
Bur. there 31 Aug. 1583.

William = Margery . . . , Sir John, Kt. = 1. Cicely Farr   Judith = Thos. Hunloke   Sarah = Fr. Morley   dau. = W. Bereblock
bur. at   bur. at   b. 1559, d.   widow of Rich.   of Dronfield   d. be-   d. before
Egham,   Thorpe,   1639. bur.   Kellefet, of   fore   1609.   James
8 April,   11 Jan.,   at Egham.   Egham. d. 22   1609.
1633.   1625.   Apr., 1612. bur.   John
at Egham.   Denham   Joan = Francis   Lyonell   George
Bishop of
= 2. Eleanor, dau. of   Denham   Joan = Francis   Winchester.
Sir Garret Moore.
bur. at Egham,
5 Oct., 1619.

= 1. Anne Cotton,   dau. d. "unchristianed"
of Whittington,   a few days after
co. Gloucester.   birth. bur. 25 Sept.,
1619.
= 2. Margaret Brooke
dau. of Sir William
Brooke, K.B. b. circ.
1642, d. 1667.

Sir John, K.B.,   Anne   = Sir William Morley, K.B.   Elizabeth = Sir Thomas Price
b. 1615, d.   b. circ.   b. circ. 1647
1660. bur. in   1643, d.   d. circ. 1701 s. p.
Westminster Abbey.   1671.

son. d. infant.   John   William   Anne   Cicely   Mary = James, 10th Earl of Derby.
bur. Egham, 28   d. un-   d. s. p.   d.   d. unm.   b. 1667
Aug., 1638.   married,   1693.   unm.   1704.   d. 1752
1683.
William, Lord Strange
d. infant.

Appendix D.

REFERENCES TO, AND IMITATIONS OF COOPER'S HILL

Anon.
   See p. 49.

Anon.
   Cooper's Hill. A Poem. Address'd to Sir Watkin Williams Wynne, Bart, London. [n.d.]

Anon.
   Three New Poems. Viz. I Family Duty . . . II The Curious Wife . . . III Buckingham House, a Poem after the Manner of Sir John Denham's Cooper's Hill, 1721.

Addison.
   "Nor Denham must we e're forget thy strains,
      While Cooper's Hill commands the neighb'ring plains."
         An Account of the Greatest English Poets to Mr. H.S.
                  (*The Annual Miscellany,* 1694, p. 325.)

Brome, Alex.
   "Thou hast subject and wit, if thou hast but a will
      Thou may'st make a poem, next that Cooper's Hill."
                  To his Friend T.S., ll. 37-38.

Buckingham.
   See Sheffield.

Butler.
   See p. 49.

Chetwood.
   I am troubled . . . that every farthing of any temporal fortune you have is upon the balance to be lost. I suppose you mean at Drapier's Hill; take care it comes up to Coopers.
                  Chetwood to Swift, Sept. 10, 1729. Swift,
                     Correspondence (ed. F. E. Ball), IV, 95.

Dennis.

Remarks upon Mr. Pope's translation of Homer, with two Letters concerning Windsor Forest, and the Temple of Fame.

The *Observations upon Windsor Forest* is a long eulogy of *Cooper's Hill,* the tone of which is sufficiently indicated by the opening sentences: "You are in the right of it: *Windsor Forest* is a wretched rhapsody, not worthy the observation of a man of sense. I shall only take occasion from it to display the beauties of *Cooper's Hill,* in emulation of which it was impudently writ."

Elwin.

"Pope considered that the 'reflections upon life and political institutions' were the distinguishing excellence of Cooper's Hill. He emulated in this respect his master's merits, surpassing him in polish of style, and fell below him in strength of thought."

Pope, *Poetry* (ed. Elwin Courthope), I, 336.

[Fage.]

St. Leonard's Hill. A Poem, Written by R. F. Gent., 1666. The earliest imitation of *Cooper's Hill* I have found.

Felton, Henry.

"Sir John Denham is famed for his Coopers-Hill, and Windsor is more honoured in being the subject of his prospect, than the hill is in being the subject of his poem. For Windsor is only the ornament of his hill, but his poem is the ornament of Windsor."

A Dissertation on reading the Classics, 1718, p. 218.

Garth, Samuel.

"They that have seen those two excellent poems of Cooper's Hill and Windsor Forest . . . will shew a great deal of candour if they approve of this."

Preface to Claremont, Works, 1773, p. 101.

Goldsmith.

"This poem . . . though it may have been exceeded by later attempts in description, yet deserves the highest applause, as it far surpasses all that went before it: the concluding part, though a little too much crowded, is very masterly."

The Beauties of English Poesy, 1767, I, 81.

Gosse.

"This poem was so decisive a victory for the adherents of the
classical school that we may call it their Marston Moor, and not too
fantastically conceive Denham and Waller, for Waller certainly
had a share in its execution, as routing the forces of the romanticists
with their ranks of serried couplets. In spite of all successive at-
tempts in the same style . . . Cooper's Hill still remains the most
celebrated, though perhaps the least read, of topographical poems.

"It is not quite true, as all the Augustan critics used to aver, that
no topographical poetry had been written in England before Den-
ham. Drayton's *Polyolbion*, and Browne's *Brittania's Pastorals* be-
long, no doubt, to altogether a different order; but it is very extraor-
dinary if Denham had never read the *Penshurst* of Ben Jonson.
There was, however, something to be distinguished between the
praise of a great peer's house and the tribute to a national river.
The *Penshurst* belonged to the old political dispensation, *Cooper's
Hill* to the new. As before, Denham showed himself extremely dex-
trous in calling public attention to his verses; they were full of
actuality. . . . There was a certain manly directness about Den-
ham, which at once recommended him to the public. In the reprints
of his poems which he himself issued, and in those which have since
been standard, the tone of *Cooper's Hill* is rigidly Royalist. But a
glance at the very rare first edition of 1642, shows that the author
revised almost every other line, and omitted whole passages which
proved him to lean towards the Neuters. At present the sudden
reference to St. Paul's and the eulogy of Waller, follow the invoca-
tion very abruptly. In 1642 these were led up to by some curious
lines, the appropriateness of which when Waller's plot was dis-
covered a few months later on, must have made Denham's ears
tingle and his hair stand on end:

> Some study plots, and some those plots t'undoe,
> Others to make 'em and undoe 'em too,
> False to their hopes, afraid to be secure,
> Those mischiefs only which they make endure,
> Blinded with light, and sicke of being well,
> In tumults seek their peace, their heaven in hell.

Of course Denham intended no reference to his friend's projects, of which he probably knew nothing; his mysterious allusions are doubtless to such double dealings as Hotham's conduct with regard to the proposed capitulation of Hull. Our author's most extraordinary indiscretion, however, occurs at the close of the first edition, which ended with these lines:

> Therefore their boundless power tell princes draw
> Within the channel and the shore of law,
> And may that law which teaches kings to sway
> Their sceptres, teach their subjects to obey.

"This was the very doctrine of the Neuters, and cannot have given Charles I any satisfaction, if a copy of his servant's poem came into his hands as he sat down in a passion to the beleaguerment of Gloucester. . . .

"On the whole, there are few poems which have enjoyed so great and so sustained a reputation as *Cooper's Hill*, which so little respond to it in the eyes of a modern reader. Yet we must not lose sight of the fact that its fame *was* sustained, and seek to discover the cause. Long after Cowley, Davenant, and their crew had sunk into neglect, Denham and Waller preserved their reputation unassailed. Prior asserts their importance, as the two pioneers of our poetry. Pope and Garth, who represent the extremity of critical acumen in an age which had begun to look without prejudice on the founders of its own fashions, spoke out clearly in praise of Denham. . . . To comprehend all this we must, in the first place, acknowledge the genuine force and sinew of Denham's rugged poem. There is sound thought in it, carefully expressed, without adornment or choice of melody, in successive blows of the sledge-hammer. After once this sort of writing had been conceived, it was comparatively easy to improve upon it, to give regularity to the stroke, grace and ease to the movement. The praise of having invented, or at least having been the first to employ in a sustained effort, a new form of English poetry must always insure Denham a niche in the history of our literature."

From Shakespeare to Pope, pp. 88-93.

Hallam, Henry.

"This argumentative school of verse was . . . much in unison with the character of that generation. . . . Cooper's Hill . . . belongs in a considerable degree to this reasoning class of poems. It is also descriptive, but the description is made to slide into philosophy. The plan is original, as far as our poetry is concerned, and I do not recollect any exception in other languages . . .

"The epithet *majestic* Denham, conferred by Pope, conveys rather too much; but Cooper's Hill is no ordinary poem. It is nearly the first instance of vigorous and rhythmical couplets, for Denham is incomparably less feeble than Browne, and less prosaic than Beaumont. Close in thought, and nervous in language like Davies, he is less hard and less monotonous; his cadences are animated and various, perhaps a little beyond the regularity that metre demands; they have been the guide to the finer ear of Dryden. Those who cannot endure the philosophic poetry must ever be dissatisfied with Cooper's Hill; no personification, no ardent words, few metaphors beyond the common use of speech, nothing that warms, or melts, or fascinates the heart. It is rare to find lines of eminent beauty in Denham; and equally so to be struck by any one as feeble or low. His language is always well-chosen and perspicuous, free from those strange turns of expression, frequent in our older poets, . . . the expletive *do* . . . seldom occurs in Denham, and he has in other respects brushed away the rust of languid and ineffective redundancies which have obstructed the popularity of men with more native genius than himself."

Introduction to the Literature of Europe, 1842, III, 30-31.

Hay, Williams.

"Mount Caburn is a spiritless imitation of Cooper's Hill, a bad copy of the noblest original. This prospect does not afford a Thames, a Windsor, or a London which are the peculiar embellishments of the other, and subjects worthy the great poet who sung them."

Introduction to Mount Caburn, A Poem, 1730.

Herrick.

To M. Denham, on his Prospective Poem. Complete Poems (ed. Grosart), 1876, II, 220.

Johnson.

"Cooper's Hill is the work that confers upon him the rank and dignity of an original author. He seems to have been, at least among us, the author of a species of composition that may be denominated *local poetry,* of which the fundamental subject is some particular landscape, to be poetically described, with the addition of such embellishments as may be supplied by historical retrospection, or incidental meditation.

"To trace a new scheme of poetry has in itself a very high claim to praise, and its praise is yet more when it is apparently copied by Garth and Pope; after whose names little will be gained by an enumeration of smaller poets, that have left scarce a corner of the island not dignified either by rhyme, or blank verse.

"Coopers Hill, if it be maliciously inspected, will not be found without its faults. The digressions are too long, the morality too frequent, and the sentiments sometimes such as will not bear a rigorous enquiry."

Lives of the Poets (ed. Waugh), I, 90-91.

Paget, Thomas Catesby, Lord Paget.

"Sir John Denham's Cooper's Hill has met with universal applause, tho' its subject seems rather descriptive than instructing; but 'tis not the hill, the river, nor the stag chace, 'tis the good sense and the fine reflections so frequently interspers'd, and as it were interwoven with the rest, that gives it the value, and will make it, as was said of true wit, everlasting like the sun."

An Essay on Human Life, 1736, preface.

Pope.

"Bear me, O bear me to sequester'd scenes,
The bowery mazes, and surrounding greens;
To Thames's banks, which fragrant breezes fill,
Or where ye Muses sport on Cooper's Hill.

(On Cooper's Hill eternal wreaths shall grow,
While lasts the mountain, or while Thames shall flow)

.   .   .   .

Here his first lays majestic Denham sung;
There the last numbers flow'd from Cowley's tongue."
                                    Windsor Forest, ll. 261-272.

"Who now shall charm the shades where Cowley strung
His living harp, and lofty Denham sung?"
                                    Ibid., ll. 279-280.

"This is one, among a thousand instances of Homer's indirect
and oblique manner of introducing moral sentences and instruc-
tions. These agreeably break in upon his reader even in descriptions
and poetical parts, where one naturally expects only painting and
amusement . . . I must do a noble English poet the justice to
observe that it is this particular art that is the very distinguishing
excellence of Cooper's Hill; throughout which the descriptions of
places and images raised by the poet are still tending to some hint,
or leading into some reflection upon moral life or political institu-
tion, much in the same manner as the real sight of such scenes and
prospects is apt to give the mind a composed turn, and incline it
to thoughts and contemplations that have a relation to the object."
                    Pope, *The Iliad of Homer*, 1763, III, 169, note.

Scott, John.
    "Perhaps few poems have received more indiscriminate applause
yet possessed less intrinsick merit than Denham's Cooper's Hill."
                        *Critical Essays on Some of the Poems of
                        Several English Poets*, 1785, p. 1.

Scott allows the poem little if any merit. It is difficult to account
for his animosity and the bitterness of his tone. Much of his criti-
cism is wide of the mark. He points out with justice, however, Den-
ham's frequent lapses from grammatical exactitude.

Sheffield, John, Duke of Buckingham.
    "If yet a just coherence be not made
    Between each thought; and the whole model laid

So right that ev'ry line may higher rise
Like goodly mountains till they reach the skies . . .
'Tis epigram, 'tis point, 'tis what you will,
But not an elegy nor writ with skill,
No Panegyrick nor a Cooper's Hill."

An Essay on Poetry, 1691, ll. 106 ff.

Somerville, William.

"Tread with respectful awe
Windsor's green glades, where Denham, tuneful bard,
Charm'd once the list'ning Dryads with his song
Sublimely sweet."

The Chace, 1735, Bk. III, ll. 346-349.

Swift.

"Then, with a long spear he [Homer] slew Denham, a stout
Modern, who from his father's side derived his lineage from
Apollo, but his mother was of mortal race. He fell, and bit the
earth. The celestial part Apollo took, and made it a star; but the
terrestrial lay wallowing upon the ground."

Battle of the Books, Prose Works (ed. Temple Scott), I, 178.

Taine, H. A.

Taine has three pages of eulogy of the poem, of which the following
may serve as an example:

"Tous ces sujets sont appropriés à la noblesse et aux limites de
l'esprit classique, et déploient ses forces sans révéler ses faiblesses
. . . L'agrément s'y joint à la solidité; l'auteur de Cooper's Hill
sait plaire autant qu'imposer."

Histoire de la Littérature Anglaise, 1863, II, 532.

Vaughan.

"Cotswold and Cooper's, both have met
With learnèd swains, and echo yet
Their pipes and wit."

Mount of Olives, stanza 2.

Ward, James.

"Shall Cooper's Hill, majestic rise in rhyme,
Strong as its bases, as its brow sublime?

Shall Windsor Forest win immortal praise,
Itself outlasting in its poet's lays?
And thou, O Phoenix Park! remain so long
Unknown to fame, and unadorn'd in song?"

Phoenix Park, ll. 1-6. (*Miscellany Poems, Original and
Translated, by several hands*. Concanen, 1724).

Welsted, Leonard.
"The rabble's cry, untaught by reason's rules,
Nor truth to traitors gives, nor wit to fools; . . .
The marsh becomes not, hence, a limpid rill;
Nor Windsor Forest shines a Cooper's Hill."

Of False Fame, Works, 1787, p. 201.

Wood.
"A poem it is which for the majesty of the stile is, and ever will
be the exact standard of good writing."

Athenae Oxoniensis, 1721, II, 423.

Appendix E.

"*THAMES*" *COUPLETS*, COOPER'S HILL, ll. 189-192

Imitations and References.

Anon.

> "Serene yet nervous, stately yet not proud;
> Gay but not wanton, lofty but not loud."
>
> > *The Devil, A Wife and a Poet. A Satyr. (The Grove,*
> > > *or a Collection of Original Poems, 1721.)*

Anon.

> "To Addison I first apply'd;
> Poet and orator beside;
> Much his great name to justness owes;
> When highest swell'd, he ne'er o'erflows;
> And when the dang'rous deep he shuns,
> Tho' low yet clear and sweet he runs."
>
> > *Familiar Epistle to the Earl of Sunderland.*
> > *(Miscellany Poems, Original and Translated,*
> > > *by several hands.* Concanen, 1724.)

Anon.

> "Oh! could I copy in Harmonious lays,
> Great monument! Thy pattern how to raise,
> To thee, oh Sheffield, monuments of praise,
> As thou'rt like Cooper's Hill, an equal theme,
> So would I rival Denham in his fame,
> And Sheffield should approve the generous flame."
>
> > *Three New Poems; Viz. I Family Duty* . . . 1721, p. 12.

Anon.

> "Brave without rashness, wise without deceit,
> Conscious of worth, without vain-glory great."
>
> > *Ibid.*, p. 22.

Anon.

> "Unruffled in its course a flood I spy'd
> So calm, so smooth, it scarcely seem'd to glide;

So deep, and yet so clear, that ev'ry stone
With borrow'd lustre from the bottom shone."

Bysshe, *British Parnassus*, 1714, II, 768.

Cartwright.
   See p. 53.

Dryden.
   "I am sure there are few who make verses have observ'd the
sweetness of these two lines in *Cooper's Hill:* [quotes] And there
are yet fewer who can find the reason for that sweetness."

Dedication of the Aeneid (Cambridge ed.), p. 512.

Dyer, John.
   "But stay—Methinks her lays I hear,
   So smooth! so sweet! so deep! so clear!"

Country Walk, ll. 68-69.

[Fage.]

"... or did invite
To taste of Hellicons inspiring streams,
Although perhaps not half as clear as Thames."

St. Leonard's Hill, 1666, p. 1.

Gosse.
   "These are marvellous lines; they are among the memories of
our language; and if Sir John Denham had been habitually lifted
on this graceful and pure level of eloquence, most later poets, at
all events those of his own order, might have addressed to him the
same adroit compliment. But there exists a mystery about these
lines. In collating the first edition I was amazed to find them en-
tirely absent, and they do not occur until the second edition of the
poem, published in 1643. . . . Nor is the versification of the poem
in any other instance so fine and regular as in the celebrated quat-
rain, which, for want of better information, we must continue to
consider the most brilliant example of second thoughts in the Eng-
lish language."

From Shakespeare to Pope, p. 91.

Gray.

> "Now the rich stream of music winds along,
> Deep, majestic, smooth and strong."
>
> *Progress of Poetry*, ll. 7-8.

Hallam, Henry.

"The comparison by Denham between the Thames and his own poetry was once celebrated.

"[Quotes the couplets and Johnson's criticism.] But the ground of objection is, in fact, that the lines contain nothing but wit, and that wit which turns on a play of words. They are rather ingenious in this respect, and remarkably harmonious, which is probably the secret of their popularity; but as poetry, they deserve no great praise."

Introduction to the Literature of Europe, 1842, III, 31, note.

Hill.

"I am sorry the Man of Ross, who is so beautifully your *theme*, is not, like the Thames to Sir John Denham, your example also."

> Pope, *Letters* (ed. Elwin Courthope), V, 47.

Hughes.

> "For see where beauteous Thames do's glide
> Serene, but with a fruitful tide;
> Free from extreams of ebb and flow,
> Not swell'd too high, nor sunk too low."
>
> *A Thought in a Garden.* (*Poems and Translations
> by several hands*, 1714, p. 154.)

Jacob, Hildebrand.

> "Tho' blind, yet bold; tho' dumb, you teach to speak;
> Strong without bones; and thro' your triumph weak."
>
> *The Silent Flute*, ll. 33-34.

Johnson.

"The four verses, which, since Dryden has commended them, almost every writer for a century past has imitated, are generally known:

[Quotes.]

The lines are not in themselves perfect; for most of the words, thus artfully opposed, are to be understood simply on one side of the comparison, and metaphorically on the other; and if there be any language which does not express intellectual operations by material images, into that language they cannot be translated. But so much meaning is comprised in so few words; the particulars of resemblance are so perspicaciously collected, and every mode of excellence separated from its adjacent fault by so nice a line of limitation; the different parts of the sentence are so accurately adjusted; and the flow of the last couplet is so smooth and sweet; that the passage, however celebrated, has not been praised above its merit. It has beauty peculiar to itself, and must be numbered among those felicities which cannot be produced at will by wit and labour, but must arise unexpectedly in some hour propitious to poetry."

Lives of the Poets (ed. Waugh), I, 91-92.

Knapp, Francis.

"Let me ne'er flow like thee! nor make thy stream
My sad example or my wretched theme."

To Mr. Pope on his Windsor Forest,
ll. 52-53. (*Windsor Forest*, 1720.)

Mallet, David.

"Great without swelling, without meanness plain,
Serious, not simple, sportive, but not vain;
On Trifles slight, on things of use profound,
In quoting sober, and in judging sound."

Of Verbal Criticism, 1733, ll. 221-224.

Mason, John.

"I shall conclude my Remarks on the Iambic Measure with observing, that from the Principles before advanced, we may be able to account for the peculiar Elegance of that celebrated Distich of Mr. *Denham's* in his *Cooper's Hill,* which hath been rendered so famous by Mr. *Dryden's* proposing it as a Sort of Problem to exercise the Wits of Grammarians, to discover the true Source of its Harmony.

Tho' deep, | yet clear; | tho' gen|tle, yet | not dull;

Strong with|out rage; | without | o'er flow|ing full.

Mr. *Hughes* supposes that all the admired Music of these Lines arises from the free and unforced Quantity of the Syllables, the Propriety of the Pauses, diversifying the Grammatical Structure of the Sentences, transporting the Order of the Words, and closing the Couplet with the emphatical Word *full;* and then concludes, *if there be any other mystery in these lines, I own, it is beyond my skill to discover it.* Now I apprehend there is a further Mystery in them, which indeed he was not aware of, arising from the Order and Quality of the Poetical Numbers; in the Choice and Disposition of which the Poet was extremely happy. For he hath introduced into these two Lines every one of the dissyllable Feet; the Iambic and Pyrrhic in the first, and the Trochee and Spondee in the second. So that it hath all the Advantage of Harmony which Variety of Numbers can give it. Nor is he less happy in the Disposition of these Numbers. For in the first Line, excepting the fourth Foot, they are all Iambics; the last Part of each falling not only on accented Syllables, but emphatical Words, and those in Contrast too, makes the Sound and the Sense most perfectly accord. The fourth Place is possessed by a Pyrrhic, which is always an agreeable movement. . . .

"The second Line begins with a Trochee; which gives Motion, as it were, to the River; but is immediately checked by the Spondees and Iambics that alternately follow. So that the stately Flow of the Numbers expresses that of the River they describe

And the Sound is still an Eccho to the Sense.

"In a Word then, the Beauty of this Distich consists in two Things, *viz.* the Elegance of the Stile, and the Harmony of the Verse.—The Elegance of the Stile arises from the Transposition of the Words, the Propriety of the Pauses, and the Contrasts of the Description; and the Harmony of the Verse arises from the Variety and Disposition of the Numbers, happily adapted to the Emphasis of the Words, and the Nature of the Subject; as I have just shewn. And this I take to be a true Solution of this Poetical Problem, which there needs no other *Ædipus* to unriddle than a little Insight into the Power of Numbers and the Principles of Verse."

An Essay on the Power of Numbers, 1749, p. 59.

Meredith.

" 'So, then, life is going smoothly,' said Emma.
'Yes, at a good pace and smoothly: not a torrent—
Thames-like, "without o'erflowing full." ' "

Diana of the Crossways, 1885, II, 142.

Monboddo, James Burnet, Lord.

"In monosyllables he [the poet] has a greater liberty [of accentuation], but which he ought not to abuse by laying the accent upon insignificant monosyllables . . . On the contrary, it is a great beauty of verse, when the monosyllable, on which the accent is thrown, is a word that not only will bear an emphasis, but requires it . . . And this is one of the beauties of that celebrated distich of Mr. Denham, in his *Cooper's Hill*, which Mr. Dryden proposes as a problem to exercise the wits of the critics, to discover the reasons why it is so harmonious.

[Quotes.]

Where the emphasis, as well as the accent, falls upon the monosyllables *deep, clear, strong, rage*, and *full*. But this is not the only beauty of those lines. For, in the *first* place, There are the antithesis of *deep* and *clear*—*gentle* and *dull*—*strong* and *without rage*—*full* and *without o'erflowing*. 2ndly, If these antitheses had been all expressed in the same manner, I should have thought there were too many of them, and that the composition was too uniform. But there is only a similarity in the two first of them; which being carried no further, I think, is a beauty. And the expression of the two in the second line is different not only from those in the first, but from one another. These are beauties of composition independent of the versification. But *lastly,* There is a further beauty in the versification besides that already observed, namely, that the second line begins with a Trochee, that is, with an accented syllable, in place of an unaccented, with which the first line begins. This gives a flow to the second line very different from that of the first, and gives a beautiful variety to the whole, which

otherwise the four antitheses, notwithstanding the change of expres-
sion, would render a little too uniform in the structure."

Of the Origin and Progress of Language,
1774-1809, II, 389-390, note.

Pope.

"So soft though high, so loud and yet so clear,
Ev'n list'ning angels leaned from heav'n to hear."

The Temple of Fame, ll. 374-375.

"Flow, Welsted, flow! like thine inspirer, beer,
Tho' stale, not ripe, tho' thin, yet never clear;
So sweetly mawkish, and so smoothly dull;
Heady, not strong; o'erflowing, tho' not full."

Dunciad, Bk. III, ll. 169-172.

Prior.

"But her own king she likens to his Thames,
With gentle course devolving fruitful streams;
Serene yet strong, majestic yet sedate,
Swift without violence, without terror great."

Carmen Seculare for the year 1700, ll. 280-283.

Say, Samuel.

"The like contraste to each other, I imagine, must be added to
the many accounts that have been given of the pleasure which
every reader is sensible of in that celebrated[1] distich in Cooper's

---

[1] The late Mr. Hughes, in a sketch for an Essay on the Harmony of Verse
(which was never finished), endeavors to account for the beauty of this distich
in the following manner:

"As the harmony of these lines has all the perfection that can arise from the
unforc'd quantity of the syllables, so is that harmony varied by the stops, the
diversifying the grammatical structure of each sentence, and the different placing
of the accent on the words. It may seem very minute to explain this particularly;
but because Mr. Dryden has somewhere mentioned the musick of these lines as a
riddle which few cou'd explain, and has kept that secret to himself, it may not
be amiss to offer at a solution of it.

"I shall say nothing of the natural and unforc'd quantities in these two lines,
(which are immediately obvious to every reader) but only that by this means
the verse is smooth, and there is no need to distort any word in the pronouncing
to make it stand in the verse. The four pauses are also musical, each containing

Hill, which Mr. Dryden has render'd so remarkable by proposing the true reason of it as a problem to torture the grammarians. For nothing can be more different than the sounds, and the numbers or movements in the two verses, as will appear to the ear itself, and by measuring the time in the feet of either, that are oppos'd to the other.

$$\text{Th\=o' d\=ep, y\u{e}t cl\=ar; th\=o' g\=entle, y\u{e}t n\u{o}t d\=ull;}$$

where the verse moves as slow, and silent, or as gentle as the river: All in iambics, if we call 'em so, that are nearer to spondees, excepting in one place, where it had been a manifest impropriety.

But stronger ideas requir'd numbers stronger and fuller: and such is the following verse.

$$\text{Str\=ong w\u{i}th\=out r\u{a}ge; w\u{i}th\=out \=o'erfl\=owing, f\u{u}ll.}$$

It begins with a trochee, which gives motion to the river; but check'd by a spondee of two very long times, oppos'd to the shorter times of that which stands in the same place, in the preceding verse; as the trochee here is oppos'd to a spondee of longer sound in the former. The like we may observe in the true or genuine iambic in the third foot, which is oppos'd to the gentler spondee above it: And as the weakest sounds fall, as the ideas require they should, on the fourth and fifth feet in the first; so the sounds, that fill and arrest the ear, stand in the fourth movement here,

an entire sentence; but this musick wou'd not be so perfect if the grammatical structure of each sentence was the same; as if, for example, it run thus:

Tho' deep, yet clear; tho' gentle, yet lively;
Tho' strong, yet calm; tho' full, yet restrain'd.

This, tho' the quantities of the syllables were kept as exactly as at present, would not make so musical a verse. But (as it is in Denham) the second sentence is varied from the first by the negative; the third from both the preceding; and the last sentence from the third by the participle, and the transposing the order of the words; and the closing the couplet with the emphatical word 'full' compleats the harmony:

[Quotes.]

If there be any other mystery in these lines, I own, it is beyond my skill to discover it."

and yet are clos'd in the most agreeable manner, as the law of
the distich generally demands, with a real iambic, or sounds that
approach the nearest to it. And the last half of the former verse
has no beauty in my opinion, but what is owing to this opposition,
and its agreement with the image it represents."

Poems on Several Occasions, 1745, pp. 151-153.

Sedley.

"*Chaste,* without *Pride;* tho' gentle yet not soft,
    Not always cruel, nor yet kind too oft."

A Pastoral Dialogue. (*A Collection of Poems, viz.,*
                    The Temple of Death, 1701.)

Swift.

"Nor let my votaries show their skill
    In aping lines from Cooper's Hill;
    For know I cannot bear to hear
    The mimicry of 'deep, yet clear.'"

Apollo's Edict, ll. 46-49.

Wesley, Samuel.

"The little glimpse that Dryden gives is more
    Than all our careless writers knew before;
    A few chance lines may smooth and roundly fly,
    But still no thanks to us, we know not why.
    He finds examples, we the rule must make,
    Tho' who without a guide may not mistake?
        (a) 'Tho' deep yet clear, tho' gentle yet not dull
            Strong without rage, without o'erflowing full.'
    If we that famous riddle can unty,
    Their brightest beauties in the pauses lie,
    To admiration vary'd; next to these
    The numbers justly order'd charm and please:
    Each word, each happy sound is big with sense,
    They all deface who take one letter thence.
        (a) Mr. Dryden's riddle in his Preface to Virgil."

An Epistle to a Friend, concerning
                    Poetry, 1700, pp. 14-15.

Appendix F.

I

COLLECTED EDITIONS

1668. POEMS/AND/TRANSLATIONS,/WITH THE/SOPHY./ Written by the Honourable/Sir *JOHN DENHAM*/ Knight of the *Bath./LONDON,*/Printed for *H. Herringman* at the Sign of the/ Blew-Anchor in the *Lower-Walk* of the/*New-Exchange.* 1668.

1671. POEMS/AND/TRANSLATIONS,/WITH THE/SOPHY./ Written by the Honourable/Sir *JOHN DENHAM*/Knight of the *Bath./The Second Impression./LONDON.*/Printed by *J.M.* for *H. Herringman* at the Sign of/the *Blew-Anchor* in the *Lower-Walk* of/the *New-Exchange.* 1671.

(1676?) Listed by Sir Sidney Lee in the Dictionary of National Biography. I can find no copy of, or reference to, such an edition.

1684. POEMS/AND/TRANSLATIONS,/WITH THE/SOPHY./ Written by the Honourable/Sir *JOHN DENHAM,*/Knight of the *Bath./The Third Impression./LONDON,*/Printed by *J.M.* for *H. Herringman;* and are/to be sold by *Jos. Knight* and *Fr. Saunders,*/ at the Sign of the *Blue Anchor* in the/*Lower Walk* of the *New-Exchange.*/ MDCLXXXIV.

1703. POEMS/AND/TRANSLATIONS,/WITH THE/SOPHY./ Written by the Honourable/Sir *JOHN DENHAM*/Knight of the *Bath./The Fourth Edition.*/To which is added,/*Cato-Major* of Old-Age./*LONDON,*/Printed by *T.W.* for *H. Herringman* and Sold by/*Jacob Tonson* at *Grays-Inn* Gate in *Grays-Inn-/Lane,* and *Thomas Bennet* at the *Half-Moon* in/St. *Paul's* Church-yard. 1703.

1709. POEMS/AND/TRANSLATIONS;/WITH THE/SOPHY,/A /TRAGEDY./Written by the Honourable/SIR *JOHN DEN-HAM,*/Knight of the *Bath.*/THE FIFTH EDITION./*LONDON:* /Printed for *Jacob Tonson,* within *Grays-Inn*/Gate, next *Grays-Inn* Lane. 1709.

1719. POEMS/AND/TRANSLATIONS;/WITH THE/*SOPHY,*/ A/TRAGEDY./Written by the Honourable/Sir *JOHN DEN-HAM,*/Knight of the BATH./The SIXTH EDITION./*LON-DON:*/Printed for *Jacob Tonson,* at *Shakespear's/Head,* over-against *Katharine-street*/in the *Strand.* 1719.

1769. POEMS/AND/TRANSLATIONS;/WITH THE/SOPHY,/ A/TRAGEDY./Written by the Honourable/Sir JOHN DEN-HAM,/KNIGHT of the BATH./The SEVENTH EDITION,/ LONDON./Printed for T. Davies, in Russel-street, Covent-Gar-/den; J. and F. Rivington; W. Johnston; G./Kearsley; T. Becket; and J. Robson./ M,DCC,LXIX.

1771. POEMS/AND/TRANSLATIONS;/WITH THE/SOPHY,/ A/TRAGEDY./WRITTEN BY THE HONOURABLE/SIR JOHN DENHAM,/KNIGHT OF THE BATH./GLASGOW:/ PRINTED BY ROBERT & ANDREW FOULIS/M.DCC.LXXI.

1773. *The British Poets.* Edinburgh. Printed for A. Kincaid and W. Creech and J. Balfour.

1779. *Works of the Poets of Great Britain and Ireland* etc. Edited by Samuel Johnson.

1779. *The Poets of Great Britain.* Edited by John Bell.

1780. THE/POETICAL WORKS/OF/SIR JOHN DENHAM./ CONTAINING HIS/MISCELLANIES | SONGS
                    EPISTLES | TRANSLATIONS/
&c &c &c/ (Quotation from Somerville)/PERTH./Printed and sold by R. MORISON and SON,/Booksellers./ *Anno* 1780.

1795. *A Complete Edition of the Poets of Great Britain.* Edited by Robert Anderson.

1807. *The Works of the British Poets, collated with the best editions.* Edited by Thomas Park.

1807. *The Poets of Great Britain.* Edited by Samuel Bagster.

1810. *The Works of the English Poets.* Edited by Alex. Chalmers.

1819. *The Works of the British Poets with lives of the authors.* Edited by Sanford.

1822. *The British Poets, Including Translations*. Chiswick, Printed by C. Whittingham.

1857. *The Poetical Works of Edmund Waller and Sir John Denham*, etc. Edinburgh. Edited by Rev. George Gilfillan.

II

COOPER'S HILL

1642. COOPERS/HILL./A Poëme./ (Device)/ London Printed for *Tho. Walkley*,/ and are to be sold at his shop at the Signe/of the Flying Horse between York-house/and Britaines Burse. 1642.

1643. COOPERS/HILL./A Poëme,/(Device)/ *Printed in the yeare M.DC.XLIII.*

1650. COOPERS/HILL/ A Poeme./ The Second Edition with/Additions./*Written by* JOHN DENHAM *Esq;*/(Device)/LONDON/ Printed for *HUMPHREY MOSELEY*,/ and are to be sold at his Shop, at the Signe/ of the Princes Armes in St. *Pauls*/Church-yard. 1650.
(In the British Museum copy 1650 is crossed out, and Jan. 21, 1649, written in.)

1655. COOPERS/HILL./ Written in the yeare 1640./ *Now Printed from a perfect Copy; And/ A Corrected Impression./ By* JOHN DENHAM *Esq;*/(Device)/ *LONDON,*/Printed for *Humphrey Moseley,* and are to be/sold at his Shop, at the Signe of the Princes/ Armes in St *Pauls* Church-yard. 1655.

(1660) (Cooper's Hill. A Poem. The third edition with additions. By John Denham Esquire, with a Prologue and Epilogue to the Sophy; and Verses to Mr. Richard Fanshaw, Esq., upon his ingenious Translation of Paster Fido into English. London for Humphrey Moseley 1660. 4to.
Kennett, White, *A Register and Chronicle Ecclesiastical and Civil,* 1728, p. 299.)

1676. *COOPERS HILL*/ LATINE REDDITUM./AD/NOBILISSI-
MUM D^{num}/GULIELMUM D^{num} CAVENDISH,/Honoratissimi
Domini/GULIELMI/COMITIS DEVONIAE/ Filium Unicum./
(Device: the Sheldonian Theatre) /OXONII,/ E THEATRO
SHELDONIANO. MDCLXXVI.

1709. *COOPERS-HILL.*/A/POEM,/Written by the Honourable/Sir
JOHN DENHAM,/Knight of the *Bath.*/(Device)/LONDON:/
Printed and Sold by *H. Hills,* in *Black-fryars,* near/the Water-side.
1709.

III

POEMS

1642. THE/SOPHY./As it was acted at the Private House in Black
Friars/by his Majesties Servants./LONDON,/Printed by *Richard
Hearne* for *Thomas Walkley,* and/are to be sold at his shop at the
Signe of the/Flying Horse betweene Yorkhouse/and Britaines
Burse. 1642.

1643. *Mr.* HAMPDENS *Speech occasioned upon the Londoners Peti-
tion for Peace* [broadside]. The copy in the British Museum is
dated March 23, 1643.

1651. THE/ANATOMY/OF PLAY,/Written by a worthy and/
Learned Gent./Dedicated to his Father, to/shew his detestation
of it./(Device)/London, Printed by *G.P.* for *Nicholas Bourne*/
and are to be sold at the South entrance/of the Royall Exchange.
1651.

For reference to a possible 1645 edition, see Johnson, *Lives of
the Poets* (ed. Napier, I, 78, note). This may be the edition re-
ferred to by Aubrey: "Sir John Denham wrott an essay against
gameing to shew his detestation of it to his father, printed by N.
Brookes, at the Angel in Cornhill. I have it about 3 or 4 sheets 8vo.
His name is not to it, but I know 'twas his; and a kinsman of his,
that was one of his father's clarkes, gave the copy to Brookes, and
Sir John Denham owned it to me."

Aubrey, *Brief Lives* (ed. Clark), I, 221, note 2.

1656. THE/DESTRUCTION/OF/TROY,/AN/ESSAY/UPON THE/SECOND BOOK/OF/*VIRGILS AENEIS.*/Written in the year, 1636./*LONDON:*/Printed for *Humphrey Moseley,* at his shop at the sign of/the Princes Armes in S. *Pauls* Church-yard,/ 1656.

1659. A/PANEGYRICK/*ON*/HIS EXCELLENCY/The LORD GENERAL/GEORGE MONCK:/Commander in Chief of all the Forces/IN/*ENGLAND,*/*SCOTLAND,*/AND/*IRELAND.*/*LON-DON,*/Printed for *Richard Marriot* in Fleet-street, 1659. This poem is in the British Museum in the form of a broadside.

1660. THE/PROLOGUE/TO HIS/MAJESTY/At the first PLAY presented at the Cock-pit in/WHITEHALL,/Being part of that Noble Entertainment which Their MAIESTIES received *Novemb.* 19./from his Grace the Duke of ALBEMARLE./(Text)/*LON-DON,* Printed for *G. Bedell* and *T. Collins,* at the/*Middle-Temple Gate* in *Fleet-street.* 1660. The British Museum copy has the date Nov. 23, added in manuscript.

1667. ON/*Mr.* ABRAHAM COWLEY/*His Death, and Burial amongst the/Ancient Poets.*/By the Honourable Sir *John Denham.*/ (Folio Sheet)/Licensed *August* 15, 1667. *Roger L'Estrange*/*London,* Printed for *H. Herringman,* at the Blew Anchor/in the Lower Walk of the New Exchange. 1667.

1669. *CATO MAJOR*/OF/OLD AGE./A Poem./By the Honourable /Sir *JOHN DENHAM*/Knight of the *BATH.*/(Device)/In the *SAVOY,*/Printed for *Henry Herringman* at the Sign of/the *Anchor* in the Lower-Walk of the/*New Exchange.* 1669.

1678. Horace./A/Tragedy./Translated from Monsieur Corneille./The Fifth Act Translated by/Sir John Denham./In the Savoy:/Printed by T. N. for Henry Herringman at the Sign of/the Blew-Anchor in the Lower Walk of the/New Exchange, 1678.

Heading: By the most deservedly admired/ Mrs. Katherine Philips, etc.

1710. *CATO MAJOR*/OF/OLD AGE./A POEM./By the Honourable/Sir *JOHN DENHAM*,/Knight of the *Bath.*/(Device)/*LONDON:*/Printed and sold by *H. Hills*, in Black-Fryers, near the Water-side, 1710./(Price three Pence.)

1714. A/VERSION/OF THE/PSALMS/OF/*DAVID*,/Fitted to the TUNES Used/in CHURCHES./By the Honourable/Sir *JOHN DENHAM*,/Knight of the *Bath.*/*LONDON*,/Printed for J. BOWYER at the Rose in *Ludgate-/street*, H. CLEMENTS at the Half-Moon in *St./Paul's Church-yard*, T. VARNUM and J. OSBORN/ at the *Oxford*-Arms in *Lombard-Street.* 1714.

This book was edited by Heighes Woodford, who in his dedication to the Earl of Derby, the husband of Denham's granddaughter, says, ". . . your Lordship will be my voucher how the original copies of Sir John Denham came first into my hands, and that they had lain a considerable time with the Right Reverend Father in God, George, Lord Bishop of Winton."

For comment on these poems, see:

Felton, Henry, *A Dissertation on Reading the Classics*, etc., 1718, p. 219 ff.

Mayne, Jasper, *Upon Sir John Denham's Translation of the Psalms* (Bodleian Library, MS. Eng. Poet. e. 4).

Watts, Isaac, *The Psalms of David imitated in the language of the New Testament*, etc., 1719, preface, xxv.

Woodford, Samuel, *A Paraphrase upon the Canticles . . . with other occasional Compositions in English Verse*, 1679, p. 146. *To the Honourable Sir John Denham, upon his new Version of the Psalms*. Dated 1668.

There are references to them in MS. Ballard XII, No. 115, and MS. Ballard XV, No. 52, in the Bodleian Library.

n.d. A/RELATION/OF A/QUAKER,/That to the Shame of his Profession, Attempted to/Bugger a Mare near Colchester.

IV

MANUSCRIPTS

Cooper's Hill.
  MS. Harleian 367.
  MS. Harleian 837. British Museum.

Dialogue between Sir John Pooley and Mr. Tho. Killigrew.
  MS. Ormonde.
  MS. among the papers of the Marquis of Ormonde at Kilkenny
  Castle.

On Mr. Tho. Killigrew's return from his Embassy.
  MS. Clarendon.
  Calendar of Clarendon Papers, II, 143. Bodleian.

Verses on the Cavaliers imprisoned in 1655.
  MS. Clarendon.
  Clarendon State Papers, April-December, 1655. Bodleian.

On the Earl of Strafford's Trial and Death.
  MS. Stowe 970.
  MS. Egerton 2421. British Museum.

Elegy on the Death of Judge Crooke.
  MS. Harleian 6933.
  MS. Egerton 2421. British Museum.

Translations of Virgil.
  MS. Hutchinson. See p. 41.

INDEX

Addison, 55.
Aeneid, 41.
Anatomy of Play, The, 6.
Aristotle, 60 (2).
Ascham, Roger, 52.
Ashburnham, Mr., 13.
Astcot, 101.
Aubrey, John, 2, 4, 21.
Aubrey, William, 100.
Ausonius, 49.

Bamfield, Col., 14.
Baron, Robert, 46 n.
Beaumont, 30.
Berkeley, Sir John, 12, 13.
Black Prince, The, 48.
Bolton, Duke of, 137 n.
Boswell, Humfrey, 14.
Brecknox, Capt., 9.
Bristoll, Lord, 18, 190.
British Princes, The, 32.
Broderick, Mr., 17.
Brooke, Penelope, 21.
Brooke, Sir William, 21.
Buckingham, Duke of, 16, 18.
Butler, Samuel, 19, 28 n., 49.
Byron, Richard, Lord, 137 n.

Carbery, Earl of, 16.
Carey, Lucius, Lord Falkland, 35 n.
Cartwright, William, 30, 53, 54.
Case, Thomas, 132, 134.
Cato, 60, 202.
Cato Major, 1, 41, 43.
Caulier, 138.
Cavendish, Lady, 23.
Charles I, 6, 7 (2), 8 (3), 12 (3), 13, 32, 47, 48 (2), 53, 59, 60.
Charles II, 7 (2), 14 (3), 18, 19, 21 (2), 59, 60.
Chaucer, 29, 31.
Chidleigh (Chudleigh), Gen. James, 130 n., 131.
Cicero, 41, 202, 203.

Cleveland, 28 n.
Cockram, Sir John, 108 n.
Conway, Lord, 24.
Cooper's Hill, 6, 7, 8, 11, 16, 30 (2), 36 (2), 38, 40 (2), 42 (2), 47 ff., 53, 54, 55, 56, 57.
Corneille, 41.
Cornwallis, Sir Frederick, 138.
Coventry, Thomas, Lord, 137 n.
Coventry, Sir William, 137 n.
Cowley, 14, 31, 60.
Craven, Lord, 59.
Crofts, William, Lord, 14, 107 n.
Croke (Crooke), Sir George, 156 n.
Cromwell, 15.

Davenant, Sir William, 28, 29, 32, 113 n., 317 n.
Demosthenes, 203.
Denham, Ann, 4, 4 n., 14.
Denham, Anne Cotton, 4, 4 n., 9, 10, 11.
Denham, Elizabeth, 4, 4 n., 14.
Denham, Sir John, father of the poet, 3, 5, 6.
Denham, Sir John, his will, 1; physical appearance, 2; family, 2, 3; schooling, 3 ff.; first marriage, 4; children, 4, 5; at Oxford, 3, 4; at Lincoln's Inn, 5; son dies, 6; father dies, 6; inheritance, 6; called to bar, 6; Royalist opinions, 6 ff.; sheriff for Surrey, 8; Gov. Farnham Castle, 8; prisoner in London, 9, 11, 12; birth of Ann, 10; intercedes for Wither, 10; goods sold, 10; at Dartmouth, 11; exchanged for Harris, 11; at Exeter, 11; in France, 12, 14; compounds, 12, 13, 15; to Charles I, 12 ff.; aids escape of Charles I, 13; aids escape of Duke of York, 13, 14; in Scotland, 14; in Poland, 14; returns to England, 15; with Pembroke, 15; arrested, 16; abroad with